DO NOT REMOVE
CARDS FROM POCKET

ALLEN COUNTY PUBLIC LIBRARY

FORT WAYNE, INDIANA 46802

You may return this book to any agency, branch,
or bookmobile of the Allen County Public Library.

DEMCO

SOVIET DEFECTORS

SOVIET DEFECTORS
The KGB Wanted List

VLADISLAV KRASNOV

HOOVER INSTITUTION PRESS

STANFORD UNIVERSITY   STANFORD, CALIFORNIA

The Hoover Institution on War, Revolution and Peace, founded at
Stanford University in 1919 by the late President Herbert Hoover,
is an interdisciplinary research center for advanced study on
domestic and international affairs in the twentieth century. The
views expressed in its publications are entirely those of the
authors and do not necessarily reflect the views of the staff,
officers, or Board of Overseers of the Hoover Institution.

Hoover Press Publication 323

Copyright 1985 by the Board of Trustees of the
Leland Stanford Junior University

First printing, 1986

Manufactured in the United States of America

90 89 88 87 86   85   9 8 7 6 5 4 3 2 1

Library of Congress Cataloging in Publication Data

Krasnov, Vladislav.
  Soviet defectors.

  Bibliography: p.
  Includes index.
    1. Civil rights—Soviet Union.   2. Defectors—Soviet Union.
3. Political persecution—Soviet Union. 4. Soviet Union—Politics and
government—1945-   .
I. Title.
JC599.S58K73   1985   323.4′092′2   85-17661
ISBN 0-8179-8231-0

Design by P. Kelley Baker

In Memory of My Mother,
Ekaterina Ivanovna Krasnova

CONTENTS

FOREWORD

How odd it is that the Soviet regime has drawn near to the biblical age of three score years and ten without, until the publication of this book, a single scholarly work on defection by its subjects having appeared. Vladislav Krasnov is thus a pioneer in a new, small, but important area of Soviet studies.

He is an admirable pioneer—calm, fearless, objective, literate, numerate, systematic, undeterred by obstacles or sacred cows. He knew what he wanted to do and set about doing it. The result, as readers will see, is rewarding. But he rightly insists that his treatment is far from exhaustive.

To start with, Krasnov wisely limits himself to the period since 1945. This makes the topic manageable and leaves the earlier Soviet years, when defection was an equally sensitive issue, to a pioneer of the future. Beyond this, painstaking research in a dozen or so countries around the Soviet periphery would clearly build up more complete data on defection, to supplement what Krasnov has accumulated on 470 individuals for 1945–69 and on approximately 200 individuals for 1969–84. Regarding the former period he was able to exploit a lucky break: a top-secret list of defectors and Western agents for whom the KGB was searching had fallen into the hands of an emigre organization. But for the years 1969–84 he had to rely mostly on the information he could gather from various press sources.

In his mapping of this neglected territory, Krasnov is suitably methodical. He defines with precision what he means by a defector; he surveys, briefly but vividly, the present literature in the field, which consists mostly of defectors' memoirs; he examines the attitudes and motivations of the principal parties involved—the defectors themselves, the receiving governments, and the KGB; he discusses perceptively his statistical tables on the age and nationality of defectors, their year and method of defection, the countries they choose, their previous occupations, and so on; and here, as elsewhere, he takes care not to stretch his data beyond what they will bear, appealing indeed to future researchers to focus on the many gaps and uncertainties to which he points.

On occasion, Krasnov the objective scholar does not hide his humane values and his critical view of the insensitive or even negligent ways in which governments have sometimes handled defectors. He documents the vulnerability of defectors and their natural resentment when their motives, which are often dissident and patriotic, are unjustly suspected.

In addition, while fully aware of the dangers posed by phony or "planted" defectors, Krasnov argues convincingly that too little is done to eliminate unnecessary obstacles to defection or to exploit the unique and valuable resource it supplies. If defections and defectors' stories were publicized more vigorously, he says, several benefits would ensue. The government of Finland, for example, would come under greater pressure to terminate its present agreement with the Kremlin to return defectors to the USSR. The increased publicity would make it harder for Soviet agents to continue to harass defectors or even sometimes to kidnap or murder them. World peace would become more secure, as interviews, articles, and books by defectors would undermine the effect of Soviet propaganda and have a salutary impact on Western opinion. Finally, defections by senior officials like Arkady Shevchenko and Michael Voslensky might occur more regularly, and this would give the West a better understanding of the Kremlin's carefully concealed processes of decisionmaking.

We might note here in passing that in 1983 The Jamestown Foundation was set up in Washington, D.C., to promote goals very similar to those advocated here by Krasnov. Also—and this is my own long-range speculation—if high-level defections become more frequent in the years ahead, the cumulative damage done to Soviet diplomacy and espionage, and thus to the morale of the Soviet elite as a whole, could perhaps turn into a tangible factor pushing the leadership toward liberal reform.

This brings me to some final remarks about Krasnov's interpretation of the dynamic trends in Soviet defection. Having demonstrated statistically that the average rate of defection was markedly higher in the drab Brezhnev era than in the more hopeful years of Khrushchev, he speculates that this trend will continue in the future, since the USSR's domestic problems are so intractable.

To my mind, this is persuasive. Since the late 1970s the mood of Soviet society has become increasingly sour and tense. Social, economic, and political problems have mounted; the debilitating war in Afghanistan has dragged on.

By 1982, open dissent had become impossible and legal emigration had been virtually halted. As few emigrants and defectors have been returning to the Soviet Union, the message has come through that settling in other countries is at least possible—if only one can somehow *get* there.

In these circumstances, the desperation in a number of disaffected communities long barred from emigration has been growing. In 1984, for example, the Gorelkin family of Pentecostals from Vilnius took the unprecedented risk of attempting a collective escape on foot, even though two of them were in poor health. Five adult children and their parents (who were approaching 60) trekked for twelve days through the mountains of southern Georgia. Avoiding the border patrols that annually catch hundreds of escapers near the USSR's perimeter, and cutting their way through frontier fences, they miraculously reached Turkey and freedom.

Conceivably, of course, Mr. Gorbachev's Politburo will in due course ease social tensions, restart emigration, reinvigorate the economy, and withdraw the "limited contingent of Soviet troops" from their temporary duty in Afghanistan. But while such welcome developments might indeed reduce the rate of defection, they would surely not halt it. For as Krasnov suggests in this pathfinding book, defections will go on occurring until the day Russia is free. And that, for the time being, is the stuff of dreams.

Peter Reddaway,
London School of Economics
and Political Science

ACKNOWLEDGMENTS

This study could not have come about without the help of several individuals and institutions. My heartfelt thanks go, first of all, to Professor Edward E. Ericson, Jr., of Calvin College and Dr. Milorad Drachkovitch of the Hoover Institution, who encouraged me to start this project. William H. Bowen of Dallas has my special thanks for standing solidly behind the project from its inception.

I am grateful to the Hoover Institution for a summer 1978 research fellowship and for its ongoing cooperation with my endeavors, including my trip to Europe in the summer of 1979. Hilja Kukk expertly assisted me in exploring the Hoover Library; Charles Palm introduced me to the Archives; and Dr. Richard Staar helped me to reach out beyond local resources.

I am grateful to NTS chairman Aleksandr Artemoff for making accessible to me the principal source for this study and to the research staff of Radio Liberty for supplying me with additional information.

I am grateful to the Slavic Research Center in Sapporo, Japan, for providing me with the opportunity to use the facilities of Hokkaido University's Computer Center. I am particularly indebted to Masatomo Togashi, Mrs. Akaishi, and Professor Kubo in making the computer talk to me.

Professors Michael Pleck of the University of Illinois and Bill Belovicz of the Monterey Institute of International Studies were very helpful in organizing the computer basis of my study. The practical assistance of Charles Moore and John Caske of the Hoover Institution was likewise invaluable.

An Earhart Foundation grant in the summer of 1981 enabled me to write the first draft. In 1985, a visiting grant for research at the Kennan Institute for

Advanced Russian Studies of the Woodrow Wilson International Center for Scholars provided me with an opportunity to update my bibliography and appendixes by using the rich resources of the Washington, D.C., area, especially the Library of Congress.

Finally, I am indebted to my student, Peter Schultz, for the editing and typing of the first draft; to Susan Tousey for the typing of the final draft; and to Peter Reddaway of the London School of Economics, Robert Crowley, and B. Alexander for reading the manuscript and offering valuable suggestions. Special thanks are due to Dr. Lennard Gerson of Nassau Community College for helping me smooth out the manuscript. The final responsibility for the text rests with me.

Everyone has the right to leave any country, including his own, and to return to his country.

Everyone has the right to seek and to enjoy in other countries asylum from persecution.

The U.N. Declaration of Human Rights

[No person seeking territorial asylum] shall be subjected to measures such as rejection at the frontier . . . or compulsory return to any state where he may be subjected to persecution.

The U.N. Declaration on Territorial Asylum

The participating States,
Desiring *to contribute to the strengthening of peace and understanding among peoples and to the spiritual enrichment of the human personality . . .*

Make it their aim *to facilitate freer movement and contacts, individually and collectively, whether privately or officially . . . and to contribute to the solution of the humanitarian problems that arise in that connection.*

The Helsinki Accords

NOTE ON TRANSLITERATION

For the transliteration of Russian quoted words, phrases, and titles, the Library of Congress system, with the omission of diacritical marks, was used. It corresponds to System II, recommended for this purpose, in J. Thomas Shaw's *The Transliteration of Modern Russian* (New York: MLA, 1979).

In transliterating personal names, System I was used in the text and Appendixes. However, exceptions were made in the text for the authors, publications, and publishers whose spelling in English has already been established, such as Peter Deriabin (not Pyotr Deryabin), Andrei (not Andrey) Sakharov, *Baby Yar*, and *Possev*. Notes and Bibliography follow the publishers' spelling (e.g., Georges Agabekov, not Georgy Arutyunov). Inevitably, the same names may appear as Allilueva, Guzenko, Victor, Pyotr, or Elena in the Appendixes, but as Alliluyeva, Gouzenko, Viktor, Peter, or Yelena in the text, Bibliography, and Notes.

INTRODUCTION

The subject of this book is Soviet defectors (*perebezhchiki*)—those people who have left the USSR in violation of Soviet law and against the wishes of the Soviet government. They may have crossed Soviet borders, jumped a Soviet ship, or failed to return home from a sojourn abroad; in any case, they have sought political asylum in other, noncommunist countries. Defectors ought to be distinguished from the hundreds of thousands of others who have voted their disapproval of the Soviet regime by their feet. These others are usually referred to as the three waves of emigration; they include (1) the émigrés who left Russia in the wake of the Revolution and Civil War; (2) the refugees and Displaced Persons (DPs) who, at the end of World War II, found themselves outside Soviet borders and chose to remain in the West; and (3) the current exodus of Soviet citizens of primarily Jewish origin to whom Soviet authorities grudgingly issue exit visas to Israel. Defectors also ought to be distinguished from the small number of those who were exiled, such as Aleksandr Solzhenitsyn; deprived of Soviet passports while traveling abroad, such as the cellist Mstislav Rostropovich; or left the USSR as a result of political arrangements, such as the dissident Vladimir Bukovsky, who was freed from jail and brought to the West in a swap for an imprisoned Chilean communist leader. Although the Soviet regime has been plagued by defections since it came to power in 1917, the present study is limited to postwar defectors.

In spite of the fact that a number of Soviet defectors in recent years—most notably Stalin's daughter Svetlana Alliluyeva, MIG-25 pilot Viktor Belenko, U.N. Undersecretary General Arkady Shevchenko, chess grand master Viktor Korchnoy, ballet stars Natalia Makarova, Mikhail Baryshnikov, and Aleksandr Godunov—were catapulted into the limelight of the free world media, the majority of defections have attracted either scant or no attention at all. Even though defectors themselves have written a number of books and articles, their writings are almost exclusively concerned with their own cases. There have been no systematic studies of the phenomenon of defection, and if there were, they were certainly not made available either to scholars or the public at large. The story of postwar defection thus remains largely untold.

Although I have been interested in the subject ever since my own defection in 1962, until recently I could not even contemplate undertaking the present study. The chief obstacle was the lack of sources. In the January 17, 1977, issue of *U.S. News & World Report*, I ran into an article, "In War, in Peace: Flight from Communism Goes On." It contrasted the "legal" flow of refugees with "the illegal or 'black' stream of escapees," that is, those defectors who "brave bullets and mine fields, climb barricades, elude tough border patrols, swim swift rivers and sail for weeks in leaky boats through stormy seas to reach sanctuaries." The consensus of the magazine's reporters from a number of European and Asian countries was that it is nearly impossible to obtain sources on the "black stream" of defectors. Even "their precise number is a tightly guarded secret," the article stated. On the one hand, "Communists won't admit that anyone wants to escape from their rule" and, on the other hand, "some western governments refuse to disclose details of the exodus for fear of disrupting relations with Communist governments." It was clear that the study to which I aspired would be a nearly impossible task. On my part, I was further handicapped as a defector. For the simple reason that defectors are usually—though, in most cases, erroneously—associated with espionage and international intrigue, I could not expect free world governments to be cooperative with me, someone whom they would rather suspect.

However, in the very same month that the *U.S. News* article appeared, *Possev*, a Russian émigré monthly published in Frankfurt, West Germany, began the publication, in several issues, of a list of some 600 names of Soviet defectors. *Possev* said that its list was based on a secret KGB publication that contained a lot more than just the names. The KGB publication was, in effect, a sort of wanted list produced for distribution among high-ranking KGB operatives inside the USSR and abroad. One of its volumes was smuggled out and found its way into the hands of the NTS (the Russian initials stand for National Labor Union of Russian Solidarists), the anticommunist Russian émigré organization that publishes *Possev*. Although the *Possev* List (see Appendix 1A) contained only names, *Possev* promised to send to each listed person a copy of his or her entry as it actually appears in the KGB publication. Having found my name on the *Possev* List, I requested a copy of my entry. When it arrived, I was not only satisfied as to its authenticity, but I was also impressed with its wealth of information.

I then conceived the idea of using the KGB records, which henceforth will be referred to as the KGB Wanted List, as the principal source for my present study. After my proposal was accepted at the Hoover Institution, I negotiated with the NTS and eventually was allowed to use the volume of the KGB Wanted List in their possession and to extract data from the 470 entries on postwar defectors. For the protection of the privacy of the entrants, all names were deleted. (A copy of that extract is now deposited in the archives of the Hoover Institution and henceforth will be referred to as the Hoover File.) I then fed the data from each entry into a computer for the purpose of statistical analysis. A discussion of the results forms Part Two of this book.

I realized, however, that for a better understanding of postwar defection, I needed some additional sources. Valuable as it was, my KGB source had its limitations. It had plenty of information on the scope of defection, including geographic and annual distribution, and it gave detailed characterizations of defectors, but only from a KGB viewpoint. It did not provide any information on their motives, aspirations, and ideas. Nor did it shed much light on their encounter with the reality on this side of the Iron Curtain. Moreover, my source did not extend beyond the year 1969.

In my search for such other sources, I wrote letters to the CIA, the Immigration and Naturalization Service, and the State Department, requesting whatever information they could share with me. Neither the CIA nor the INS would oblige. The State Department, however, offered to send me a copy of a series of interviews with defectors conducted by its staff between 1951 and 1960. Unedited and in typewritten form, these interviews were published by the State Department under the title "The Soviet Union as Reported by Former Soviet Citizens" and released for limited distribution among scholars "in order to make available to students of Soviet affairs basic data for their research from sources not readily accessible." Although these interviews could not shed light on the post-1969 period for which I lacked sources, I accepted the offer and asked the State Department to send a copy for the Hoover Institution's archives. I found them a very valuable complementary source for the study of defection during the 1940s and 1950s.

I was not too surprised at the lack of cooperation on the part of U.S. governmental agencies in the project from which, I felt, the United States could only benefit. I knew that even the Freedom of Information Act could not help me, because of my defector background. Besides, I realized that there was a legitimate government concern with the protection of defectors' privacy. Still, I was most disturbed by the discovery that the State Department interviews with defectors were discontinued in 1960 and apparently never resumed. This confirmed my suspicion, which I had held for a long time: American interest in defectors, never too great, has been on the decline since the late 1950s, when the Soviet government began loudly to profess its love for peaceful coexistence, détente, and such. Even the Simas Kudirka incident in 1970 could not reverse this trend.

Indicative of this trend was *The New Republic*'s article appropos the defection of Arkady Shevchenko in April 1978. The article was entitled "The Unwelcome Defector: An Embarrassment for Both Sides." The author, who claims to be an insider in Washington, stated that gone were the days of the cold war, when a defector "was welcome in the West as live ammunition in the great propaganda battle—a proof of tyranny on the Other Side, and of freedom on ours." By contrast, "in these days of détente [a defector] is viewed as an embarrassment, a liability, a factor that can adversely affect the precarious balance of U.S.-Soviet negotiations over a wide range of issues." He then revealed a secret of which the Carter Administration, with its professed concern for human rights, should be ashamed: "U.S. officials no longer keep a tally of defectors; guidelines call for minimizing their importance, avoiding publicity."[1]

Revelations like the above only strengthened my determination to extend my project beyond 1969, throughout the détente era to the present. Even though for the post-1969 period I had to rely chiefly on news stories available to the general public, I have attempted in this study to create a comprehensive, if fragmentary, picture of postwar defection from the USSR.

The purpose of this study is twofold. First, I hope that it will break ground for future scholarly studies of defection in the context of the dissident and human rights movement and as a form of opposition to the regime. Realizing that such studies could never be fully successful without a broader and more varied source base, I hope this book will encourage defectors to come forward and share their knowledge, experience, and ideas with both specialists and the general public. I am convinced that whenever public attention is drawn to something that the Soviet government would rather hide, distort, or destroy, the public is the winner, as its understanding of the USSR increases. I am also convinced that defectors themselves would gain greater security through greater publicity.

Second, I intend this study as a fact book that will break the monopoly of government bureaucrats on dealing with defectors and will open the matter of defection—whenever it does not involve national security risks, and most often it does not—to public scrutiny. Such a fact book would do what the government has failed to do: it would help (1) to establish a public tally of past, present, and future defectors; (2) to emphasize their importance for our understanding of the USSR; and (3) to assure future defectors all the publicity they deserve, since publicity has proved to be the only guarantee that their human rights are not tossed into a bureaucratic wastebasket under the pretext of preserving "the precarious balance."

The need for such a fact book seems especially great in the mass media.

The media has been rather tame in reporting Soviet defections, apparently out of the same "diplomatic" fear of disrupting "the precarious balance." As a result, the general public has a skewed perception of defectors as either ambitious ballet dancers or disgruntled KGB agents. Whenever defection has involved plain Soviet folks—sailors, soldiers, or students—media reporting has been either scant or nonexistent. What is worse, such reports, when they do appear, have been routinely saturated with errors: not only have the names been misspelled, patronymics used in place of last names, or last names used in place of first, but Russian nationality has been assigned to Armenians and Estonians. It may not have been entirely the fault of reporters, because most frequently they had to rely on information grudgingly released by government bureaucrats; still, the media can be faulted for not doing their homework.

Consider, for instance, the following aside that was tacked on at the end of the UPI report concerning the defection of Arkady Shevchenko on April 11, 1978:

> In 1943 Col. George Kravitsky, chief of an overseas office of the KGB secret police, defected, wrote the book *I Chose Freedom*, which became a bestseller, and later died under mysterious circumstances in New York.

Apparently written with a good intention of putting Shevchenko's defection into historical perspective, this comment can only confuse a newspaper reader because all facts in it are so mixed up that one cannot even tell who the defector in question was. If it was Walter Krivitsky, he defected in 1937, wrote the book *I Was Stalin's Agent*, and died in 1941—perhaps under mysterious circumstances, but in Washington, not New York. If it was the author of *I Chose Freedom*, his name was Viktor Kravchenko, but he was not a KGB colonel, defected in 1944, and died in New York in 1966.

Such inaccuracies, spurred by sensationalism, make the general public suspect that every defector is either a KGB agent or a double agent. In fact, very few of them are. But all of them are on the KGB Wanted List. They are on that list for the simple reason that, unable to emigrate from the USSR, they exercised their right "to leave any country, including [their] own," as it is proclaimed in the United Nations Declaration on Human Rights, of which the Soviet government is a signatory. So, the thesis of this book is: Defection from the USSR is, first and foremost, a human rights problem that should be treated as such; it is caused by the failure of the Soviet government to guarantee to its citizens the right of emigration, and it will persist as long as the Soviet government does not bring its laws and practices into conformity with the international obligations it took upon itself by signing such documents as the U.N. Declaration on Human Rights and the Helsinki Accords on Security and Cooperation in Europe. To be sure, the United States and other free countries, which have traditionally granted political asylum to defectors, should always be on guard against possible Soviet attempts to breach their security by planting Soviet spies in the guise of defectors. But they stand to gain a lot more—both politically and from the national security perspective—by treating defectors not as potential spies about whom the public must know nothing, but, most important, as fellow human beings craving the same basic human rights that Westerners take for granted.

Of course, there are some other reasons why defectors are wanted by the KGB. For one thing, they create adverse publicity for the USSR by the mere fact of defection, especially if it is reported, and thus undermine Soviet propaganda efforts to sell communism to other countries. Moreover, many defections have been chiefly motivated by a desire to tell the truth about life on the other side of the Wall, and a number of defectors have actually done so by writing and speaking publicly. This too undermines Soviet propaganda and damages their aggressive designs. Unfortunately, the West has shown little interest in what defectors have to say, even though, in my opinion, their revelations about the Soviet system have been and will be no less vital for the preservation of peace in the world than any Soviet military and espionage secrets that some of them may have divulged.

The main reason for this lack of receptivity to defectors' messages was suggested by Susan Sontag in her February 1982 speech in support of the Solidarity movement in Poland. She spoke, I believe, for the intellectual establishment of this country when she said about its past attitudes:

> We had identified the enemy as fascism. We believed in, or at least applied a double standard to, the angelic language of Communism . . . The emigres from Communist countries we didn't listen to, who found it far easier to get published in the *Reader's Digest* than in *The Nation* or the *New Statesman*, were telling the truth . . . The result is that many of us, and I include myself, did not understand the nature of the Communist tyranny.[2]

This is a very significant admission, and I hope Ms. Sontag is right when she goes on to say, "Now we hear them." I also hope that this book will help them to tune in to defectors.

Now, a few words about how this book is organized. It consists of three parts—Part One, "Soviet Defectors in the Public Record"; Part Two, "The KGB Wanted List, 1945-1969"; and Part Three, "Defections from 1969 to the Present"—as well as a Conclusion and Appendixes. Part One introduces the reader to the body of literature on defectors that was produced during the postwar period. It is divided into three chapters. The first chapter examines a few books written by specialists in the West about Soviet defectors. The second chapter summarizes a number of autobiographical accounts written by defectors themselves. Although these books were written for general readers and received some attention at the time of their publication, they are now largely forgotten. This is regrettable because these accounts have not lost their relevance to the present day. The third chapter deals with interviews conducted by the U.S. State Department with Soviet defectors. Even though these interviews have been available to Sovietologists, they remain unknown to the general public and, I suspect, to a great number of specialists. The purpose of Part One is to acquaint the reader with the flesh-and-blood reality of the human beings behind the data presented in Parts Two and Three.

Part Two, "The KGB Wanted List, 1945–1969," deals with the principal source for this study, the most comprehensive KGB record of Soviet defectors that is available in the West. After a description of the source and presentation of a sample of its entries, several chapters are devoted to a discussion of the statistical analysis of the data that were extracted from the KGB records and fed into a computer. The main objective of Part Two is to determine, on the basis of these data, the scope, character, and patterns of defection. It will address such questions as: How many defectors were there? How many of them were KGB agents, members of the intelligentsia, soldiers, or sailors? Is it true that the majority of defectors belong to such ethnic minorities as the Armenians, Estonians, or Jews? How many defectors crossed a border, jumped ship, or failed to return from a trip abroad? To which countries did they most often defect? In which countries did they settle? How many wives and children did they leave behind? Aren't many defections faked by the KGB in order to plant spies? Is there any truth in the Soviet allegations that defectors have criminal backgrounds? What punishment can they expect if they return, or are returned, to the USSR? What is the KGB Wanted List for? Toward the end of Part Two there will be a discussion of the dynamics of defection, that is, whether and how the patterns of defection have changed during the reigns of Stalin, Khrushchev, and Brezhnev. In view of the statistical nature of Part Two, some readers may find it advisable to read only the chapter summaries and the last two chapters of this section.

Part Three, "Defections from 1969 to the Present," begins where Part Two leaves off, around April 1969. It should be kept in mind, however, that Part Three differs, and not just chronologically, from Part Two. It is based solely on my own list of defections (see Appendix 3), which I compiled mostly from newspaper accounts and other public records. Since the data provided in news stories are different from the police-record type of data of the KGB Wanted List, there was no way to create a uniform data file for the post-1969 period or a composite file for the entire postwar period. Therefore, my findings in Part Three must be considered rather tentative. Nonetheless, I attempted to trace both continuity and new trends of the post-1969 defection as compared to the previous period. Although Part Three deals with defections that fall mainly under Brezhnev's rule, one can assume that it tells as much about Yuri Andropov, who was the KGB chief during that period. Part Three is chiefly concerned with interrelationships between defections and such political events of the post-1969 period as détente, the Kudirka incident, the Helsinki Accords, the rise and decline of the dissident and human rights movement, and the Jewish emigration.

The Conclusion puts defection into historical perspective as a uniquely twentieth-century phenomenon, characteristic of totalitarian communist regimes. I argue that the human rights denied to defectors in their home country have not always been assured in their host countries either. I also argue for the need to institute and implement a new U.S. policy toward defectors that would both assure defectors' human rights and maximally satisfy U.S. national security interests.

Insofar as this is a fact book, it is supplied with several Appendixes to which, I hope, readers will pay more than casual attention. In any case, they are not just for specialists. Besides the *Possev* List of defectors, which was extracted from the KGB Wanted List, there are several other lists that I have compiled from public sources. Among these are a list of those defectors missing from the *Possev* List, a list of abortive attempts at defection, a list of those who returned or were forced to return to the USSR, a list of defection by hijacking ships or planes, and a composite list of post-1969 defections.

Following the Index is a questionnaire form that old and new defectors are asked to fill out and mail to The Jamestown Foundation, 1708 New Hampshire Avenue, N.W., Washington, D.C. 20009, so that the source base for this book can be updated, corrected, and improved.

I

SOVIET DEFECTORS
IN THE PUBLIC RECORD

1

What Has Been Written About Soviet Defectors?

Gordon Brook-Shepherd's *The Storm Petrels*

Precious little has been written about Soviet defectors. As far as the defectors of the period prior to World War II are concerned, the first and only book I am aware of was published in 1977 in England. Titled *The Storm Petrels: The Flight of the First Soviet Defectors*, it was authored by Gordon Brook-Shepherd, a British journalist. [1] It relates the stories of five select trailblazers of that long line of Communists who chose freedom: Boris Bazhanov, Stalin's one-time personal secretary, who crossed the border to Iran on New Year's Day of 1928; Georges Agabekov (actually Arutyunov), the chief Soviet spy in the Middle East, who led the manhunt for Bazhanov before he himself defected in France in June 1930; Grigory Besedovsky, the acting Soviet ambassador to Paris, who escaped from the embassy in October 1929; Walter Krivitsky, the illegal resident in Holland in charge of Soviet agents in several European countries, who defected in October 1937; and Alexander Orlov, a secret service chief, who had presented Stalin with the entire gold reserves of Spain, 600 tons (still in the USSR), only to run for his life in July 1938.

Although all five had told their stories in their own books, Brook-Shepherd's volume is more than a simple recapitulation of their memoirs. Drawing, in his words, "from a wide range of Western official sources" and from interviews with some of those storm petrels who were still alive "on both sides of the Atlantic," most notably Bazhanov, he created his own picture of prewar defection. (Bazhanov died in France in January 1983.)

Brook-Shepherd realizes that these five were not the only defectors of the period and, in fact, he refers to a half-dozen other defectors in his book. Still, his book gives no idea of either the history or the scope of the prewar defections. Moreover, though indexed, his book lacks a bibliography and is poorly footnoted, and therefore is ill-adapted for scholarly use. However, he has turned a sympathetic ear to his defectors, and the book is animated by his awareness of their historical significance and relevance to the present day. "They were not only the political heralds of the Cold War," writes Brook-Shepherd. "By what they revealed and what they did in exile, this handful of forgotten men helped to shape the course of that great East-West conflict which is still with us."[2]

Even though the author himself "devoted hardly any space to drawing morals from these stories," he concludes his book rather effectively by letting Bazhanov speak for all the storm petrels by quoting from his personal letter:

> You know, as I do, that our civilization stands on the edge of an abyss... Those who seek to destroy it put forward an ideal. This ideal [of communism] has been proven false by the experience of the last sixty years...the problem of bringing freedom back to Russia is not insoluble...the youth of Russia no longer believe in the system, despite the fact that they have known nothing else. If the West [develops its] confidence and unity, [it] can win the battle for our civilization and set humanity on the true path to progress, not the twisted path of Marxism.[3]

This will be so only if the message of the defectors is listened to more attentively than it was before World War II.

COLONEL HINCHLEY'S *THE DEFECTORS*

Only a little more attention has been paid to postwar defectors. In 1967, Vernon Hinchley, a colonel of British intelligence, published *The Defectors*.[4] Although he does not directly say so, he seems to have an insider's view on some defections, and he has accumulated a considerable amount of information. Nonetheless, his book is of little use to scholars and not easy reading for anyone because it is poorly organized, makes no reference to sources, and lacks an index.

Above all, the book suffers from lack of understanding of defection as a phenomenon characteristic of totalitarian communist regimes. Hinchley paradoxically defines a defector as someone "who changes sides legally" and who finds his closest kin in a traitor "who changes sides illegally."[5] Treating defection as a "two-way traffic," East-to-West and West-to-East, Hinchley illustrates his point by citing a few examples of both. In the West-to-East traffic he includes such British agents of the KGB as Guy Burgess, Donald MacLean, and Kim Philby, as well as the nuclear physicist Bruno Pontecorvo, whom he defines as a "nonpolitical" defector "who left Harwell for Moscow for the very sensible reason that he was offered a better job."[6] He also includes in this category three Americans: William H. Martin and Bernon F. Mitchell, both of whom fled to the USSR in 1960, and Sergeant Glen Rohrer, who escaped from Camp King, West Germany, in 1965. The East-to-West traffic he exemplifies with Viktor Kravchenko, Igor Gouzenko, Oksana Kasenkina, Vladimir and Evdokia Petrov, Oleg Lenchevsky, Nikolai Khokhlov, Bogdan Stashinsky (whose name he misspells as Starkinsky), and Aleksandr Kaznacheev.

Hinchley apparently sees no difference between the two groups. It does not occur to him that whereas the West-to-East group chiefly consists of KGB agents who were recruited in the West and escaped to the USSR when their spying activities were about to be exposed, the East-to-West group consists of people who never were pro-Western spies but decided to defect to the West more for reasons of conscience than anything else. Strictly speaking, Hinchley's use of the term "defectors" for the West-to-East traffic is inappropriate because those Westerners who cannot stand "capitalism," for whatever reason, do not need to defect at all: they can simply buy a one-way ticket to any Soviet bloc country.

Toward the end of his book, Hinchley expands on his initial definition thus: "The defector is an individual, usually mature, talented and above average in intelligence, who for years has worked honestly and approvingly for his native country" and then happens to "decide that he would be better off, either intellectually or economically" in some other country, and so "he changes sides." This may be taken as a compliment by some, but I doubt whether any Soviet defector would wish to be interrogated, and have his fate decided, by a professional intelligence officer such as Hinchley. I think a defector would rather entrust his or her fate to any Englishman on the street, who would certainly show more understanding and sympathy.

In fact, Hinchley admits that he has little sympathy for those to whom he devoted his book. Drawing the bottom line under his West-East potpourri of defectors, he puts them down as "mentally tough introverts to whom natural loyalties mean little." Not believing them capable of being "the life and soul of a cocktail party," Hinchley concludes: "All I have against the average defector is that I could never like him very much."[7] Of course, he is free to dislike anyone, but he should not have written his book at the level of cocktail party banter. After reading it, one wonders whether, for Hinchley, Russia's communist revolution took place at all.

JOHN BARRON'S *KGB:*
THE SECRET WORK OF SOVIET SECRET AGENTS

Incomparably more valuable, and more sympathetic toward defectors, is John Barron's *KGB: The Secret Work of Soviet Secret Agents*, published in 1974.[8] Although it is not a book about defectors per se, it tells more about them than any other book. Conversely, without the information provided by defectors, Barron could not have revealed so much about the secret work of the KGB. Barron readily acknowledged his indebtedness to a number of defectors "without whose trust, courage, and intelligence the work never could have been accomplished."

Vividly narrated by a seasoned journalist, Barron's book is good reading for the general public. At the same time, it has all the merits usually associated with scholarly studies: it is thoroughly researched and footnoted; sources and bibliography are listed; and relevant appendixes, an index, charts, and photographs are provided. Moreover, throughout the book Barron usually corroborates the evidence from any particular source with that from other sources, and he convincingly argues his points. I find his book actually superior to many academic products in that he suggests some lessons to be learned. One of them has direct bearing on the present study:

> deferential silence about KGB oppressions and depredations must be shattered. Soviet propagandists and apologists have succeeded remarkably in establishing the proposition that to condemn even the most egregious Soviet affront or injustice is somehow to "fan the flames of the cold war." The reverse is true. Silent acquiescence positively encourages the kind of KGB actions that are the essence of the cold war by suggesting to Soviet rulers that these actions have no deleterious consequences.[9]

Insofar as the majority of defectors are both victims and prey of the KGB (even though only a small number of them were actually former KGB agents), Barron's advice was an inspiration for the present study.

THE HARVARD PROJECT

Unfortunately, scholars, including Sovietologists, have paid very little attention to the study of defectors. This was apparently due to the fact that, at least since the establishment of the official USA-USSR exchange of scholars at the end of the 1950s, it has been somehow thought that work about defectors would fan the flames of the cold war. So, whatever scholarly work on defectors was undertaken was done mostly before the onset of peaceful coexistence (later named détente) at the end of the 1950s. Most notable is the Harvard Research Project on the Soviet Social System, which was put together in 1950 and was initially underwritten by the U.S. Air Force.

The admirable idea of the project was to tap a new and abundant source of information about the secretive communist state, namely, the thousands of refugees from the USSR, some of whom were still crowding transit camps in West Germany while others had already resettled in the United States. On the basis of data gathered by this project, a number of books were written by American scholars, including *How the Soviet System Works*, by Raymond A. Bauer, Alex Inkeles, and Clyde Kluckhohn, and *The Soviet Citizen: Daily Life in a Totalitarian Society*, by Inkeles and Bauer. The latter, not published until 1959, contains the main body of statistical data from the project. That body of data was collected with the help of a detailed questionnaire, to which there were about three thousand respondents, and 329 "extended life-history interviews." The main thrust of the questions was to establish a statistical basis for learning about the prevailing attitudes of Soviet citizens to various aspects of Soviet political, cultural, social, ethnic, and economic life.

Although the majority of the respondents belonged to the category of the so-called Displaced Persons (DPs)—that is, those who during the war were either forcibly brought to Germany by the Nazis or fled the USSR of their own free will—there were among them some postwar defectors. As the authors acknowledge, the DP group "was supplemented by an appreciable but generally decreasing flow of persons fleeing from the Soviet occupation forces, from Soviet missions in western countries, and by an occasional person who fled directly from the Soviet Union, crossing through the intervening Iron Curtain territories in the course of his flight."[10]

It is not clear how many defectors there were among the three thousand questionnaire respondents. However, among the 329 extended interviews, 91 were conducted "with postwar refugees," that is, defectors. It is significant that the Harvard Project did not shun the defectors and appreciated their information. That information certainly contributed to the insights into the Soviet system that were gained as a result of the project. In the conclusion to *The Soviet Citizen*, Alex Inkeles sums up one of those insights:

> In the balance hangs the decision as to what the dominant cultural and political forms of human endeavor will be for the remainder of this century and perhaps beyond. It is perhaps only a little thing that separates the Soviet world from the West—freedom. Inside the Soviet Union there are some who ultimately are on our side. But they are a minority, perhaps a small one. Their ranks were first decimated by Stalin and later thinned by the refugee exodus. We had therefore better turn our face elsewhere, rest our hopes on other foundations than on the belief that the Soviet system

will mellow and abandon its long range goals of world domination... If we are not equal to the task, we will leave it to the Soviet Union to set a pattern of human existence for the next half-century.[11]

This was written more than two decades ago. In the years since, in spite of the rise of the dissident and human rights movement in the USSR, Soviet leaders have been successful in setting "the pattern of human existence" for many more millions of people throughout the world, thus proving the West not quite equal to the task of preserving freedom. Among several reasons for this failure of the West, one, not the least important, must be that the West has been putting more trust in the promises of the Soviet leaders than in the warnings of the defectors.[12]

2

WHAT HAVE DEFECTORS
WRITTEN ABOUT THEMSELVES?

Now we shall review a selection of thirteen major books produced by defectors themselves. The first six books—those by Viktor Kravchenko, Igor Gouzenko, Oksana Kasenkina, Grigory Klimov, Grigory Tokaev, and Peter Pirogov—focus on the Stalin era. The next five—written by Peter Deriabin, Nikolai Khokhlov, Vladimir and Evdokia Petrov, Aleksandr Kaznacheev, and Yury Krotkov—shed light on the USSR under Stalin and Khrushchev. The last two books—those by Leonid Vladimirov and Aleksey Myagkov—spotlight the USSR under Brezhnev.

In selecting these authors and books from a larger pool of literature produced by defectors, primary consideration was given to the ones whose descriptions are coextensive with the available KGB records, that is, those that fall between 1945 and 1969. It is hoped that these descriptions will provide a human dimension to the statistical language of Part Two, where the KGB Wanted List is discussed.[1] However, even though the majority of the selected authors are on the KGB Wanted List, no direct personal parallels will be drawn out of respect to the privacy of the individuals involved.

VIKTOR KRAVCHENKO'S *I CHOSE FREEDOM*

Chief engineer of a number of large steel plants and construction projects, Viktor Kravchenko was one of the heroes of the Stalinist industrialization. He met and sat in council with such Soviet leaders as Sergo Ordzhonikidze, Lazar Kaganovich, Ivan Tevosyan, and Aleksey Kosygin. When he was sent in 1943 to Washington as a member of the Soviet Purchasing Commission, which handled lend-lease operations, his recommendation was signed by Anastas Mikoyan. Although he had defected before the end of the war, his book, *I Chose Freedom*,[2] published in 1946, belongs to the postwar period, for it has established major themes and set the tone for much of the writing by postwar defectors.

When Kravchenko decided to break with the Soviet government on April 3, 1944, he did not turn himself in to the U.S. government; instead, he placed himself "under the protection of the American public opinion." He talked to the *New York Times*, which indeed published the news of his defection the next day. That was a wise decision, and it may have saved his life, because in the conditions of the wartime alliance the U.S. government would most likely have returned him to the USSR. It was also a symbolic decision, because many other Soviet defectors have thought of themselves as defecting not to any particular government but to the free world at large.

Kravchenko made it a point of honor not to disclose whatever military-related secrets he may have had, focusing instead on his principal disagreements with the Soviet regime. In a statement to the *Times*, he pointed out the unnaturalness of the alliance of Western democracies with Stalinist tyranny, warned the West against the two-facedness of Soviet foreign policy, and denounced the Soviet government for its failure to fulfill the promises made to the Soviet people during crucial moments of the war:

> While professing to seek the establishment of democracy in countries liberated from fascism, the Soviet government at home failed to take a single step toward granting elementary liberties to the Russian people.
>
> In the territories cleared of the Nazi invaders, the Soviet government is re-establishing its political regime of lawlessness and violence, while prisons and concentration camps function as before.
>
> The hope of political and social reforms cherished by the Russian people at the beginning of the war have proven to be empty illusions.[3]

The above charges against the Soviet government make Kravchenko a forerunner of the first wave of postwar defectors. They also anticipate the principal demands of the current dissident and human rights movement. By defecting, Kravchenko "had chosen a precarious freedom as against a comfortable enslavement."[4] He was fully aware of "the frightening consequences" of his action. During his first few years in freedom, he was constantly hounded by Soviet agents in the United States. Receiving death threats, he frequently changed addresses. Nonetheless, he went on writing his book in order to tell the truth about certain "great chunks of the Communist reality" that "have completely escaped American attention." These unknown "chunks" included "slave labor, police dictatorship, the massive periodic purges, the fantastically low standard of living, the great famine of 1932–33, the horrors of collectivization, the state-organized child labor."[5] As Aleksandr Solzhenitsyn would later acknowledge, Kravchenko's revelations about the Soviet system were just as important as his own, but they were largely ignored.[6]

Kravchenko's greatest disappointment after defection was the discovery of a strong pro-Soviet lobby in American intellectual circles.

> I was to learn slowly and incredulously, [that] those who venture to tell some truth about the Stalin tyranny, who speak up *for* the Russian people and against their oppressors, are discounted and dismissed and sometimes pilloried as "anti-Russian." I became aware that my resolve to escape into the free world and to use the freedom to defend my people would not be so simple as it had seemed at a distance. I realized that I must expect to be denounced and ridiculed by precisely those warm-hearted and high-minded foreigners on whose understanding and support I had counted.[7]

This unwillingness of the West to learn the truth about the USSR was to become a prominent theme of the later defectors. Like Kravchenko, they were to discover that "Stalinist propaganda in the outside world has been more successful than any of us in Russia suspected." When, at the instigation of the Soviets, a French communist weekly challenged the truthfulness of Kravchenko's book and suggested that it had been written by an American security service, Kravchenko filed a libel suit in a French court. The USSR sent several Soviet citizens to France to testify on behalf of the communist defenders. In effect, the trial set Kravchenko against the USSR. In March 1949, the court ruled in his favor. Never again did the Soviet government dare to challenge the truthfulness of a defector's testimony.[8]

A compulsion to tell the truth was both the paramount motive for Kravchenko's defection and the chief inspiration of his life in freedom. Having obtained his freedom, he never forgot about the bitter fate of his unfortunate compatriots and remained convinced that

> an understanding of the Russian reality by the democratic world is the precondition for my country's liberation from within. The weight of world opinion, the leverage of its spiritual support, now serving the Kremlin's despotism, must be diverted to quicken and aid the Russian aspirations for freedom.[9]

But while remaining a true Russian patriot, Kravchenko did not forget his duty toward the free world. He never tired of reminding it, as Solzhenitsyn and Sakharov do now, that no lasting peace is possible until "the liberation of the Russian masses from their tyrants." In February 1966, Kravchenko was found shot in his New York apartment, where he lived under an alias. His death was ruled a suicide. Ironically, the same newspaper that gave him a lease on life in the free world remembered him in an obituary not as one of the first to tell the truth about the USSR but as a man who had contributed to the hysteria of the cold war. It took another decade before "the weight of world opinion, the leverage of spiritual support" began to shift in favor of human rights in the USSR.

IGOR GOUZENKO'S *THE IRON CURTAIN*

Kravchenko's allegations about the two-facedness of the Soviets toward their Western allies were soon proven correct by another defector. On September 5, 1945, Igor Gouzenko, a cipher clerk at the Soviet Embassy in Ottawa, turned himself in to Canadian authorities. He was accompanied by his pregnant wife and their two-year-old son. At first, incredulous Canadian officials refused to believe his story. Only after they had examined the 109 secret documents that he had taken from the Embassy's safe did they realize that since World War II the Soviets had been operating a spy ring aimed at obtaining American and British atom bomb secrets. Gouzenko's defection was so significant for safeguarding the security of Western democracies that one contemporary observer exclaimed, "Perhaps never before in history has a 'little man' become a figure of such international consideration and importance."[10] Suffice it to say that Gouzenko's testimony led to the indictments of nuclear physicists Allan Nunn May and Klaus Fuchs, both of whom spied for the USSR in Britain, and Fred Rose, a member of the Canadian Parliament.

While hiding from Soviet agents somewhere in Canada "under an alias and, perhaps, in disguise," Gouzenko went on to write a book, *The Iron Curtain*, which was published in 1948. Only twenty-six years old at the time of defection, Gouzenko did not possess as much experience or knowledge of the inner workings of the Soviet system as Kravchenko. However, he portrayed largely the same picture of arbitrary purges, brutal collectivization, famine, poverty, and slave labor.

Like Kravchenko, he was deeply impressed by the panic in Moscow in October 1941, when the Germans stood at the gates of the capital. For a few days, civil order completely broke down; the Muscovites watched with hatred and despair as party and secret police officials tried to be the first to flee the capital. At that time, remarks Gouzenko, even "the Germans seemed to be secondary with many who were heaping their hatred on [the fleeing] NKVD people."[11]

Gouzenko devotes much attention to the sudden turnabout of Soviet propaganda after Stalin realized that the war could not be won under the worn-out communist slogans of "proletarian internationalism" and "class struggle."

"The words 'Communism' and 'Soviet' disappeared. Instead everything was spoken of as 'Russian.' Marxism was forgotten."[12] This sudden identification with Russian nationalism, observes Gouzenko, was completely hypocritical, because the communist rulers continued to manipulate the country from the sanctum of their privileged existence. Gouzenko insists that the Soviet regime is contrary to the true national aspirations of the Russian people, even though it knows how to exploit and distort Russian patriotism for its own ends.

Another prominent theme is that of social inequality in the allegedly classless Soviet society. "Never before has Russian soil supported such a class of parasites,"[13] writes Gouzenko about the opulent lifestyle of the Soviet elite, whom Milovan Djilas later decried in his book, *The New Class*. The theme of social inequality was later developed into a book by another defector, thanks to whom the term *nomenklatura* became standard among Western Sovietologists seeking to understand the Soviet power structure.[14]

Gouzenko's observations about the success of Soviet propaganda among opinion makers in the West are similar to those of Kravchenko:

> For a long time after my arrival in Canada, I delved into press files and 'I Saw Russia' books. I was constantly amazed that so many seemingly reputable literary minds could have been so pathetically duped by the Soviet propaganda ruses.[15]

He was particularly amazed to discover that among those duped were a large number of Jews. Gouzenko knew from his own experience that neither Soviet Jews nor their Western co-religionists were looked upon kindly at the Embassy or anywhere else in high Soviet institutions. To this topic he devotes a whole chapter, "The Soviet and the Jews," which is especially worth reading now, when the mass exodus of Soviet Jews from the USSR has become a manifest chapter of world history.

Gouzenko's book was prefaced with editorial praise of "the profound, unusual and daring tribute paid our free way of life by Igor Gouzenko. He deliberately risked his life to espouse what we so casually accept as our birthright. By this very act he helped to safeguard our great heritage of freedom."[16] As to the accuracy of Gouzenko's testimony, it was confirmed by "the highest tribunals of Canada." Both Gouzenko and his wife were included in the KGB Wanted List, and both were condemned, in absentia, to death. In June 1982, Igor Gouzenko died near Toronto, Canada, of natural causes, at the age of sixty-three.

OKSANA KASENKINA'S *LEAP TO FREEDOM*

In her bid for freedom, Oksana Kasenkina, a fifty-two-year-old biology teacher assigned to teach the children of Soviet diplomats in New York, leaped out of a third-floor window at the Soviet Consulate on August 12, 1948. As a result of the fall, she nearly lost her life, but she was saved by American doctors. Her *Leap to Freedom*, as she titled her book (published in 1949), would have been unnecessary were it not for the State Department, which had prevented the serving of the writ of habeas corpus for her release from de facto imprisonment at the Consulate after her previous unsuccessful attempt at defection. In her book, Kasenkina accuses the State Department of caving in to Soviet blackmail "implying a danger of war."[17]

Although considerably older than either Kravchenko or Gouzenko, Kasenkina was influenced by both in her decision to defect, thus proving that defection can be contagious. Once she accidentally picked up a Russian émigré newspaper and found an article about Kravchenko. What affected her most was not Kravchenko's description of Soviet horrors, with which she was familiar first-hand, but "that the world at large had no idea" of them. "It was excruciating to learn," writes Kasenkina, "how widely the Soviet Union was considered some sort of latter-day paradise!"[18] When she later sneaked out to see *The Iron Curtain*, a film about Gouzenko, her decision to reach out for "wonderful, ecstatic freedom" matured.

Kasenkina was not a disillusioned child of the revolution, as Kravchenko was. Nor did she bring with her any secrets, as Gouzenko did. She was a plain person who suffered through the horrors of Soviet reality as millions of others did. She was old enough to remember, with gratitude, the Hoover Relief Administration's efforts to save starving Soviet citizens in the early 1920s. In 1933 she lost her only daughter in "a man-made famine" that devastated the Ukraine in the wake of Stalin's collectivization. In 1937 her husband perished in the purges. Then the war swallowed her only son. It was only thanks to her teaching excellence that she was chosen to join the Soviet mission in New York in 1946. Her description of the lifestyle of Soviet diplomats, including Andrei Gromyko and his family, can be profitably read even now.

A deeply religious person, Kasenkina saw communism in apocalyptic terms as "an insane worship," in which Russia is but "a vast sacrificial altar, claiming believers and non-believers [in communism] alike."[19] Until her death in 1960 in Miami, Florida, Kasenkina hoped "that Christianity will once more become united, a step so vital and essential for the ultimate defeat of totalitarian Communism."[20]

PETER PIROGOV'S *WHY I ESCAPED*

Three months after Kasenkina's leap to freedom, the contagion of defection struck the Soviet air force. On October 9, 1948, Peter Pirogov and Anatoly Barsov (also known as Borzov) flew their fighter plane from the Western

Ukraine to the American occupation zone in Austria. The two made the attempt only after they had heard on a Voice of America broadcast that, in conjunction with Kasenkina's defection, "Secretary of State [George] Marshall declared that within the territories of the United States the police could not interfere in a man's private life without trial."[21]

After coming to the United States, the bachelor Pirogov adjusted well and immediately set out to write a book, *Why I Escaped*, published in 1950. Barsov, on the other hand, who had left behind a wife and toddler son, fell prey to the promise of forgiveness readily offered by the Soviet Embassy in Washington and returned to the USSR. A later defector reported that Barsov was executed without having seen his son.[22]

The book's chief interest lies in the fact that its author is, in the words of his translator, "in every sense, a typical Russian and a true product of the Bolshevik system." Born into a peasant family in 1920, Pirogov ran the usual gamut of Soviet indoctrination, becoming first a Leninist Pioneer, then a Komsomol (Communist Youth League) member and a party candidate. The indoctrination, however, did not obliterate his memory of how, after collectivization, the Russian peasant "walked the fields of Mother Russia, head bowed, lips tightly sealed, and his God burning in his heart."[23]

Having served in the Soviet armed forces from 1939 until his defection, Pirogov sheds much light on the mood of Soviet soldiers prior to, during, and after the war. Especially interesting is his description of the situation in the Far East, where he served part of the war. According to Pirogov, there, on the borders of Manchuria, "the mixed population, composed of every possible racial group, hated the regime even more than people in the rest of the country" and only waited for a Japanese invasion to rise against the system of concentration camps.[24]

Toward the end of the war, Pirogov wound up in Germany, where he was dismayed by the plundering, looting, raping, and senseless slaughter of civilians by Soviet troops. After the war, Pirogov found himself doing the bidding of those who during the war had stayed in the rear: he had to take part in the suppression of the population in the Western Ukraine. He reached the height of his career on May Day, 1948, when he took part in the air show over Moscow, led by Stalin's son, Vasily. Pirogov frankly admits that, though he was a distinguished flier, he was bestowed the honor because he had cooperated with SMERSH (a Russian acronym for that branch of the Soviet security police that was charged with spying on the Soviet armed forces) in spying on his fellow soldiers.

A few months later, Pirogov dared to challenge Soviet air defenses. He was fully aware of the risk he was taking. He knew that any airplane deviating from its prescribed course would be shot at. Nonetheless, he took the risk. For him, it was a gesture of defiance against those "who stole our fatherland from us, who converted it into a huge concentration camp, who appropriated to themselves our victory at the very moment when we brought the enemy's banners to the doors of the Kremlin."[25]

GRIGORY KLIMOV'S *THE TERROR MACHINE*

Grigory Klimov belongs to the largest category of postwar defectors: those who ran away from Soviet occupation forces in Germany. Although he defected in January 1947, at a time when many Soviet defectors were routinely turned back to the USSR by Western allies, he managed to stay on, and in 1951 his book, *Berliner Kreml* (The Kremlin of Berlin), was published in West Germany. The title refers to the township of Karlshorst near Berlin, where the headquarters of the Soviet Military Administration (SMA) of Germany were located. In 1953, the book appeared in English under the title, *The Terror Machine: The Inside Story of the Soviet Administration in Germany*.[26]

Klimov was able to tell the "inside story" thanks to his former work at SMA headquarters as a staff officer, interpreter, and supervisor of the electronics industry in East Germany. From the very beginning he was advised that the SMA is but "the most advanced line of the post-war front." Attending the meetings of the Allied Control Commission in Berlin, he was struck that whereas the Western allies "welcomed us as joint victors and sincere allies in war and peace...we, on the other hand, regarded the 'Allies' as the opposing party...They believed that Marx and Lenin were dead. But now the shadows of these two men stood behind us."[27]

As far as Klimov was concerned, he had some other shadows to worry about—those of the secret police, the MVD (the Russian initials stand for the Ministry of Internal Affairs). Klimov reports how Marshal Zhukov, whom soldiers loved "as the savior of our fatherland," was replaced in March 1946 by Marshal Sokolovsky, who was more subservient to the Kremlin. From that time on, Anastas Mikoyan was the actual "viceroy," and the real power in Karlshorst belonged to MVD General Ivan Serov. With bitterness, Klimov describes how former combat soldiers in the SMA were gradually replaced by party hacks and the security police who had stayed in the rear during the war.

The MVD was also at work terrorizing the Germans into submission to the three men who were to form the future government of East Germany: Grotewohl, Pieck, and Ulbricht. The Germans nicknamed this triumvirate the GPU (one of the previous names of the Soviet secret police) for their cooperation with the Soviets.

Having come to the same conclusion as Pirogov, namely, that the hard-won victory over the Nazis was stolen by Stalin and his henchmen in the party and secret police, Klimov decided that he had no future in his fatherland. He argues that his disillusionment was typical of thousands of Soviet soldiers, and he goes so far as to say that "Every Soviet citizen who has seen Europe is lost to the Soviet regime."[28] Were it not for "a secret agreement between the American governor and the Soviet command, under which both parties bound themselves to hand over deserters,"[29] Klimov says, the West would have been flooded with Soviet army deserters. Klimov's own encounter with the American authorities after his defection has left a bitter taste with him that especially shows in his later writings.

GRIGORY TOKAEV'S *STALIN MEANS WAR*

A former professor at the Zhukovsky Air Force Engineering Academy, Tokaev was one of the foremost Soviet experts on aerodynamics. When he defected with his wife and daughter in November 1947, he was adviser on aviation matters to Marshal Sokolovsky, the head of SMA in East Germany. In his 1951 book, *Stalin Means War*, Tokaev described the subjugation of East Germany as "a microcosm of Stalin's plan for world conquest."[30]

As an aviation expert, Tokaev was intimately involved with the so-called Sänger Project. Sänger was a German scientist who in 1944 had approached Hitler with the proposal to develop a "piloted rocket plane." The Nazis did not have time for such experiments, but when a copy of Sänger's manuscript fell into Soviet hands, it caught the fancy of the Kremlin. As a person familiar with Sänger's writings, Tokaev was summoned to Moscow. There he was briefed at a number of meetings in the Kremlin attended by Politburo members and such dignitaries as Dmitry Ustinov (who died in 1984 as Defense Minister) and Artyom Mikoyan, the son of Anastas Mikoyan and one of the designers of Soviet MIG fighters. In spite of Tokaev's less than enthusiastic appraisal of the feasibility of the project, at the final meeting Stalin himself gave his go-ahead for the formation of a special commission for the purpose of producing a rocket plane "capable of dropping atomic bombs over New York and London."[31] Ivan Serov, the MVD boss of East Germany, was put in charge of it, and Tokaev was appointed his deputy. Thus Tokaev become involved in the "brain search" operations, in which he implicates the highest hierarchy in the Kremlin. The operations included the attempts to abduct the German aircraft designers, Sänger and Kurt Tank.

It was in the process of trying to lure Kurt Tank into coming to Moscow that Tokaev began to feel that he himself was being entrapped by MVD agents who suspected him of conspiring with Tank. When he was again summoned to Moscow, he knew that "a return to the capital would be suicide," and he decided to defect. He decided to defect not only to save his life but also because "it seemed vital to me that the world should be warned of the conspiracy being hatched against it in the Kremlin."[32] However, knowing that the Allies "had handed back quite a number of defectors,"[33] he did not even seek their assistance, but instead defected through the intermediary of a third country.

Tokaev is the only postwar defector who not only suggests the existence of organized opposition to Stalin's regime but also claims that he himself belonged to an underground group that had followers in the highest ranks of the party, the armed forces, and the MVD. In contrast to previous authors who were either ethnic Russians or expressed a Russian self-awareness, Tokaev is a proud son of the Ossetians, a small, predominantly Muslim, nation in the North Caucasus. He suggests that the underground group to which he belonged was opposed to the postwar Soviet drift toward "a fusion of the old Russian chauvinism and Marxist-Leninist phraseology."[34]

In his book *Soviet Imperialism*, published at the time of Khrushchev's peaceful overtures to the West, Tokaev warned against accepting them at face value. He also predicted that the Soviets "will endeavor to split the western nations by stirring up local and national hatreds, such as that between the French and Germans, or between Europe and the United States." "By playing on these feelings," he explained, "Soviet diplomacy hopes to obtain a peaceful disruption of western defenses, after which the border countries will be brought piecemeal under Soviet influence and control without a major conflict of any kind."[35]

Tokaev lives in England and teaches aerodynamics at a university. He remains on the KGB Wanted List.

PETER DERIABIN'S *THE SECRET WORLD*

Within a year of Stalin's death in March 1953, the Soviet State Security[36] itself was riddled with defections. One of these defectors was Major of State Security Peter Deriabin, who escaped from his post at the Soviet Embassy in Vienna, Austria, on February 15, 1954. He was then thirty-three. Unlike the previous authors, Deriabin was an insider of the secret police apparatus. He described it in his book, *The Secret World*, published in 1959.[37] A peasant's son, he left behind him a long and varied career. He had taught history in high school and fought in World War II as an officer and political commissar, before he graduated from a SMERSH school at the end of the war. From that time on he rose from a case officer and surveillance chief in a provincial town to a personnel chief for the Kremlin's bodyguards, party secretary and deputy chief of the Austro-German section of the Foreign Intelligence headquarters in Moscow, and chief of the SK (Sovetskaia Koloniia) section charged with the surveillance of Soviet citizens in Austria.

His disillusionment grew with each successive step of his career. As political commissar he hated deceiving his soldiers about phony Soviet victories when these soldiers had no air cover. As a cadet at the SMERSH school, he was revolted at the task of rewrapping butter stamped "Made in USA" with wrappings bearing a Soviet trademark. A party member since 1941, he knew that he owed his career to slavishly following the party line. While serving with the Kremlin's bodyguards, he enrolled at the Institute of Marxism-Leninism and then saw "the crookedness of the current Soviet ideology even when judged by Marx's own premises."[38] Tired of the dirty job of spying on his colleagues, he asked to be transferred to Foreign Intelligence. But there, too, he had to do the dirty work. He was involved, for instance, in the planning of the kidnapping of Dr. Walter Linse, the head of the Association of Free German Jurists, in West Berlin on July 8, 1952. Ironically, when he was transferred to Vienna, Deriabin's last assignment was to investigate the defection of one of his charges in Vienna, a certain Skachkov. While investigating the defection, he felt that "the lie was reaching the point beyond endurance" and absconded himself.

The book reflects Deriabin's varied experience with both domestic and foreign spying. Appended with charts and copies of official documents, it offers a systematic overview of the structure and mode of operation of various branches of the State Security system. Deriabin emphasizes that "The basic goal of the State Security is to control the thoughts and curb the individual aspirations of the Soviet people, harnessing them to the regime's prescribed goals."[39] The task of preventing defections across the borders is entrusted to border troops, numbering over 200,000 men.[40] "Not to be confused with border patrols which exist in every free country," Deriabin explains, these "are set apart from the regular army and operate on the frontiers of the Iron Curtain as a law unto itself."[41] Even inside Foreign Intelligence there is a special section whose main functions are, first, "to infiltrate, sabotage, and destroy all active organizations of Soviet citizens who have managed to escape their native country" and, second, "to persuade or bludgeon" them into returning to the USSR.[42]

While in the West foreign intelligence is usually understood in the restricted sense of gathering military and political information about a hostile country, "to the Soviet mind, intelligence makes policy, or at least State Security does." Deriabin calls it "an active aggressive political arm of the regime," and he describes its purpose as "not only to acquire information and to prevent others from acquiring information, but to manufacture information, destroy sources of foreign information, terrorize, assassinate, and proselytize, as occasion demands." In short, its purpose is "to subvert the political and social life of a foreign country."[43]

His book appeared during the heyday of Western illusions about Khrushchev's de-Stalinization and peaceful coexistence drive, and Deriabin admits that there has been a significant decrease in the scale of violence and intimidation perpetrated by the State Security. Nonetheless, he warns that "the beast has changed his spots slightly, but he has not gone away."[44]

NIKOLAI KHOKHLOV'S *IN THE NAME OF CONSCIENCE*

On February 18, 1954, three days after Deriabin's defection in Vienna, Nikolai Khokhlov, captain of state security and the commander of a traveling executioners' squad, entered the apartment of a Russian émigré leader in Frankfurt, West Germany. Khokhlov told him that he had been sent to kill him but instead decided to defect. Khokhlov gives an account of his defection in the book *In the Name of Conscience*, published in 1959.[45] Unlike Deriabin, whose career covered different branches of State Security, Khokhlov worked all his adult life in Special Bureau Number One, or Spetsburo, which Deriabin describes as "the most sinister office of the State Security's Foreign Intelligence branch." The Spetsburo was responsible for acts of violence overseas. Explains Deriabin, "Whenever possible, the State Security gets local gangsters to do its overseas dirty work. But in delicate cases, one or two Spetsburo officers are dispatched from Moscow to do the regime's job."[46] Khokhlov's "delicate" assignment was to "liquidate" Georgy Okolovich, the leader of NTS, a Russian émigré organization headquartered in Frankfurt.

Khokhlov was well prepared for the assignment. Recruited to the State Security in 1941, he was one of the first Russians trained for operations behind front lines in a German army uniform. He took part in one of the most spectacular *partizan* exploits of World War II, the assassination of Wilhelm Kube, the Nazi governor of Belorussia. After the war, Khokhlov was sent on several covert missions in Romania, Austria, Italy, France, and Denmark. After Soviet control over Eastern Europe was secured, Khokhlov took part in the implementation of a new order given to the Spetsburo: "To establish combat operations for weakening the network of military bases of the American Command in Europe."[47] However, in the wake of Stalin's death and especially after the uprising in East Berlin in June 1953, Stalin's successors came to fear the possibility of popular revolt inside the USSR and shifted the emphasis to "the struggle against anti-Soviet organizations both within the USSR and abroad."[48]

High on the list of those anti-Soviet organizations was the NTS, which was described as "the only émigré organization actively functioning on the territory of the Soviet Union . . . sending their people for underground propaganda of an armed revolt."[49] On January 9, 1954, Khokhlov received final instructions and blessings from Aleksandr Panyushkin, then head of Foreign Intelligence, and was off to Frankfurt under the assumed name of Walter

Oesch, a Swiss citizen. He was to lead a team of two other agents ordered to kill Okolovich.

Now Khokhlov faced a moral dilemma: either let the man be murdered by his team or defect. He knew that if he failed to carry out his orders, he would imperil his own safety in the USSR. He also knew that when he hunted the Nazis, he hunted enemies of the Russian people. But Okolovich was a Russian patriot. During his stay in Germany, Khokhlov came across *Possev*, one of the NTS publications, and when he saw the two slogans of NTS, "For Russia" and "God is in Truth, Not in Force" (the latter ascribed to St. Aleksandr Nevsky), he came to feel that "NTS was my organization."[50]

Thus, Khokhlov's chief motivation for defection was not merely to obtain freedom for himself, but to join the NTS in its struggle for the liberation of Russia from communism. In this he was influenced by his wife Yanina, to whom his book is dedicated and who emerges as its true heroine. An engineer by education, she proved impervious to Marxist-Leninist indoctrination at school and managed to retain a deeply Christian outlook on life that she inherited from her parents. When informed about his deadly mission, she not only advised him against taking a man's life but made it clear that she would consider him a coward unless his defection was motivated by a desire to fight for the liberation of all people under communism. Her advice was self-sacrificial, for she knew she would face the bitter fate of a defector's wife left behind.

In a sense, Khokhlov defected then not to the United States but to NTS. However, when, on the advice of Okolovich, he approached the American authorities in Frankfurt and offered his cooperation in foiling a Soviet spy ring in West Germany, they refused to give credence to his story. Only after he had coaxed the Americans into arresting the other assassins (who later corroborated his story in court) did they begin to take him seriously, but it was too late. On April 13, 1954, Dr. Aleksandr Trushnovich, member of the NTS and chairman of the West Berlin Rescue Committee, was kidnapped and taken to the Soviet zone. Khokhlov also accuses the Americans of bungling a plan to extricate his wife and son from Moscow.

In spite of his bitter disappointment with American officials, he came to the United States and for two years used every opportunity to tell the truth about the USSR. The U.S. government dispatched two diplomatic notes to Moscow on behalf of his family, but he never saw his wife and son again. After the uprising in Hungary in 1956, he returned to Europe to "make my direct contribution to the revolutionary movement in the battle for the liberation of Russia." On September 15, 1957, during a conference in Frankfurt, he was poisoned with radioactive thallium that Soviet agents managed to slip into his coffee cup. Fortunately, he drank but a sip, and the American doctors were able to save his life.

In 1958 Khokhlov went to South Vietnam to help the Ngo Dinh Diem government to set up an anticommunist guerrilla movement. However, when it became clear that the Americans would block any attempt to expand operations to North Vietnam, he resigned his position in 1961. In 1963 he went to South Korea to take charge of NTS broadcasting to Russia. Again his discussions with South Korean officials on the matter of setting up an anticommunist guerrilla movement displeased the Americans. He then gave up his hope of the Americans ever allowing him to actively resist communism, and he returned to the United States to further his education. He earned his Ph.D. in psychology and is now a professor at a state college in California, where he specializes in parapsychology.

Khokhlov's interest in parapsychology is not accidental, for he fears that the free world is unable to counter Soviet moves for the control of the hearts and minds of free people. He puts his trust in the "eternal laws" as they are expressed "in the tablets of Moses, the precepts of Christ, the lines of the Koran, and the sayings of Buddha." Says Khokhlov: "The world is built upon them. The Soviet power has attempted to subvert them to its own use. But this is against the laws of the cosmos, and that is why the Soviet power is bound to go to its doom. For men are the children of God, and not of the party or the state."[51] Khokhlov remains on the KGB Wanted List, and there will be a discussion of his published entry in Part Two.

VLADIMIR AND EVDOKIA PETROV'S *EMPIRE OF FEAR*

While Khokhlov was struggling to convince the Americans of his credibility, in another corner of the world Australian intelligence was trying to induce the defection of Vladimir Petrov, consul and third secretary of the Soviet Embassy in Canberra, who had shown an unusual amount of curiosity about the land of the kangaroo. Only after he had finally defected on April 2, 1954, did Petrov reveal that he was actually a lieutenant colonel of the MVD and chief of spy operations in Australia. Two weeks later he was joined in defection by his wife, Evdokia, who had combined her secretarial duties to the ambassador with covert duties as captain of the MVD.

The Petrovs' case is perhaps the least ideologically motivated case of defection. Neither Vladimir nor Evdokia was driven by the same passion to tell the truth that motivated Kravchenko's defection. Unlike Khokhlov, they did not face the moral dilemma of either killing someone or defecting. They certainly did not defect in order to fight against communism. The overriding reason for their defection was fear, the title of their jointly written book, *Empire of Fear*, published in 1956. "Fear is the essential instrument of Communist domination," say the Petrovs. "Fear is the master wherever the power of the

Kremlin can make itself felt. That fear ruled our lives in the Embassy at Canberra and drove us to seek refuge and freedom from fear in Australia."[52] Having freed themselves from fear, the Petrovs say, "we did not set out to write an anti-Soviet book, but to tell a true story, whatever picture might emerge."[53] Only by telling the truth, they felt, could they help the West to understand the reality of the USSR and to find "something better and stronger, which can free the whole world, and the people of Russia, from the bondage of fear."[54]

Vladimir Petrov's twenty-one-year career in the secret police began in 1933 when he became a cipher clerk in the OGPU building on Lubianka Square. He was soon to learn about the intricacies of Soviet spying during the Spanish Civil War. In 1937 he got his first foreign assignment as cipher chief at Soviet Military Headquarters in Sinkiang, China. There he took part in the suppression of the uprising of the native Muslims against the Soviets and their puppet Chinese government in Sinkiang. Upon his return to Moscow, he was awarded with the order of the Red Star. Working at NKVD headquarters in Moscow in the late 1930s, he was a silent reader of the messages of mass terror in his own country. At the beginning of the war he was made chief of cipher communications for the whole Gulag system, and for that job he was rewarded in 1942 with another foreign assignment, this time to Sweden, where he stayed until 1947. While in Sweden he handled the recruitment of "illegal" agents and, after the end of the war, the repatriation of Soviet citizens interned in Sweden. Above all, he was charged with the job of spying on the Embassy personnel, including the ambassador herself, Madame Aleksandra Kollontai. In 1947 Petrov was transferred to the Committee of Information (K.I., Komitet Informatsii), headquartered in Moscow, where he supervised spying on the crews of Soviet ships sailing on the Danube River through several East European countries. Evdokia, whom he married in 1940, followed him in these assignments, doing similar jobs at a lower level.

In 1951, both of them were rewarded with appointments to the Embassy in Canberra. Under cover of diplomatic immunity, Consul Petrov organized the "illegal" spy network, of which he was acting resident from February 1952 until his defection. The term "illegal" is used for those agents who work without the "legal" cover of diplomatic immunity. "The vital importance of the 'illegal' system," explains Petrov, "is that it can continue to operate in time of war, after diplomatic representatives have been withdrawn."[55] In addition to spying on Australia, Petrov did his usual job of spying on the Embassy personnel. However, after the demise of Beria in July 1953, both Petrovs found themselves without the usual support of their chain of command, MVD headquarters in Moscow. They were even accused of trying to form a "Beria faction" at the embassy. They knew that the accusations were groundless, but fear of returning to Moscow proved crucial in their decisions to defect.

"In all my twenty-one years as a professional State Security Officer," says

Petrov, "I never came across one authentic case of foreign espionage in the Soviet Union in peace-time." Nonetheless, "thousands were accused of espionage and shot." His conclusion echoes that of Deriabin: "the vast machinery of State Security in the Soviet Union is chiefly employed not against foreign espionage . . . but against the Soviet people themselves."[56]

That the Petrovs did not originally intend to defect does not mean that they had not seen any evil in the Soviet system. On the contrary, Vladimir, who is of peasant origin, describes collectivization as a holocaust visited by Soviet rulers on their native land. The theme of nostalgia for the prerevolutionary way of life of the Russian peasants counterpoints the theme of fear. Both Petrovs seem to be more representative of average Soviet citizens than the other authors. Their story makes one wonder how many "internal defectors" may be found in the USSR, not just in labor camps but in the ranks of State Security.

In 1956, when many in the West were hopeful of fundamental changes in the USSR, the Petrovs argued that "the Soviet government, having seized power by revolution, has set up a machine unique in its elaboration to ensure that no second revolution shall be possible." The Petrovs, who were part of that machine, saw "little hope of a spontaneous popular revolt among the divided and intimidated masses of the Soviet people."[57]

Ten years later, in 1966, one still could expect neither any fundamental changes from within the system nor a revolt. But the names of Pasternak and Solzhenitsyn were known throughout the world, and the trials of Daniel and Sinyavsky were met with universal indignation. In another ten years, Andrei Sakharov was the Nobel Peace Prize winner, and an American President openly proclaimed his support for human rights in the USSR. But the warning to the West that the Petrovs issued then remains timely now: "The rulers of the Soviet Union respect only one thing—strength . . . [And they] have no respect at all for those whom they can intimidate or deceive."[58]

As of 1969, both Petrovs were on the KGB Wanted List, both condemned to death.

ALEKSANDR KAZNACHEEV'S *INSIDE A SOVIET EMBASSY*

Unlike Vladimir Petrov, who was trained as a KGB operative but worked abroad posing as a diplomat, Aleksandr Kaznacheev was trained as a diplomat but was involved in KGB work abroad. He defected from the Soviet Embassy in Rangoon, Burma, on June 23, 1959, and his book, *Inside a Soviet Embassy*, was published in 1962.[59]

The book's chief significance lies in the fact that, only twenty-seven years old when he defected, Kaznacheev was a product of the post-Stalin era and the first major defector to offer insights into Khrushchev's policy of "peaceful coexistence." Moreover, as a specialist on Southeast Asia with knowledge of both Chinese and Burmese, Kaznacheev sheds much light on the history of the Sino-Soviet conflict and on Soviet strategy vis-à-vis Third World countries.

Kaznacheev studied at the Moscow Oriental Institute. When the institute was closed, as an outstanding student of Chinese, he was transferred to the elite Moscow Institute of International Relations, from which he graduated in 1957. The goal of the institute, says Kaznacheev, was not only to produce well-educated specialists in international relations "but to make them the first-line fighters on the cold war's numerous fronts." There was much emphasis on language training, in his case Burmese, Mandarin, and English, because "there can be no good cold-war fighter without a thorough knowledge of some foreign languages," explains Kaznacheev.[60] Still, about 60 percent of the total curriculum was devoted to Marxist-Leninist indoctrination.

In spite of the indoctrination, the mood of the country after Stalin's death was such that "the neo-Leninist illusions that Russia should return to the principles of Lenin and pure Communism began to spread among intellectuals and youth." However, Khrushchev's denunciation of Stalin's crimes and the political unrest in Poland and Hungary "destroyed neo-Leninist illusions and had the most profound effect on all Soviet people." Kaznacheev recalls that the students of Moscow University's physics and mathematics department greeted the Hungarian revolution by sending to the Central Committee of the CPSU a resolution containing "some incredible demands: jamming of foreign broadcasts must end; Western newspapers and other publications must be allowed free entry into the country; and—most unbelievable!—a two-party system must be introduced in the Soviet Union."[61] As I myself was at the time a student at Moscow University, I can only confirm Kaznacheev's observations about the restiveness of the period that eventually gave birth to the dissident and human rights movement.

Due to his knowledge of a little-known language, Kaznacheev was assigned abroad immediately upon his graduation. Although, unlike Petrov, he served at the lower ranks, he had a good opportunity to observe the inner workings of the Embassy as he did "all the dirty paper work." Moreover, after his recruitment by the KGB in 1958, he became a member of Political Intelligence (Politicheskaia Razvedka), whose primary objective was "penetration and subversion of local regimes, direct and active participation in the struggle between different political parties."

For a while, the Soviets tried to pursue a so-called friendly neutrality policy in Southeast Asia. They gave economic assistance to native regimes as long as they remained anti-Western, "friendly-neutral" toward the USSR, and legalized indigenous Communist parties. "We gave up the idea of Communist armed rebellion and instead encouraged the native Communists to set up legal organizations and penetrate the nationalist political parties, with the aim of peaceful takeover through parliamentary processes."[62] However, Peking refused to adhere to this policy until a secret "gentlemen's agreement" was made, according to which the Soviets recognized the whole of Southeast Asia—Vietnam, Cambodia, Laos, Malaya, Thailand, and Burma—as the Chinese sphere of influence. In return, the Chinese recognized India, Afghanistan, and all of Asia to the west of them as the Soviet sphere. However, as early as 1958-1959, it became clear that the agreement would not work and that "Southeast Asia is going to be the main trouble spot in our relations with China."[63]

Kaznacheev devotes considerable attention to such methods of Soviet "psychological warfare" as planting news (produced by a KGB office in Moscow and translated by him into Burmese) into local newspapers as if the stories had originated in neighboring countries. Although he describes Soviet propaganda as "crude" and "primitive," he admits that "for an underdeveloped country such approach seemed to work." Referring to the American approach of publishing "nothing but information, leaving it to the reader to make the final judgment," Kaznacheev says that such an approach would not work in an underdeveloped country "where the majority of the people are still lacking political experience and sophistication." Thus, in Burma, Soviet propaganda went practically unchallenged. "We in the Soviet Embassy only wondered if Americans would ever recognize the irrefutable fact that propaganda is one of the strongest weapons in political and psychological warfare."[64]

Although Kaznacheev had ceased to believe in communism even before he went to Burma, he explains his defection by falling in love with the Burmese way of life, Buddhist philosophy, and Oriental mysticism in general.[65] One might even say that he defected not to the West but to the East. In his opinion, despite Soviet propaganda success in developing countries, the Marxist-Leninist ideology is just as inimical to native philosophies of the Third World as it is to Western democracies. It was only for security reasons that Kaznacheev could not stay in his beloved Burma and sought political asylum in the United States. That Burma remains an independent country is due in no small degree to his revelations about Soviet designs on this part of the world.

Condemned to death by a Moscow criminal court for revealing "secret information about the work at a Soviet embassy," Kaznacheev remains on the KGB Wanted List.

YURY KROTKOV'S *I AM FROM MOSCOW*

Yury Krotkov was an established Soviet playwright whose name has been familiar to me since high school. He was best known in the USSR for his anti-American play, *John, Soldier of Peace*, which was widely staged throughout the country. Therefore, his defection in England in September 1963 was as shocking to the Soviet establishment as it was exhilarating to me, especially since it came within a year after my own defection. Like myself, he belongs to a growing category of defectors who may be called "nonreturners" (*nevozvrashchentsy*), that is, those Soviet citizens who travel abroad with official permission but then choose not to return to the USSR.

Krotkov's first postdefection book, *I Am From Moscow*, appeared in 1967.[66] Unlike other authors, Krotkov tells little about his personal background,[67] but it is clear that he belonged to the privileged few, since his father was a sort of court painter for Stalin. He focuses instead on the month preceding his selection for a tourist trip to England. Although Soviet tourism is formally sponsored by Intourist, Krotkov says it is actually under the control of three organizations: the Central Committee of the CPSU, which selects the candidates; the Ministry of Foreign Trade, which supplies them with convertible currency; and the KGB, which provides the security clearance for those chosen, watches their steps abroad, and interrogates them upon return. The selection process is so rigorous that Intourist usually winds up with the same "safe" people who are unlikely to defect because they have a high stake in Soviet society. They usually belong to the cream of the Soviet intelligentsia, even though some token "distinguished workers" and "masters of socialist fields" (peasants) are also included.

Krotkov goes on to describe two types of Soviet tourism abroad: ordinary and special. Whereas the ordinary tourist groups have no particular assignment other than showing the flag, the special groups are sent to represent the Soviet view at various cultural, political, commercial, and athletic events. "The Union of Soviet Societies for Friendship with Foreign Countries staffs its own special groups which, besides tourism, conduct propaganda work abroad, something which is considered . . . a most honorable mission."[68] As I myself was a member of such a special propaganda team sent to Sweden, I can confirm the truthfulness of his description of the selection process, including an appearance before the Exit Commission of the Central Committee, "just like diplomatic officials."

Even after landing on foreign soil, a Soviet tourist continues to feel perilously close to home, because he or she is constantly watched by disguised KGB agents, who either come along with the group or are supplied by the Soviet Embassy of the host country. This means, of course, that even a nonreturner's defection usually involves more than simply failing to return: one has to escape from fellow travelers who jealously watch each other, since they are liable for not reporting an intended defection or not interfering with it when it occurs.

"A defector . . . what kind of a phenomenon is he?" asks Krotkov. He explains that the need to defect arises directly from the absence of the right to emigrate. "A Russian cannot emigrate in the normal way. That simple act, the ancient common prerogative of all people, is, according to Soviet law, a form of treason, a betrayal of the motherland; in other words, the most heinous of crimes." Although Krotkov admits that there are some "publicity seekers and opportunists" among defectors, he insists that the essence of defection is determined by those defectors whose primary motives are ideological. Lest one underestimate the "historical phenomenon" of defection, Krotkov calls it "the most vulnerable spot in the policies of the Communist leaders" and "proof of the existence of an insoluble conflict" in the system itself.[69] "If the borders of our motherland are closed," says Krotkov, "all is not right with our motherland. After all, even Hitler did not forbid emigration."[70] Defection is a form of individual resistance to the attempt of Soviet leaders "somehow to lock up the spirit of freedom." Krotkov indicates the scope of this resistance by saying that his own defection was inspired not by Rudolf Nureyev, a ballet dancer whose defection in the early 1960s created a sensation, but by millions of the Displaced Persons who, after World War II, refused to return to the USSR.

Krotkov's own motives for defection include a desire to be "a genuine, creative writer." Not having "sufficient strength of spirit" to engage in "active struggle," as his hero Boris Pasternak did, Krotkov chose defection "so that I can at least say to myself: 'I have ceased lying and being a coward... Now I am a human being,' for, until now, I have not been a human being."[71]

LEONID VLADIMIROV'S *THE RUSSIAN SPACE BLUFF*

Werner von Braun, the late head of the American space program, hailed Leonid Vladimirov's book, *The Russian Space Bluff: The Inside Story of the Soviet Drive to the Moon*, published in 1973, as "fascinating, informative and worthy of a wide readership in the United States."[72] The author's real name is Leonid Finkelshtein; he was an editor of a popular science magazine before he defected from a Soviet tourist group in London on June 22, 1966. As he explains, he replaced his Jewish name with the Russian-sounding pen name, Vladimirov, in order to facilitate his work back in the USSR, and he has taken it along into defection. He is the first in our series to defect during Brezhnev's rule.

The book follows the development of the Soviet space program from 1957, when the first Sputnik was launched, to 1966, when Vladimirov defected. In a flashback, Vladimirov describes the origins of Soviet research into jet propulsion in the early 1930s and recounts its survival (barely) of the purges of 1937–1938, its continuation in special research prisons during the war, its reinforcement with German rocket designs and designers after the war, and its maturation in secret research settlements founded by Stalin's State Security chief, Lavrenty Beria.

Vladimirov claims that, at the time of his defection in 1966, he "knew for certain that the USSR had quietly abandoned all dreams of engaging in a 'moon race' with the United States" and that the Americans "would be the first to set foot on the Moon." Surprised that "everybody in the West believed the reverse to be true,"[73] he set out to write a book whose principal thesis is in the title. Contrary to a common view in the West that the Soviets were in space thanks to the alleged superiority of their technological and education base, Vladimirov argues that this was so in spite of Soviet technological backwardness.

Paradoxically, he asserts that the Soviets "were never ahead in space."[74] Even when the first Sputnik was launched on October 4, 1957, says Vladimirov, the Soviets were lagging behind the Americans in two crucial areas of space technology: the booster power of their rocket engines and electronic guidance systems. Whatever Soviet achievements, they were mostly made "thanks to a rigid and unrestrained dictatorship" by the Soviet rulers whose guiding principle was to "beat the Americans at all cost." The rulers forced the pace of the Soviet space program in order to score propaganda victories and thus bluff the world about the real situation in Soviet science and technology.

Why were the Soviets so keen on bluffing? And why were they so anxious to hide their technological backwardness? Besides the obvious reason that technological backwardness thwarts their propaganda efforts to sell communism at home and abroad, Vladimirov gives two other reasons. One is that the veil of secrecy allows them to copy "without let and hindrance what is new in science and technology in the West without having to pay for it in hard currency."[75] Another reason is to blackmail the free world into concessions by creating the false impression that the Soviet war machine relies on an indigenous technological base. In fact, argues Vladimirov, the Soviet war machine largely depends on the innovations of Western technology that they steal through espionage or obtain legally through trade and cultural exchange.

Vladimirov also argues that the Soviet space bluff fits well within overall Soviet foreign strategy. Thus, the first Sputnik not only helped to divert attention from Khrushchev's damnation of Stalin's reign of terror, but also made the free world quickly forget about Khrushchev's own suppression of the Hungarian revolution. The second manned space flight, that of German Titov on Vostok-2 in August 1961, was deliberately timed "to draw the attention of world public opinion away from the Berlin Wall," which was then under construction.

Just as the defectors before him had been disbelieved in their accounts of Stalin's reign of terror, so Vladimirov was disbelieved in his account of Soviet space research, and his book did not appear in English until seven years after his defection. However, the combined efforts of all the previous defectors and later of *samizdat* and *tamizdat* dissident authors gradually made the West a bit more receptive to what new defectors say. As Vladimirov admits, "had it not been for the appearance of [Solzhenitsyn's] *The First Circle* many people might not have believed what I say."[76]

ALEKSEY MYAGKOV'S *INSIDE THE KGB*

Aleksey Myagkov was not even born when Kravchenko defected. He was a schoolboy when Deriabin, Khokhlov, and the Petrovs stood at the end of their Soviet careers. Born in 1945 into a family of ordinary Russian peasants, Myagkov joined the military in 1952, when he became a cadet at a paratroopers' school in Ryazan. He was commissioned a lieutenant in 1966 and stationed at an airborne division near Kaunas, Lithuania. The reality of the Soviet military soon shattered his "youthful dreams about the integrity and manliness of the profession of an army officer."[77] However, since a Soviet career officer is expected to serve for life, he saw no other way to quit than by joining the KGB. After graduating from KGB School No. 311 in Novosibirsk, he was sent on a tour of duty with Soviet troops in East Germany in February 1969. For five years he was attached to the 82nd Motorized Rifle Guards Regiment. Although he wore an army uniform, he belonged to the KGB chain of command, where he advanced to the rank of captain. On February 2, 1974, he was assigned his usual "watchdog" duty during a visit to West Berlin by a group of Soviet army officers, but "the watchdog slipped the leash" and defected.

His book, *Inside the KGB: An Exposé by an Officer of the Third Directorate*, was published in England in 1976. Chiefly focused on the post-1969 period, which is not covered by the KGB Wanted List, Myagkov's book substantially complements and updates the picture of Soviet military control of East Germany and KGB control of the Soviet military that has emerged from the writings of earlier defectors.

Myagkov estimates that there were about 1,500 KGB staff officers working in the German Democratic Republic, divided basically between two branches of the KGB. About 900 of them belonged to the First Directorate, whose main task is espionage abroad, and the remaining 600 were under the Third Directorate, to which Myagkov himself belonged and with which he is more familiar. Although its main task is officially described as counterintelligence against Western espionage, in reality the Third Directorate is chiefly preoccupied with domestic spying in order to protect the troops against the corrosive influence of internal dissension. In essence, the Third Directorate is a successor of the wartime SMERSH, whose activities were described by Pirogov and Deriabin. Myagkov's observations coincide with the Petrovs' conclusion that the State Security system "is chiefly employed not against foreign espionage . . . but against the Soviet people themselves." Explains Myagkov, "While it is difficult to catch a spy—the majority of counter-espionage workers have seen them only on the cinema screens—there is no lack of 'anti-Soviets' and other 'internal enemies' of the regime,"[78] even though KGB officers occasionally have to invent them in order to fulfill "production quotas" and thus advance their careers.

Myagkov gives several examples. A lieutenant colonel was relieved of his army post for criticizing the Soviet electoral system in a private conversation overheard by a KGB *seksot* (informer). Lyudmila Birasten, the wife of a Jewish officer, was falsely accused of "speculations" (illegal trade), and her husband was promptly transferred to the Far East because the KGB had received a directive from then-KGB Chairman Andropov to get rid of Jews in the Soviet troops in East Germany.

The emphasis on domestic spying did not prevent the KGB from expanding espionage abroad. Myagkov puts the number of Soviet agents recruited from among FRG citizens at about 2,000. He also suggests that détente was followed by an increase of Soviet espionage efforts in the West. He cites a top-secret order by Andropov to increase recruitment in West Germany at the time when the FRG-USSR treaty of mutual cooperation was signed in 1970.

Describing the living conditions of Soviet conscripts, Myagkov compares their service to "a term of imprisonment." Though he knew of no cases of defection across the border, he reports a sharp increase in the number of "spontaneous" desertions and suicides, and he attributes that increase to the fact that "human patience is simply exhausted."

In spite of the abominable life of Soviet conscripts, Myagkov believes they can still be relied upon in a critical situation. Barely hiding sarcasm, he argues that precisely because they cannot stand their "imprisonment" in the barracks, Soviet soldiers would "enjoy expeditions even more, as it was during the occupation of Czechoslovakia." They enjoy giving vent to their aggressive feelings against their enemies, and "it matters little who those enemies are, Czechs, Germans, Poles, or Americans."[79] Myagkov seems to suggest that even though Soviet leaders are either unable or unwilling to alleviate various frustrations of their soldiers, they know how to channel them against "external enemies."

Myagkov notes an increase in opposition to the regime, and suggests that such well-known dissidents as Solzhenitsyn and Sakharov are only the tip of a submerged iceberg of discontent. However, the well-known dissidents are "exceptions" in that they are protected by world public opinion, "while thousands upon thousands of unknown people perish between the KGB millstones." Although he respected "such brave souls" and hoped that some day "monuments will be erected in their honor,"[80] he did not see any real possibility for himself to resist the regime from inside. He chose instead to "inflict a great harm" on the regime by defecting. He does not think he betrayed his country, because the Soviet regime is in itself "a threat not only to the peoples of the Soviet Union but also to the majority of countries of the world. To defend such a regime is treachery, to fight it, no."[81]

Each of our authors was driven to defection by a combination of reasons: fear of repression, desire to tell the truth, hope for a better life, pursuit of freedom, or an urge to protest and fight back against the system that threatened to obliterate their personalities. For each individual, the decisive reason appears to have been different: from Kravchenko's compulsion to tell the truth about Soviet realities to Krotkov's more modest wish to stop living a life of duplicity; from the Petrovs' fear of repression to Khokhlov's desire to join anticommunist forces. All of them loved their country, and none felt that by defecting they were betraying it. On the contrary, they were convinced that by defecting they not only affirmed their human identity but also performed a patriotic duty toward Russia. Defection was not an easy choice for any of them. All had to take great personal risks and were lucky just to have an opportunity to defect. They knew that if they failed they would face the death penalty or, at the very least, ruin the rest of their lives; if they succeeded, they would never see their loved ones again. They also knew that the shadow of retribution would hang over their heads to the end of their lives. The uniqueness of their books stems from the strength of their characters and convictions as well as the intensity of feeling and thought that were required to make the decision to defect. By writing their books, they have validated their reasons for defection.

These authors have told many things about the USSR that nobody else could tell. Virtually all revelations the early defectors made about life in the USSR under Stalin were met in the West with disbelief and outright rejection; but these revelations were later confirmed by other sources, most notably in Khrushchev's anti-Stalin speech at the Twentieth Party Congress in 1956. There are no reasons to suspect that more recent defectors' information about the USSR under Khrushchev and Brezhnev is less truthful. They may have occasionally erred in judgment and detail, but none of them can be accused of deliberately lying about the USSR. That is why Soviet leaders, after their defeat at the Kravchenko trial in France in 1949, have never tried again to challenge the truthfulness of defectors' testimony in open court. That is why Aleksandr Solzhenitsyn, who normally does not favor those who voluntarily abandon their country, paid a tribute to defectors like Kravchenko, who wrote his books in spite of Soviet threats on his life. In a 1983 interview describing the dilemma expatriate Russian writers must face, Solzhenitsyn drew a parallel between Kravchenko and himself: "Thirty years ago, Kravchenko defected, revealing to the West the terrible things that were going on; people preferred to listen to Bertrand Russell. Eight or nine years ago I described what was really happening—and again, except for a few, the West paid no attention."[82]

More important for the purpose of our study, however, is not what these authors wrote about the USSR, but what they wrote about the West or, rather, their encounter with the West. This encounter has never been easy. Contrary to the widely held belief that Soviet defectors have always been "welcome in the West as live ammunition in the great propaganda battle" against communism, defectors themselves testify that this was not so even during the most tense spells of the cold war. In fact, several authors describe the bitter experience of discovering that Western authorities in general and the U.S. government in particular were often either unprepared or unwilling to grant them refuge and protection from Soviet agents. This was true not only for Kravchenko, but also for Gouzenko, Kasenkina, Tokaev, and Khokhlov, the last three cases occurring well into the cold war period. Defectors have been virtually unanimous in reproaching the West for its failure to expose the falsity of Soviet propaganda and to counter it with their testimony.

From Kravchenko and Gouzenko to Vladimirov and Myagkov, the defectors have been disappointed to discover that Soviet propaganda has been successful in fostering in the West illusions about the USSR. They felt that their stories were largely disbelieved because Soviet propaganda, aided and abetted by some leading Western opinion makers, was largely believed. As a result, all of them had to overcome considerable difficulties in getting their message across to the West.

That message can be summed up as follows: first, the Soviet regime does not have a popular mandate to rule and is contrary to the national aspirations of the Russian and other peoples populating the USSR; therefore, it can rule only by lies, intimidation, and violence. Second, the communist internationalist ideology was proven bankrupt during World War II when the regime had to appeal to Russian national patriotism in order to survive; it has since been exploiting Russian patriotism to its own communist ends, which are as alien to the Russians as to any other nationality. Third, there is no reason to believe that a regime that owes its existence to the domestic use of lies, intimidation, and violence would rely on different means in its foreign policy. Fourth, since no legal opposition to the regime is tolerated, defection is just about the only way to oppose it or express one's individuality; once in freedom, it is a duty of a defector to speak his mind because, in the words of Kravchenko, "an understanding of the Russian reality by the democratic world is the precondition for my country's liberation from within." Moreover, it is the defectors' duty to warn the West that strength, not concessions, is the only way to stave off Soviet expansion.

That message anticipates, of course, the message that the West was to hear from inside the USSR with the beginning of the dissident and human rights movement in the late 1960s. It particularly anticipates Aleksandr Solzhenitsyn's warning to the West, which he made in his speech at the AFL-CIO meeting in Washington on June 30, 1975: "The Communist leaders respect only firmness and have contempt for persons who continually give in to them."[83]

3

WHAT DID SOVIET DEFECTORS SAY?

We now turn to interviews with 43 Soviet defectors published by the State Department during the 1951–1960 period in a series of reports collected under the title "The Soviet Union as Reported by Former Soviet Citizens."[1] The reports are rather extensive and seem to follow the interviews closely. According to a prefatory note, "The statements of the sources are not edited except for the deleting of identifying data."[2] Especially valuable are the interviews with individual defectors. There is no explanation as to how the interviewees were selected, but a great majority of them are officers who defected from the Soviet armed forces in Germany. Some defected before 1951, others shortly before the time when the interviews were conducted. Among the latter interviewees are three Armenian youths who defected after 1957 and one merchant seaman who defected in 1960.

Each report is organized, more or less, in the following order of topics: Personal Data; Motives and Conditions of Defection; Employment Experience; Information on Various Branches of Soviet System, such as the Army, Secret Police, and Party; Information on Domestic Conditions of the USSR, such as Social Welfare, Culture and Education, Religion and Church, National Differences and Problems; Attitudes Toward the Soviet System and the USA; and Political Aspirations and Predictions of the Source about Russia's Future.

Below, a selective review is presented of those topics that are more relevant to the present study: (1) Motives of Defection, (2) Attitudes Toward the Soviet Regime, (3) Morale of the Soviet Army, (4) Nationalities Problems,

(5) Aspirations for a Future Russia, (6) Attitudes of the Sources Toward the USA and Suggestions for Its Foreign Policy.

MOTIVES OF DEFECTION

Nearly all interviewees indicated a combination of ideological, political, and moral objections to the Soviet system as the most decisive reason that drove them to defection. A former MGB lieutenant spoke for many when he said: "The principal motive impelling one toward defection is disgust with the Soviet system as one which stifles initiative, promotes inefficiency and indifference, and which makes a decent standard of living impossible." Although he admitted that for some defectors "material considerations are, perhaps, the most important," he spoke with scorn of those who had defected only because of them. As for himself, he insisted that he had defected "for purely political reasons," but asked his interviewers not to overlook the lack of "spiritual freedom" in the USSR as an important factor in any decision to defect. When asked about the factors militating against defection, he mentioned "fear of being caught, uncertainty as to one's future in the West, reluctance to leave one's native land, family and friends, and the fear of the possible consequences of defection for relatives."[3]

To the general disgust with the Soviet system, several interviewees added such personal reasons for defection as being unable to marry an East German girlfriend (the Soviets do not allow fraternization with the population of subjugated countries) or a threat of transfer from East Germany to remote parts of the USSR where the conditions of service are much worse.[4] Since none could even question the system, much less oppose it in any legal way, defection seemed a last resort of self-expression. Practically all interviewees could be called ideological defectors. Only one of them, a lieutenant colonel who had graduated from a law institute in Moscow, refused to call himself so. He classified himself as a "realist" and "materialist" and cited "a drinking incident" that could have led to his "dismissal and disgrace" as the prime motive for his defection. But even though he would have preferred to stay in the USSR, he was just as disgusted with the regime whose aim, he said, was the creation of a "1984 society."[5]

ATTITUDES TOWARD THE SOVIET REGIME

None of the interviewees felt that their views of the Soviet system were unusually negative. To the contrary, many of them emphasized that their views were typical of the majority of Soviet people. In any case, the majority of interviewees seemed to agree with the following statement of a former chief engineer of a Soviet-run factory in East Germany:

> The Soviet system is basically unsound. It is an experiment which has failed. The initials VKP [which at the time stood for the name of the Communist Party] should be translated *Vtoroe Krepostnoe Pravo* (Second Serfdom). The Communists do not believe in their professed ideals but simply use their ideology to deceive the masses. This had been true of Lenin and was still more true of Stalin...Eighty to 90 percent of the Soviet people are opposed to the regime. This includes probably half or more of the Communists.[6]

A tank lieutenant, who grew up in a *sovkhoz* in Bashkira, estimated that "all peasants" and about 80 percent of the workers were opposed to the regime.[7] Another Russian officer of peasant stock, who grew up in Buryat Mongolia in Siberia, fought at the battle of Stalingrad, and after the war filled "a series of responsible engineering positions" in East Germany, testified that "it was safe to say that 100 percent of the peasants are opposed to the Soviet Union." According to him, the peasants often recall "their good life under the Czars, when few laws were in effect and there was an incentive to work."[8]

A Jewish sergeant, who had fought with the Soviet army during World War II and earned a medal "for bravery" and party membership, also held the belief that "life under the Czarist system was better." He gave the following assessment of the attitudes of various social classes to the regime:

> The peasants offer the greatest resistance to Soviet controls. They are the best element among the people and they would be the first to join the ranks of a power opposing the Soviet Union. Among the workers and intelligentsia it would be more difficult for a foreign power to elicit support [even though] there are elements in the intelligentsia who are becoming disillusioned and would take advantage of an opportunity to assist in the elimination of the Soviet system.[9]

As to the reasons for the failure of the Soviet government to satisfy the Soviet people, the interviewees were nearly unanimous that this failure has to do with communist ideology, which the government can neither renounce nor adhere to. According to a captain from Leningrad who had served in the Soviet army for ten years and had been a party member:

> The practice of the Soviet regime does not in any way correspond to the theories which it professes to follow. Marxism-Leninism is a system of sacred texts which cannot be revised, but which have no relation to reality.

The captain believed that "the Politburo has excellent information about the real situation in the country," but had no choice except to continue to "deceive its subjects and keep them in ignorance." Why? For the simple reason that "if they knew the truth about life abroad and the truth, for that matter, about what is going on inside their own country, there would be a revolution."[10]

MORALE OF THE SOVIET ARMY

As far as the morale of the Soviet people in general and the Soviet armed forces in particular is concerned, the interviewees were virtually unanimous that "it would be very low in the event of war with America." That opinion was expressed by a major who had a college education and served as an army veterinarian from 1939 until his defection in the late 1940s. He based his opinion on his observations at the front:

> In the early months of the war, the morale of the Red Army had been very low. Mass surrenders had taken place but the barbarous and inhumane policy of the Germans had united the Soviet people and elevated the morale of the army. At first, there was no hatred of the Germans and there was even a tendency to believe their propaganda leaflets.[11]

The American interviewers point out that the major "did not think that the hatred aroused by German atrocities had been extended by the Soviet people to foreigners in general." According to him, "the Soviet people knew the difference between national socialism and American democracy."

The major's opinion was seconded by several other defectors. The tank lieutenant was convinced that "if the Germans had been clever they would have won the Russian masses to their side." He speculated that in the event of war with America, the morale of the Soviet army would be even lower than during the initial stage of the war against the Nazis. In any case, he "did not think many Soviet people would willingly fight against the United States" because they "draw a sharp distinction between American and German political principles."[12] The Jewish sergeant speculated that "in the event of war, the number of deserters would triple the number which deserted in the past war." As to the satellite countries, "their armies would fight only with guns at their backs" and "would desert by the thousands to the Western side."[13] Another defector, an aviation expert who was a party member and had been engaged in the dismantling of German plants before he defected, strongly emphasized "that there are many Soviet citizens, officers, soldiers, and even generals who do not wish to return to the Soviet Union." He felt that many more soldiers would have defected, were it not for the fact that they don't speak German and "mistrust the Germans, many of whom work for the Soviet police."[14] The officer engineer from Buryat Mongolia was one of several to point out another deterrent: "As late as 1948 they did not know whether the Americans or British would accept them."[15] Their testimony coincides with that of Klimov and Tokaev.

The low morale of the army reflected the general negative attitude of the populace, especially the peasants, toward the regime. The captain from Leningrad explained it by the fact that the majority of conscripts were "recruited from the peasantry," and the peasants hated the Soviet regime mostly because of collectivization. According to him, "discipline in the Soviet Army, particularly in Germany, rests mostly on force and fear." He spoke for many when he concluded, "the Soviet Union is not at present ready for a major war. This is because the people do not wish to fight for the Soviet regime."[16]

NATIONALITIES PROBLEMS

As to the nationalities problems in the USSR, nearly all interviewees testifed that they exist to a far greater extent than one might surmise from Soviet propaganda claims. Several defectors, including those of Russian origin, admitted that the Russians often exhibit at least "a mild feeling of superiority" over the non-Russians and in return are hated, in varying degrees, in every national republic.

Several defectors expressed the view that one of the strongest national antipathies that exists in the USSR is the antipathy the Slavic population of the country, especially the peasants, feels toward the Jews, whom they often "hold responsible for the revolution" and otherwise accuse of being cunning or failing to contribute their share during the war.[17] That view was somewhat contradicted by the testimony of the only two interviewees of Jewish origin. As had been mentioned, the Jewish sergeant was not only awarded a medal for bravery, but also shared the opinion of many Russians that life under the czars had been better than under the Soviets. The other interviewee of Jewish origin, a captain of the Army Medical Corps, felt that anti-Semitism mostly "emanates from the top rather than from the bottom." He illustrated his point by relating such actions of the Soviet government as the closing of the Jewish publishing house *Der Emes*, the arrest of the Jews who volunteered to fight on the side of Israel, and the introduction of a quota for Jews wishing to be admitted to universities. He did not deny, however, "the possibility of the resurgence of anti-Semitism on a wide scale" if it is instigated by the government.[18]

As to the anti-Russian feelings on the part of minorities, the consensus was that they were strongest in Central Asia and the Caucasus.[19] However, virtually all interviewees made it clear that anti-Russian feelings were mainly caused by the realization on the part of the non-Russians that the Russian language and the Russian settlers were used to subjugate them under the communist political system, which they hated. Thus, the Jewish sergeant who had visited his brother in Uzbekistan reports that conditions there are "far worse" than before the revolution. "The Uzbeks say that under the Czar there was only one governor who supervised them. Now the Russian overlords are everywhere and completely dominate life in Uzbekistan."[20] A defector from Kabardinia, a small, predominantly Muslim, people from the North Caucasus, testified that during the war "a large majority of the Kabardinians (at least 80 percent) were opposed to the Soviet regime." But, though they "greeted the Germans warmly," they actually "wanted a return of the freedom which they enjoyed under the Czars." According to him, before the revolution, "the Kabardinians and Russians lived side by side in the Caucasus in complete harmony, with no feeling of superiority exhibited by the Russians."[21] The three young Armenians, who defected across the border after the first Soviet Sputnik, also testified that "Armenians distinguish between the Russian people, who are blamed for their passivity under oppression, and the Russian Communist Party, which is hated as the instrument of the tyranny." They emphasized that "the entire population of Armenia desires liberation from communist rule."[22]

At least one defector, a Russian, conceded that "relations even between Ukrainians or Belorussians and Great Russians were not very friendly."[23] Nonetheless, the prevailing view was that "the Slavs are the backbone of the USSR."[24] That view was shared not only by the Russian defectors but also by the only one with a strong Ukrainian identity, a former lieutenant colonel, described as "an intelligent man, with considerable power of analysis," who "does not engage in loose talk." He testified that "on the whole, the Russians and the Ukrainians got along better than any other two Soviet nationalities" and that "there was no sharp feeling of difference" between the two. "He seemed to be of divided mind himself as to whether the Ukraine . . . should be a separate, independent state," says the report, but perhaps "inclined slightly toward a negative answer."[25]

The Ukrainian's views were corroborated by the Jewish medical captain who testified that in the armed forces particularly, "the Ukrainians work well with the Russians." In fact, the captain seemed to imply that both Ukrainians and Belorussians are favored over the Russians, as far as a military career is concerned, and estimated that the two peoples constitute "40–50% of the officer and sergeant cadres." He also testified that among the Ukrainians he had met, "the feeling of separatism was negligible." Not many defectors would agree with him that "the nationality question does not exist as such," but the captain spoke for all when he said that "the people's hatred of the regime subordinates any dislikes and discriminations which may exist among themselves."[26]

ASPIRATIONS FOR A FUTURE RUSSIA

The Ukrainian lieutenant colonel seemed to express a general consensus when he said that he "saw no great difference between Russians and other peoples of the world so far as their aspirations and values were concerned." Not believing that the Soviet regime is capable of improving itself, he was convinced that "the [Soviet] system would have to be abolished."[27]

As to a future political and economic system, opinions were more divided. The prevailing view was expressed by the aviation expert, who said that even though "people still talk of life before the Revolution. . . , they do not want a return to the Czars." In fact, "most Russians do not know what they want politically except they would like to see the end of police control." Confident that eventually "they would find a way to establish some kind of democratic life," he insisted that "there must be free exchange of ideas" with other countries and that "intellectual freedom must be granted to scientists and scholars."[28] The chief engineer expressed the hope that "under a good political system the State would not be all powerful but would act only to maintain order and protect legitimate rights," including "freedom of enterprise as well as democratic civil liberties."[29]

The tank lieutenant was more specific in stating that "the ideal form of government would be a government of the American type." When asked to define it, he said that democracy means that "everybody should be equal," that "the Russian people would be able to change its government every four years," and that "workers should have the right to strike."[30] Although the aviation expert saw the United States as "the only workable economic system," he felt it was a mistake to call it capitalism and suggested that "perhaps another name could be found to fit the American system under which a person owns his own property and has an incentive to work."[31]

All interviewees agreed that the Soviet system must be abolished, but opinions were divided as to the means of achieving it. Some, like the Jewish captain, felt that, remote as it might be, "The idea of revolt must . . . be implanted in the masses. . . Once [it] is established, the people will work out their own means of resistance." Although he personally had some misgivings about the NTS, he thought its principles "were good" and praised it for offering an "image of a government for tomorrow, something positive to which the people can look forward."[32] The aviation expert, on the other hand, felt that "any talk of a real resistance movement in the Soviet Union is pure nonsense." Still, he seemed to agree with the captain that "the organization and help must come from the outside; the rallying point must be beyond the Soviet frontiers."[33] The chief engineer felt that "the only hope of salvation for the people of Russia is the possibility that there will be a war which would rescue the Soviet people."[34] Though started by the Soviets, the war would eventually bring about a downfall of the Soviet regime, provided Western democracies do not make the same mistakes that Hitler made, in identifying the Russian people with the regime.

ATTITUDES OF THE SOURCES TOWARD THE USA AND SUGGESTIONS FOR ITS FOREIGN POLICY

As we have seen, the defectors' attitudes toward America were overwhelmingly respectful and friendly. Typically, they expressed confidence in the superiority of American technology, thought highly of the morale of U.S. armed forces, and saw the American political system as a model that a future Russia should emulate. They felt no doubt that their attitude reflected that of the majority of Soviet people. In the opinion of the chief engineer, the greatest reserve of goodwill was created during World War II, when millions of plain Soviet folks experienced America's help first-hand. According to the chief engineer, "they knew that their armies were being fed American food, were using American equipment, and were wearing American cloth in their uniforms." Despite all the efforts of Soviet propaganda to minimize it, says the chief engineer, "this aid had aroused gratitude as had American aid given by the ARA [President Hoover's American Relief Administration] during the famine" in the wake of the civil war.[35] The existence of goodwill toward America was the chief reason why many interviewees felt that Soviet troops would be even less willing to fight the Americans than they were during the initial stage of the war against the Germans.

Still, several defectors expressed doubt about whether America would be able to capitalize either on its technological superiority or goodwill among Soviet people in resisting Soviet expansion in peace time. Nor were they sure that America would not repeat Hitler's mistake in the event of war. They especially faulted U.S. foreign policy for its lack of firmness in dealing with the Soviet Union and for a naive belief in solving international problems by negotiations alone. As the chief engineer summed up his advice to U.S. foreign policy makers, "the only thing that counted . . . in the struggle against the Bolsheviks was power effectively employed."[36] The "realist" lieutenant colonel, the one who refused to be called an ideological defector, was convinced that the West underestimates the willingness of Soviet leaders to assert and expand their power even at the risk of a major war. "If the Communist Party [was] willing to sacrifice millions of people for collectivization," he argued, "would it not sacrifice more for world domination? . . . When the Soviet Union feels strong enough to win a war it will start one, and no nonsense about it."[37]

Several interviewees emphasized, in the words of the Jewish captain, "the need for the West to drive home to the Soviet people the fact that it understands the difference between the people and the regime."[38] Most of them were not convinced, however, that the West makes such a distinction, and that is why they felt that the West will do no better than Hitler in the event of war. The Ukrainian lieutenant colonel was especially worried by a tendency among Western scholars "to identify Communism with the Russian people" by advancing various theories about peculiar racial traits of the Russians. He absolutely rejected such theories as "harmful and foolish," arguing that "after all, Communism was imported to Russia from the West." Sensing that his American interviewers were less interested in the defeat of communism as an ideology than in the breakup of Russia into smaller national entities, he warned against attempts to impose from the outside "any hasty or superficial solution" of the nationalities problem. "A foreign power," he went on, "could easily break its neck on the problem."[39] Although he did not elaborate, he apparently implied that attempts to set national minorities against ethnic Russians would backfire because they would help Soviet leaders to consolidate their power by exploiting Russian nationalism.

The Jewish captain expressed a similar view when he suggested that the West would be playing a dangerous game if it tried to divide the country, should it win a war. Instead he "indicated a desire . . . that the present frontiers and boundaries would remain and that democracy would be formed with the help of the West."[40] He suggested "the use of the plebiscite" as the means of solving the nationalities problem.

Several interviewees suggested the need for the West to meet the Soviet challenge in the field of ideology and propaganda. The aviation expert, for example, praised the Voice of America (VOA) as "the most effective means of enlightening Soviet personnel in Germany," but suggested that the VOA should talk about internal problems of the Soviet regime. "If a Soviet defector spoke over the VOA to the Russians in East Germany, it would be ten times more effective than any Western diplomat who might speak," he said.[41] The Jewish captain predicted that "wars of the future will not be fought for the acquisition of land or other similar reasons, but for an ideology."[42]

To sum it up, the State Department's interviews with the 43 Soviet defectors essentially confirm and complement what has been written by our selected authors in their books. Since these interviews were apparently not intended for publication and, in any case, the defectors knew in advance that their anonymity would be preserved, their chief value is in the candidness and straightforwardness of expression. In several cases the interviewers noted that their sources were not only willing but eager to talk about ideological and political matters. When reading the reports, one has the impression that military defectors were particularly happy to have finally found someone who was interested in more than just the number of their army unit or what type of machine guns they had used.

One may argue, perhaps, that the interviewees said what the interviewers wanted to hear. This argument may have some validity in regard to answers reflecting the defectors' attitude toward the United States, especially if at the time of the interviews the defectors had not yet obtained a U.S. resident permit and hoped to get one. However, as far as their information and opinions about the USSR are concerned, one can hardly doubt their sincerity. They may have exaggerated the degree of popular discontent in the USSR, but, if they did so, it was rather due to the intensity of their feelings than to deliberate efforts to mislead the Americans.

Although the State Department's interviews shed more light on the scope of discontent among various social classes in the USSR, they tell almost nothing about the scope of defection as an expression of this discontent. All we learn from the interviews is that, in the opinion of the defectors, many other Soviet citizens would have defected, were it not for the many obstacles that prevent and deter them from doing so. We now turn to the Soviet document that will help to define more exactly the scope, as well as the social parameters, of defection.

II

THE KGB WANTED
LIST: 1945–1969

4

THE KGB WANTED LIST: A GENERAL CHARACTERIZATION

Whereas in Part One we tried to approach the phenomenon of defection subjectively, that is, through testimony provided by defectors themselves, we shall now approach it through an objective study, at least insofar as the word "objective" could be applied to the records of the organization that has been charged with the prevention of defection and the tracking down and punishing of its perpetrators. We will focus on the KGB Wanted List as a source of information about defectors. After a general characterization of the source and examination of sample entries, we will evaluate the results of a computer-assisted analysis.

The full title of the KGB source is "The Alphabetical List of Agents of Foreign Intelligence, Traitors to the Fatherland, Members of Anti-Soviet Organizations, Collaborators, and Other Wanted Criminals" (*Alfavitnyi spisok agentov inostrannykh razvedok, izmennikov rodiny, uchastnikov antisovetskikh organizatsii, karatelei i drugikh prestupnikov, podlezhashchikh rozysku*, or for short, *Rozysknoi spisok*). It is more than just an alphabetical list of names. Each entry is a summary of information contained in the KGB files on each "criminal." Such lists are known to be issued every three to six years in the form of a printed volume. Each volume contains from 2,000 to 6,000 personal entries. In the interval between issues, so-called update bulletins (*orientirovki*) are issued every two months or so. These are then incorporated in the next volume.[1]

It is noteworthy that the latest volume never completely supersedes the earlier ones. Consequently, the KGB may be using a number of different volumes concurrently. Each edition is printed in a limited number of copies, 1,500 to 1,600, each of which is registered under a serial number and bears the stamp "Absolutely Secret" (*Sovershenno sekretno*). The copies are made available only to high-ranking KGB operatives inside the USSR and abroad.

One such copy was apparently smuggled out of a KGB office and found its way into the hands of the NTS (Narodno-Trudovoi Soiuz Rossiiskikh Solidaristov), the National Labor Union of Russian Solidarists. From January 1977 through June 1978 the NTS published, in its monthly *Possev*, a list of about 600 persons thought to be defectors residing abroad.[2] This list was extracted from the smuggled KGB volume. *Possev* further offered each person whose name appeared on the list a copy of his or her entry in the KGB records. All that was required was that the individual submit a written request certified by a notary public.

Having found my name on the *Possev* List, I wrote a letter to NTS asking for the information in my entry.[3] After receiving a photocopy of my entry, I was completely satisfied as to the authenticity of the source. I was also impressed with the wealth of detail on the background, circumstances, and consequences of defection that any such entry would provide. I then conceived the idea of using the KGB source as a statistical base for my study of postwar defection. In the summer of 1979 I contacted NTS officials, asking them to donate a copy of their KGB volume to the archives of the Hoover Institution so that the data on defectors would become available for scholarly use. In response, they invited me to visit NTS headquarters in Frankfurt to examine the volume. In hopes of bringing a photocopy of the KGB list back to the United States, I accepted the invitation. However, when I arrived there, the NTS officials refused to allow me to prepare my copy until certain conditions had been met. First of all, to protect the defectors' privacy, they insisted that before a copy could be made, all personal names of defectors and their relatives must be deleted. Second, to prevent any possibility of the KGB identifying the smuggled copy, they insisted that each page of the volume be cut up and the entries reassembled at random. I would then be allowed to make a copy of this reassembled version of the text. Realizing the necessity for these extraordinary precautions, I readily accepted the NTS's conditions.

After these precautionary steps had been taken, I sorted out 470 cases of defection from among a much larger group of entries, reassembled them on 160 pages (usually three entries per page), and delivered them to the Hoover Institution Archives, where they are now deposited. The difference between the *Possev* List of about six hundred names and my 470 entries (henceforth referred to as the Hoover File) largely depends on my exclusion of those persons who can be suspected of having left the USSR during World War II.

The Hoover File covers a period of about twenty-four years, from May 2, 1945, through May 5, 1969. I chose the 1945 date in order to separate wartime defectors from those who had defected under postwar conditions. The 1969 date was set by the source itself, because the latest entry in the KGB volume registers a defection on May 5, 1969. To judge by the dates imbedded in the cancellation seals stamped over some of the entries (the defectors involved either had been presumed dead or had returned to the USSR), the volume was in use until well into 1971.

It should be pointed out that the figure 470 does not represent the total number of defections during the indicated period, but rather those who were thought by the KGB to be at large in the beginning of 1969. It excludes (1) those who tried but failed to defect, and their number may be in the thousands; (2) those who, having succeeded in defection, were subsequently returned to the USSR by Western authorities, and they may number in the hundreds;[4] (3) those who died or were killed before this edition of the KGB Wanted List was compiled; (4) those who either returned voluntarily or were forced to return by KGB agents abroad; and (5) those whose defection has remained undetected by the KGB.

Even discounting the cases of abortive defections (the first category of exclusion), the total number of postwar defectors from the USSR must be presumed to be considerably higher than 470. Nevertheless, this figure is indicative of the scope of postwar defection and is large enough to lend itself to statistical analysis.

Before analyzing the data, let us take a look at several sample entries to get a general picture of the kind of information that is contained in the KGB Wanted List. We will begin with the entry on Nikolai Khokhlov, with whom the reader has already become acquainted in Part One. Since his entry has already been published in Russian in *Possev*,[5] it is translated below in its entirety, that is, without deleting personal names.

ENTRY A

KHOKHLOV Nikolai Evgenevich, born in 1922 in the city of Gorkii, Russian by nationality, completed high school education, former employee of the KGB. Mother **Mikhailovskaia Anna Viktorovna**, sister **Khokhlova Olga Evgenievna** and half-sister, **Svetlana Evgenievna**, reside in Moscow. Wife **Timashkevich Elena Adamovna** and son live in the city of Ivanovo.

Having been sent in February 1954 to the Federal Republic of Germany on special assignment, betrayed his Motherland. On June 5, 1954, the Military Collegium of the Supreme Court of the USSR sentenced him, in absentia, to the highest measure of punishment [*VMN, vysshaia mera nakazaniia*]. A photograph and a sample of his handwriting are on file.

The dossier is filed in the Second Main Directorate of the Committee of State Security attached to the Council of Ministers of the USSR.[6]

First of all, the entry confirms the identity of Khokhlov and the credibility of his story, which he first made public at a press conference in Bonn on

April 22, 1954 (shortly after his defection) and later described in his book, *In the Name of Conscience* (see Chapter 2). At that time, there were some skeptics in the West who cautioned against taking his story at face value; they were eager to dismiss his defection either as a regrettable incident in the international chess game of the cold war or even as a concoction of the CIA.

The entry is interesting not only for what it contains, but also for what it omits. In particular, it omits the rank and stature of Khokhlov in the KGB service, as well as the nature of his "special assignment" in West Germany. The truth is that Khokhlov was one of the outstanding Soviet heroes of World War II. He was one of the first four Russians trained to operate behind front lines in German army uniforms and was a key man behind the assassination of Wilhelm Kube, the Nazi governor of Belorussia. He later fought with partisans in Belorussia and Lithuania, and after the war went on to several covert missions in Romania, France, Austria, Italy, and Denmark, advancing to the rank of captain of State Security.

As the commander of a traveling executioners' squad, he was sent to West Germany with the specific order to carry out the assassination of Georgy Okolovich, then the leader of the NTS. However, instead of assassinating Okolovich, he went to his apartment in Frankfurt only to tell Okolovich he could no longer remain in the service of the USSR. He later proved his credibility to American authorities in Frankfurt by giving them information that led to the arrest of his fellow assassins, Hans Kukovich and Franz Weber. The latter subsequently corroborated Khokhlov's story in a West German court. Khokhlov also directed the Americans to an automobile battery in which were hidden two electric pistols that fired poison bullets. These were to be the instruments of assassination.

The entry also omits any information on a subsequent attempt by KGB agents to carry out the death sentence on Khokhlov by adding radioactive thallium in his coffee during a Russian émigré conference in Frankfurt on September 15, 1957. Khokhlov barely survived this attempt on his life. In contrast to other entries, Khokhlov's entry lacks the standard physical description. The compilers apparently assumed that he had been so disfigured by the effects of the poison that there was no point in giving an old description.

The next entry belongs to the largest category of all postwar defectors— the soldiers of the Soviet occupation forces stationed in Germany and Austria after the war. It is translated below the way it appears in the Hoover File, that is, with all personal names deleted.

ENTRY B

--------, the same as --------, born in 1922 in the city of Cherkassy in the Cherkassy *oblast'*, Jewish, former member of the Komsomol, completed high school education. **Tall, sloping shoulders, long neck, light**

brown hair, grey eyes, oval face, large nose. Father --------, mother -------- live in the city of Cherkassy. Fighting at the front, he was captured in September 1942 by the Germans and kept in POW camps in German territory. Having been liberated by Soviet troops from the POW camps, from April 1945 on worked as a part-time interpreter in the service of SMERSH. In December 1945 escaped into the American zone of occupation of Germany. In 1949 lived in West Germany under the name of --------, in 1961 moved to Canada, where he has been residing in Toronto. Maintains correspondence with his relatives. In 1961 was sentenced, in absentia, to death by the military tribunal of military unit no. 48240. There is a photograph from 1966 and a sample of handwriting on file.[7]

Entry B is typical of the bulk of the Hoover File in several respects. First, the entrant belongs to the military personnel of the Soviet occupation forces in Germany. Second, it contains the physical description of the entrant, which is marked off from the rest of the text by heavy print as if to emphasize what the primary purpose of the file is. (As has been pointed out, the omission of the physical description of Khokhlov is an exception.) Third, also unlike the entry on Khokhlov, the life of the entrant B abroad has been followed through. Since the availability on file of the 1966 photograph is duly noted, it is clear that he has been the subject of a KGB search for at least 21 years after his defection. Even the fact that entrant B is Jewish does not make him atypical, as Jews occupy a rather prominent place among early postwar defectors.

Like Khokhlov, entrant B was sentenced, in absentia, to death. However, whereas Khokhlov was tried shortly after his defection by the Military Collegium of the Supreme Court, the trial of entrant B by a military tribunal was deferred for 16 years. Apparently the distinction of being tried by the Military Collegium of the Supreme Court is reserved for those who are affiliated with the KGB and who presumably committed more heinous crimes (see Chapter 7). Unlike Khokhlov, who was punished for the crime of "betraying the Motherland," in the case of entrant B the fact of defection is itself considered a crime that merits "the highest measure of punishment."

Even though entrant B's captivity in Germany, as well as his being a witness to SMERSH operations in Germany, may have aggravated his "crime," other entries show that one did not have to commit any additional crime besides defection to be sentenced to death. Furthermore, it should be noted that since entrant B escaped under Stalin, was sentenced under Khrushchev, and remained subject to search under Brezhnev, one can hardly detect any mellowing of the regime's attitude toward defectors.

ENTRY C

--------, born on December 22, 1924, in the Ukraine. **Height above average; lanky; long neck; dark, deeply set eyes; hair brown or blond; straight long nose; thin lips.**

While serving in one of the military units of the Group of Soviet Forces in Germany, escaped to West Germany, where he joined the NTS. In November 1952 took part in a conference of the Central Organization of Political Émigrés [TSOPE, Tsentral'naia Organizatsiia Politicheskikh Emigrantov] in Munich, to which he arrived from Bielefeld. In 1953 he was enrolled in NTS's Intelligence school in Bad Homburg. He was there with his wife, of either German or Czech nationality, who worked there in the kitchen. After graduating from the school, he appears to have left for the USA.[8]

This entry also belongs to a military defector. However, in contrast to entrant B, the KGB seems to know very little about the background of entrant C, and it knows nothing about the circumstances of his defection. The entry lacks such standard data as the entrant's birthplace, whether he has any relatives left behind in the USSR, and the date and place of his defection. While stating that he had served in "one of the military units" of Soviet occupation forces in Germany, the compilers apparently do not know in which one. This is uncharacteristic, because their standard practice is to identify military units by their numbers.

Thus entry C suggests the existence of a category of defectors about whom the KGB knows very little or nothing at all. Apparently, a substantial number of defections, especially those that occurred during the early postwar years, have remained undetected by the KGB. This could have happened because during the war some of the State Security records were destroyed or lost. Another reason may be that it took some time after the war for State Security to establish effective control over Soviet occupation forces and over the borders of the occupied zone.

Although the fact of defection, and thereby the *corpus delicti*, of entrant C seems to be clearly established in the eyes of his KGB hunters, the lack of information about his background may have prevented them from trying him in a military tribunal and sentencing him to the death penalty. However, a more likely reason for sparing his life is suggested by the allegations of his graduating from NTS's intelligence school. As a rule, the death penalty is meted out to those defecting soldiers who are accused of nothing except the defection itself. This was the case of entrant B. Paradoxically, those who have been accused of collaboration with various anti-Soviet groups and foreign intelligence, such as entrant C, are either sentenced to 25 years or not tried at all (see Chapter 7).

ENTRY D

--------, born in 1931 in the village of Votkino of the Khvastovichi *raion*, Kaluga *oblast'*, member of the Komsomol, fourth-grade education, a driver. **Medium height, lanky, light brown hair, split chin, long neck, protruding Adam's apple.** Sister --------, uncle -------- reside in the village of Votkino; cousins --------, and -------- reside in Leningrad; aunt -------- resides in the city of Dolgoprudnyi of the Moscow region.

While working as a civilian employee in the 26th topographic detachment of the Group of Soviet Forces in Germany on August 3, 1955, escaped to West Germany with his German cohabitant --------. In September 1957 sent a letter from Munich to his sister in the village of Votkino. According to information from our agents [*agentura*], in 1958 moved to Australia together with his cohabitant and two children. On November 26, 1957, was sentenced, in absentia, to death by the military tribunal of the military unit at field post box 48240. A photograph and a sample of handwriting is on file.[9]

Unlike the preceding one, entry D belongs to the post-Stalin era. Still, it confirms the point made earlier: that defecting soldiers who are accused of nothing except defection itself are routinely sentenced to death. There are some other features of this entry that deserve comment. First, the entrant's nationality is not indicated. This is probably due to negligence on the part of the compilers, who may have reasoned that anyone born in a Russian village, especially if he had a Russian name, must be assumed an ethnic Russian. There are dozens of such omissions, and circumstantial evidence suggests that they usually refer to persons of Russian ethnic background. Second, the entrant's low education level and the profession of driver are typical of a rather large group of defectors, as our statistics will later confirm. Third, the listing of the names of uncle, aunt, and cousins, all of whom reside in different parts of the country, shows that the KGB's surveillance efforts extend far beyond a defector's immediate family and are indeed nationwide. Fourth, the fact that entrant D was tried by a military tribunal, even though he was a civilian employee, indicates that the standard procedure for treating civilian employees of the armed forces is no different than for men in uniform. The entry is also remarkable for an unabashed admission that the entrant is being watched by KGB agents (*agentura*) and that his correspondence with his family is checked.

Finally, the reference to his escape in the company of a German "cohabitant" (*solzhitel'nitsa*) is typical of a large group of defectors from the occupation forces in Germany and Austria. Characteristically, the female companions of such defectors are always given the bureaucratic label "cohabitant." This shows that the provisions of the Helsinki Accords, which stipulate normal human communications across borders, have never been respected by the USSR, even when people of Soviet bloc countries were involved.

Entry E

--------, born in 1931 in the city of Tallinn, Estonian by nationality, former member of the Komsomol, sixth-grade education, resided in Tallinn, worked as a mechanic on the turbo-electric ship *Baltika* of the Baltic

State Steamship Company. **Of medium height, blond, ears large and stand out.** Mother --------, brothers --------, and sister live in Tallinn.

While visiting the port of New York as a member of the crew of the *Baltika*, on October 10, 1960, escaped and asked the American authorities for political asylum. On February 27, 1961, the Judicial Collegium on criminal cases of the Leningrad City Court sentenced him, in absentia, to 15 years in the ITL [Ispravitel'no-Trudovykh Lagerei, Corrective Labor Camps—V.K.]. Presently resides in the USA and is employed at an electrotechnical factory. A photograph from 1966 and a sample of handwriting are on file.[10]

Entrant E is an Estonian, and as such belongs to a relatively large group of defectors from this very small captive nation. He also belongs to a growing group of defectors who jumped ship. His sentence, 15 years in labor camps, is characteristic of penalties meted out to those who are affiliated neither with the military nor the KGB (see Chapter 7). Accordingly, he was tried neither by a military tribunal nor the Military Collegium but by a civilian court, and his punishment was lighter. Also noteworthy is the fact that he was tried not in Tallinn, Estonia, where he was born and lived and his native Estonian is spoken, but in Leningrad in the RSFSR. This happened during the "liberal" Khrushchev era, and the subsequent Brezhnev era brought no changes except updating his file with a photograph from 1966, which was either taken secretly by KGB agents in the United States or was stolen from his correspondence with relatives.

ENTRY F

--------, born in Moscow in 1943, Russian by nationality, incomplete university-level education, former student of the Institute of Oriental Languages of the Moscow State University, resided in Moscow. **Height 172 cm., strongly and athletically built, gait heavy and uneven, light brown hair, large grey eyes, wears glasses, when the glasses are off blinks a lot, nose large and meaty, ears small, hands large and sinewy, gesticulates when talking.** Wife --------, father --------, mother --------, and brother -------- live in Moscow.

Disappeared while serving as a translator on the staff of adviser of the Ministry of Mining and Industry of Afghanistan, in Kabul, during the night of October 30–31, 1967. Resides in the USA where he was recognized from a photograph by members [*sotrudniki*] of the New York mission of the Embassy of the USSR. A photograph and a handwriting sample are on file.[11]

Entry F is typical of a later vintage of defectors from the swelling ranks of Soviet personnel sent to Third World countries (allegedly, to render economic and technical assistance). They are usually better educated, are often versed in foreign languages, and are better informed about life abroad. Entrant F was in Afghanistan on official business (*sluzhebnaia komandirovka*), apparently as part of his training in one of the native languages of Afghanistan before his graduation from the university.

That the defection took place in Afghanistan, however, is unusual. Even before the Marxist revolution in 1978, Afghanistan, being infested with Soviet agents, was not a safe place in which to defect. Therefore it is not surprising that the defector quickly moved out of the country to the United States. Apparently, his defection was not made public because the compilers seem not to know anything that transpired between the time of his "disappearance" in Kabul and the time when he was recognized on the streets of New York.

The entry is rather typical of the later period in that the defector has not been tried in absentia. This may represent a new Soviet policy. However, the lack of an official verdict does not necessarily mean a softer attitude. The detailed physical description and the mention of the entrant being recognized in New York by members of the Soviet diplomatic mission hardly suggest that the hunt for defectors is off. That members of the Soviet diplomatic corps engage in other than diplomatic activities is now confirmed by an official KGB source.

The last sample entry is quoted below without deleting personal names.

ENTRY G

KRASNOV Vladislav Georgievich, born in 1937 in the city of Perm, Russian, university graduate, former editor of the Swedish Department of the State Committee of Radio and Television Broadcast at the CM of the USSR. **Medium height, light brown hair, oval face, large mouth, thin lips, straight nose, wide at the base, with large nostrils, wears glasses.** Father **Krasnov** Georgii Nikolaevich, mother **Krasnova** Ekaterina Ivanovna, brother, **Krasnov** German Georgievich, sisters **Krasnova** (**Zontova**) Zoya Georgievna, **Krasnova** (**Kokinskaia**) Liubov' Georgievna, brother-in-law **Kokinskii** Valery Borisovich reside in the city of Perm.

While visiting Sweden with a group of Soviet tourists, on October 26, 1962, turned himself in to Swedish authorities asking them for political asylum. On January 1963, appeared at a press conference before representatives of the bourgeois press with slanderous statements about Soviet reality. Resided in Sweden until January of 1966. From 1966 has been residing in the USA where he studies at a university and gives Russian-language lessons. A photograph and handwriting sample are on file.[12]

This is, of course, the entry on the author of this book. It is quoted here, in English translation, not as it appears in the Hoover File but as it appears in the KGB record (see Appendix 2A). Unlike entrant F, who is identified by the place of his studies, I am identified by my last place of work. That I graduated from the history department of Moscow University is left out, perhaps because it was considered embarrassing for the university to have such graduates. My membership in the Komsomol is not mentioned for the same reason.

The physical description appears on the whole accurate, albeit not very practical. It seems strange that the KGB does not seem to know the color of my eyes, nor the fact that I had stopped wearing glasses long before the Wanted List was compiled. Had the compilers worked with greater diligence, they would have had no trouble in finding the information from the numerous color photographs that I had sent my parents in the letters that the KGB checks. They could also have established without difficulty that the school at which I studied at the time was the University of Washington in Seattle.

As to the list of my relatives, it seems remarkable that they list my sisters by their maiden names while including the married names in parentheses. That they list my brother-in-law, whom I have never met and who married my sister after my defection, is indicative of the extent to which they go in their surveillance efforts. Still, one wonders: why not include all in-laws, aunts and uncles, nieces and nephews?

The entry is representative of the kind of defector that first came into prominence during the 1960s, namely, defectors from tourist groups. It should be noted, however, that these are not tourists in the usual sense of the word (see Krotkov's story in Chapter 2). In Soviet usage, the emphasis is not so much on *tourist* as on *group*. In my case, the tour was sponsored by the Swedish division of VOKS (Russian acronym for the All-Union Society for Cultural Relations Abroad, a KGB front organization). Members of the group were carefully selected, and their original number, 30, was eventually cut in half. Among the fifteen people chosen was a well-known surgeon from Moscow, a vice-president of Riga University, and a Heroine of the Soviet Union, a woman fighter pilot who had distinguished herself in World War II. The last was a sort of professional tourist because she had already toured in many countries demonstrating everywhere the "great achievements of Soviet women."

As far as I am concerned, I did not exactly take the initiative of applying for the trip. Rather, the VOKS officials called to inquire if the Swedish Department of Moscow Radio wanted to submit one application, and I just happened to be the one who was chosen. While on the trip, I was expected to prepare a program for propaganda broadcasts to Sweden.

As to the charge that I made "slanderous statements," it hardly deserves an answer. Incidentally, among the "bourgeois press" at the press conference were representatives from the Swedish Communist newspaper, *Ny Dag*, whom I had personally invited. The fact that I was not tried in absentia, at least by 1969, in spite of providing a Soviet court with ample *corpus delicti*, is apparently due to a new Soviet policy toward defectors, which we have already noted in connection with entry F.

These, then, are examples of entries in the KGB Wanted List. A typical entry consists of from 150 to 200 words. All personal names as well as the physical description of the entrant are set off by **boldface** print. An entry is usually divided into three paragraphs. The first paragraph commences with the last name, first name, and patronymic of the defector and contains other personal data such as the year and place of birth, education, party and Komsomol membership (if any), occupation, position or rank (if military), and last place of residence. This is usually followed by a rather detailed physical description including an estimate of height; build; color of hair and eyes; shape of nose, ears, mouth, and face; physical defects and peculiarities such as scars, birthmarks, limping, or stammering; and other distinctive features such as tattoos or the ability to speak foreign languages. The first paragraph almost always concludes with the names and places of residence of the defector's relatives—spouse, children, parents, and sometimes aunts, uncles, and cousins.

The second paragraph deals with the defection itself. Usually it includes the precise date (day, month, and year) and place (country and city) of the defection. Sometimes it contains circumstances of the defection, such as with whom the defector conspired and whether he took with him arms, money, or secrets. The defection is variously described by such words as "vanished," "betrayed Motherland," "escaped," "asked for political asylum," or "turned himself in to foreign authorities." This is often followed by a description of the defector's subsequent activities abroad, such as contacts with foreign intelligence agencies and émigré groups, and whether one made any "anti-Soviet" statements. Sometimes the "criminal" background of the defector prior to his defection is indicated by a reference to his activities during the war, such as whether he lived in German-occupied territory or was conscripted into German labor or military units. Such background data is apparently provided either to explain the motives of the defection or as evidence of the defector's additional culpability. This is frequently followed by a precise date of trial and the sentence meted out. In the absence of a trial, sometimes a statement is added that an order for arrest has been issued by a certain authority. The second paragraph usually concludes with information on the present occupation and whereabouts of the defector, whether he corresponds with anyone inside the USSR, and whether there is a photograph and handwriting sample on file.

The third and last paragraph (which we cited only in entry A) usually consists of a single sentence indicating the location of the dossier and sometimes a parenthetical reference to the first announcement of the escape. A small number of entries have been stamped over, diagonally, with a rubber stamp, indicating the cessation of the search. No reasons are given for the cancellation of the entry, but one can surmise that the defector in question died, returned to the USSR (or was forcibly returned), or was caught inside the country. The language used throughout the KGB Wanted List is rather uniform, with little individual variation. There are relatively few spelling errors, mostly related to foreign countries. For example, the compilers renamed Georgetown University the University of George Town, and the KGB editors failed to correct them.

It is clear from the quoted samples that, if analyzed statistically, the 470 entries of the KGB Wanted List could provide answers to a number of questions that are essential for an understanding of the phenomenon of defection. Among these questions are: How many Soviet citizens defected in a given year? To which countries did most of them go? How many of them crossed a border, jumped ship, or became nonreturners? What social, ethnic, or professional group produced the largest number of defectors? Is there any truth in Soviet allegations that most of the defectors have a criminal background, or that they were recruited by foreign intelligence services? What punishment can a defector expect if he returns, or is returned, to the USSR?

In the following three chapters, we shall attempt to answer these questions by a discussion of the results of computer-assisted analysis of the personal data on the wanted defectors (Chapter 5); circumstances of defections and defectors' whereabouts (Chapter 6); criminal allegations and expected punishment (Chapter 7). In Chapter 8, we shall attempt to answer, on the basis of our data, the often-asked question: Aren't many defections faked by the KGB to plant an alibi-protected spy? Finally, the findings of our statistical analysis of the KGB records will be put into historical perspective. Chapters 9 and 10 will explain how the patterns of defection changed after the construction of the Berlin Wall and under various Soviet rulers.

The discussion will be supported by references to a number of statistical charts extracted from computer printouts and included in the Appendixes. However, most of the references will be made to pages of the complete printout that is deposited in my name at the Hoover Institution Archives along with the Hoover File.[13]

5

Personal Data on Defectors

The first paragraph of the entries in the KGB Wanted List contains personal information on each defector such as sex, age, ethnic origin, education, professional background, military training, party membership, physical description, knowledge of foreign languages, and relatives left behind. The following results have emerged from our analysis of personal data on the defectors.

Sex

Of our 470 defectors, only 19 (4 percent) are women. Two interrelated reasons explain this low percentage. First, contrary to Soviet propaganda, women are customarily underrepresented in those groups that are entrusted with foreign missions. Second, the low percentage of women among defectors reflects their low percentage in such professional groups as the military, merchant seamen, and fishermen, which are the foremost sources of defectors.[1] However, in the later part of the pre-1969 period, their share began to increase (see Chapters 9 and 10). Moreover, the published accounts of post-1969 defections (see Part Three) suggest that the share of women has continued to rise, and there are no reasons to believe that, given the same opportunities, women would be less inclined to defect than men.

NATIONALITIES OF DEFECTORS

Nationality	Percentage of Defectors	Percentage of Population[a]	Ratio of Defection
Russians	42.5	54.65	0.78
Ukrainians	19.2	17.84	1.08
Jews	8.5	1.09	7.80
Estonians	7.0	0.47	14.89
Latvians	4.9	0.67	7.31
Belorussians	3.5	3.79	0.92
Lithuanians	3.3	1.11	2.97
Armenians	3.1	1.33	2.33

[a] From Zev Katz, ed., *Handbook of Major Soviet Nationalities* (New York: Macmillan, 1975), Table A.2, p. 441.

AGE

By age, the spread is between 18 and 60; the youngest defector was born in 1947, the oldest in 1900. Nearly a third of all defectors escaped when between the ages of 20 and 24, and the average age (the mean) is 28.561.[2] This rather low age apparently reflects the natural tendency of young people to be more enterprising in planning their futures and less dependent on family ties, language, and professional habits. Moreover, the fact that nearly half of all defectors came from the military, where young conscripts predominate, has undoubtedly helped to push the average age down. In the post-1969 period, the average age has tended to rise.

ETHNIC ORIGIN

By ethnic origin, of the 426 defectors whose nationality is recorded, 181 (42.5 percent) are Russians, 82 (19.2 percent) Ukrainians, 36 (8.5 percent) Jews, 30 (7.0 percent) Estonians, 21 (4.9 percent) Latvians, 15 (3.5 percent) Belorussians, 14 (3.3 percent) Lithuanians, and 13 (3.1 percent) Armenians. Among nationalities represented by one to three defectors are Azerbaijani, Georgians, Moldavians, Tatars, Avarians, Tadzhiks, Karelians, Mari, Ossetians, Kirghiz, Mordvins, Kabardinians, Komi, Germans, and Poles. Their combined number is 34 (8.0 percent)[3] (see Appendix 2B).

While it is safe to assume that no nationality in the USSR is immune to defection, the question nonetheless arises: Aren't there some nationalities that are more prone to defect than others? To answer this question, let us compare the percentages of major defecting nationalities with their percentage in the total population of the USSR during the period under study.

It would appear that only among the Russians and Belorussians was the ratio of defection negative, that is, the percentage of defectors is lower than the percentage in the population of the USSR. For the Ukrainians it was a bit higher, and for all others it was manifoldly higher, especially for the Estonians (nearly 15 times), the Jews (nearly 8 times), and the Latvians (more than 7 times). When grouped together, the Slavs—the Russians, Ukrainians, and Belorussians—constituted 65.2 percent, that is, an absolute majority of defectors. However, their share in the population of the USSR around 1959 was 76.3 percent. Consequently, their ratio of defection was negative, 0.85.

As to the Balts—the Estonians, Latvians, and Lithuanians—their share in the population was only 2.3 percent, but their share among defectors was 15.2 percent and their combined ratio of defection was 6.76. One may say that the rate of defection among the Balts was 7.95 times higher than among the Slavs, meaning that the Balts are more prone to defect than the others.

However, it would be a mistake to conclude that the rate of defections for each nationality accurately reflects the degree of dissatisfaction with or disloyalty to the Soviet regime. There are simply too many other variables that come into play and cannot be measured accurately. These variables basically fall into two categories—the opportunity for defection and the inducement to defection. The Slavs, especially the Russians, probably have a slight edge in the number of opportunities, that is, if we assume that (1) they are more trusted and therefore have a larger share in the occupation forces in Germany and in the military in general and (2) they are more often entrusted with foreign missions than other nationalities. The Balts, on the other hand, have greater inducement to defect. They have lived fewer years under communism, are more likely to have relatives or friends abroad, are more familiar with the Western way of life, and are probably more knowledgeable in foreign languages. Also, it is easier psychologically for a Balt to defect because he or she knows that the Soviet occupation of the Baltic republics is not universally recognized. Finally, Balts could expect a warmer reception as defectors because the Western officials with whom they would come into contact would understand someone escaping from the "Russians," but they might not understand why a Russian would want to leave Russia. During the first postwar years, many Russians were, in fact, returned to the USSR against their will.

A number of factors that might facilitate the Balt's decision to defect would apply, to a greater or lesser degree, to a Jew or an Armenian. Thanks to their respective diasporas, Jews and Armenians can count on finding either relatives or sympathetic nationals abroad. The existence of the state of Israel has further stimulated the Jewish impulse to defect. Interestingly enough, the rate of defection among Armenians is much higher than that among their neighbors, the Georgians. That the Georgians fared somewhat better than other nationalities under Stalin may have something to do with this. However, the fact that during World War II many thousands of Georgians fought on the German side shows that the Georgians are no more loyal to the Soviet regime than the Armenians. Apparently, the existence of the Armenian diaspora is an important factor behind their high rate of defection, as in the case of the Jews.

It may be noteworthy that the compilers of the KGB Wanted List took special care in the notation of Jewish nationality. In some cases they took pains to point out that certain defectors are Russian according to their passports, but Jewish in fact.[4]

EDUCATION

The notation of the level of education in the KGB Wanted List is extensive. There are only 27 missing cases out of 470 defectors. The breakdown of the 443 records is as follows:

LEVELS OF EDUCATION FOR DEFECTORS

Level of Education	Number	Percentage
Elementary (through fourth grade)	108	24.4
Middle (through seventh grade)	128	28.9
High school	131	29.6
College	67	15.1
Postgraduate	9	2.0
Total	443	100.0

It is clear that more than half of all defectors had no higher than a seventh-grade education. This low level of education can be explained by the fact that the largest group of defectors consisted of soldier conscripts, who often had but elementary education. Moreover, the general educational level in the early postwar period was considerably lower than it is now. As to the kind of education, it was sparsely recorded, with 358 missing cases. Out of the 112 recorded cases, 47.3 percent had technical education, 17 percent went to military schools, and 10.7 percent had studied humanities. The others had vocational training and political education.[5]

PROFESSIONAL BACKGROUND

The profession of the defectors at the time of defection or immediately prior to defection was indicated in 417 cases. In spite of the unavoidable overlapping of the professions and a certain arbitrariness of labeling,[6] it is fairly obvious that the prevalent professions were those that required a lower educational level or "low" social origin. There were 69 collective farmers (16.5 percent), 62 sailors (14.9 percent), 30 workers (7.2 percent), 29 drivers (7 percent), and 21 fishermen (5 percent). Together they constitute 211 people, over half of all with indicated professions.

The other half consists of 41 military career officers (9.8 percent); 52 intellectuals (12.6 percent); 22 translators and interpreters (5.3 percent); 20 artists (4.8 percent); 15 security officers (3.6 percent); and a few clerks, students, and athletes.[7]

The large percentage of people with peasant and worker backgrounds among the 1945–1969 defectors seems to bear out the allegations of the State Department interviewees that discontent with communism was not confined to a few informed intellectuals but spread across all walks of life and was especially rife among Soviet peasants.

THE MILITARY

The majority of the defectors, 244 (52.5 percent) out of 470, were connected with the Soviet military, mostly with the occupation forces in Germany and Austria.

Of the 244 military defectors, 171 (70.1 percent) belonged to the army, 7 (2.9 percent) to the navy, 11 (4.5 percent) to the air force, 35 (14.3 percent) were civilian employees, and 17 (7.0 percent) were in the employ of the security services attached to the armed forces.[8] The preponderance of army defectors clearly reflects the preponderance of the army in the occupation forces in Germany and Austria.

By rank, there were 31 lieutenants, 16 captains, 6 majors, and 3 officers above the rank of major. Altogether, there were 56 officers, or about 23 percent of all military defectors.[9] That means that only about one of every four military defectors was an officer. However, since only an officer's defection was likely to be reported in the press, the Western public was largely unaware of defecting soldiers. The State Department interviews did nothing to correct that impression.

One of the highest ranking Soviet army defectors was a Russian lieutenant colonel and commander of a border post (*pogranuchastok*) who escaped across the border into Afghanistan on June 7, 1953, by speeding away in his GAZ-67 car. He was charged with having taught at the American "intelligence school" at Garmisch Partenkirchen and was sentenced, in absentia, to death.[10]

PARTY AFFILIATION

Of the 130 recorded cases, there were 69 members of the Young Communist League (Komsomol) and 53 members and 8 candidate members of the Communist Party.[11] We can safely assume, however, that the actual number of defectors affiliated with elite Soviet organizations is considerably higher. In my own case, for instance, membership in the Komsomol was not recorded. This reluctance of the compilers to admit, even to themselves, that any Soviet person, regardless of his or her political affiliation, could defect, has apparently lowered the recorded number of party and Komsomol members among defectors. Nonetheless, their share among the defectors—14.7 percent for the Komsomol and 13.0 percent for party members and candidates—was higher than for the country at large. That means, of course, that the party itself, no matter how rigorously controlled, is far from defector-proof.

PHYSICAL DESCRIPTION

Physical description occupies a prominent place in the file because it serves the purpose of assisting Soviet operatives in their task of identifying and tracking down defectors abroad. However, for the purposes of this study, physical description is of little interest. It would suffice to say that the average defector tends to be of medium height, is strongly built, has blue or grey eyes (64.5 percent of all recorded cases), and blond or brown hair (over two-thirds of the cases).[12]

KNOWLEDGE OF FOREIGN LANGUAGES

Notation of foreign-language proficiency usually follows the physical description. However, the incidence of missing data for this variable is very high. In fact, only 34 defectors (7.2 percent of the total) were noted for their mastery of one foreign language or another. Although that number is too small to have much statistical significance, it may be noteworthy that among those 34, there were 23 who knew German and only 7 who were said to know English.[13] This has to do with the fact that the majority of defectors defected from the Soviet occupation forces in Germany and Austria (see Chapter 6), and they did so during the early postwar period when the main emphasis in Soviet schools was on German.

To be sure, the notation of foreign-language proficiency is rather subjective and arbitrary. In Nikolai Khokhlov's case, for instance, there is no mention of his mastery of German nor, in my case, is my knowledge of Swedish noted. Nonetheless, the KGB records reflect the fact that the overwhelming majority of defectors are ill-prepared, both linguistically and culturally, to start a new life in a new country. The defectors defect to one country or another not because they feel a cultural affinity with it but because they take an opportunity as it comes.

RELATIVES LEFT BEHIND

In addition to the 470 defectors, the KGB Wanted List contains the names of hundreds of their relatives, including spouses, children, parents, lovers, and—though less frequently—in-laws, uncles, aunts, and cousins. The notation of each relative usually consists of last name (and maiden name), first name, and patronymic and indicates in which city or village each relative resides.

Listing defectors' relatives apparently serves a double purpose. It helps the surveillance of all contacts with the defector, and—even when there are no such contacts—it blacklists the relatives, especially if they are being considered for promotion or travel abroad. Below are the results of frequency counts for the occurrence of the names of close relatives.

Spouses

There are 98 names of wives (plus one husband left behind by his defecting wife), 48 former wives, and 9 common-law wives.[14] Altogether, there are 156 persons listed who had one or another form of connubial relationship with defectors. Although the source does not spell out the marital status of the defectors, it appears that more than two-thirds of them were single and never married.

Children

Eighty-seven defectors (18.5 percent) out of 470 are known to have left children behind, as the names of their children are listed in the KGB Wanted List. Among such defectors, 61 had one child, 19 had two, 6 had three, and 1 had four children. Thus the total number of children left behind is 121.[15] This means, of course, that there are that many more people whose basic human rights are restricted and violated, in addition to the defectors themselves and their conjugal partners.

Parents

Although the KGB Wanted List usually discriminates between parents and stepparents, no such discrimination was registered on the computer cards. The results show that 267 mothers and 162 fathers were left behind.[16] The difference between the number of mothers and fathers apparently reflects the fact that the majority of defectors belonged to the generation that lost fathers in both World War II and the Stalinist purges. Although we do not have the control figures for the entire Soviet population of that period, the numbers of listed parents do not seem unusually low, which contradicts the usual assumption that defectors tend to come from broken families.

Brothers and Sisters

Three hundred thirty-five defectors (71.3 percent) out of 470 left behind at least one brother or sister.[17] Assuming that the average Soviet family of the time consisted of two children, we get the figure of at least 670 more blacklisted people whose only "crime" was to be the sister or brother of a defector.

Thus, the combined number of those blacklisted in the KGB Wanted List, in addition to the 470 defectors, consists of the following:

Spouses and lovers	156
Children	121
Parents	429
Brothers and sisters	670 (estimated)
Total	1,376 (estimated)

That means that, on the average, for every defector there are three other persons who are blacklisted in the KGB Wanted List with all the inevitable negative consequences for their human and civil rights. Even though, since Stalin's death, a defector's family members are no longer imprisoned or exiled to Siberia,[18] they continue to be discriminated against and harassed.

The case of my nephew may serve as an example of how blacklisting in the USSR affects defectors' relatives, even those whose names may not appear on the KGB Wanted List. My elder sister's son, Sergei Zontov, was only ten years old at the time of my defection in 1962. Because I lived in Moscow, my only contact with him was skiing together while vacationing in Perm, where he lived with his parents. Six years later he became a ski-jumping champion of the USSR among the juniors. As such he qualified for, and was originally included in, a Soviet team competing for the European championship in Vienna,

Austria, in 1968, but at the last moment he was not allowed to go abroad. Four years later he held a Soviet ski-jumping record, but again he was not allowed to participate in the Olympic Games in Sapporo, Japan, in 1972.

The results of our analysis of personal data contained in the KGB Wanted List are summed up as follows: (1) out of the total 470 defectors only 19 (4 percent) were women; (2) the age spread was from 18 to 60 years old with the average slightly above 28.5; (3) by ethnic origin, about two-thirds (65.2 percent) were Eastern Slavs (Russians, Ukrainians, and Belorussians), but the share of the Balts and the Jews among defectors was considerably higher than their proportion in the population of the USSR; (4) 53.3 percent had a low education (no higher than the seventh grade) and rudimentary professional training, reflecting the fact that the majority of the defectors (244 people out of 470) were serving in the military, mostly as conscripts in Soviet occupation forces in Germany; (5) a higher percentage of them were affiliated with the Communist Party and Komsomol than the average for the country; (6) only 34 defectors were noted for their knowledge of a foreign language, usually German; and (7) about one-fifth of the total abandoned their spouses and children, but the overwhelming majority left behind their parents, brothers, and sisters. Other than the fact that a typical defector of the period tended to be a young, male, soldier-conscript in Soviet occupation forces in Germany, the results of our analysis show him to be very close to a rank-and-file Soviet citizen. The significance of these figures, when compared with the more recent period, will be discussed later.

6

DEFECTION AND
ITS AFTERMATH

The compilers of the KGB Wanted List paid close attention to whatever facts were known to them about the circumstances and aftermath of each defection. Our analysis yields the following results concerning such matters as time, place, and method of defection as well as the subsequent whereabouts and occupations of the defectors.

DAY OF DEFECTION

The compilers of the KGB Wanted List took great care to register the exact day of defection, in some cases indicating the time of day as well. Still, there are 92 missing dates, 19.6 percent of the total.[1] Apparently, nearly one-fifth of all defectors escaped without giving the KGB much clue as to the timing of their escapes. Otherwise, this variable serves only a descriptive function and has no statistical significance.

MONTH OF DEFECTION

The notation of month is missing for only 21 entries (4.5 percent). Of 449 valid cases, July and August have produced the highest number of defectors, 56 and 55, respectively. They are followed by October, with 49 defectors, and by June and September, with 42 defectors each. The lowest figures within the annual cycle are registered for two winter months: 23 for January and 20 for

February.[2] These differences are apparently due to weather conditions. Good summer weather in the northern hemisphere undoubtedly facilitates escape for such categories of defectors as soldiers, sailors, and fishermen. Potential defectors are more tempted to escape in late summer and early fall because they know that they can swim in the ocean or across a river, dry their clothes in the sun, hide in the foliage, eat food crops, and spend the night in the open.

YEAR OF DEFECTION

There are only two cases in which the compilers failed to indicate the year of defection. The remaining 468 cases are distributed rather unevenly throughout a 24-year period, from May 1945 to May 1969. The annual number of defections peaks early in this period, with 59 defections in 1947, 60 in 1948, and 42 in 1949. The number declines to 8 defections in 1955 and bottoms out with 5 cases in 1958, 9 in 1959, and 8 in 1960. Toward the end of this period, the number of annual defections climbs again, reaching 20 in 1967[3] (see also Appendix 2C).

Why does the curve of annual frequencies rise to 60 defections in 1948, fall to one-twelfth that number in 1958, and then climb again to 20 in 1967? Although this fluctuation may be accidental in some cases, over the entire period of 24 years a certain pattern emerges that cannot be dismissed as accidental.

For one thing, there seems to be a definite correlation between annual frequencies, on the one hand, and whoever happens to sit in the Kremlin, on the other. It is no accident that the curve peaks under Stalin, reaches bottom under Khrushchev, and climbs again under Brezhnev. Although we shall discuss the defections under various rulers later (see Chapter 10), it should be pointed out here that the curve reflects the change in the annual rate of defection from 33.71 under Stalin to 11.21 under Khrushchev to 16.52 under Brezhnev. Thus the annual rate decreased more than three times under Khrushchev as compared with Stalin and began to climb under Brezhnev. The average annual rate for the entire period is 19.54.

But what can we say about fluctuations within each reign? Why, for instance, does the number of defectors more than double in a single year, from 28 in 1946 to 59 in 1947? One reason may be that by 1947 it became clear to many Soviet citizens, especially soldiers, that Stalin had stolen the victory from the victors, as Peter Pirogov and Grigory Klimov have so vividly described in their books (see Chapter 2). When Stalin failed to deliver on his promise of granting more political freedoms and economic benefits to the Soviet people, many of them lost all hope for reforms and looked to the outside for the possibility of a better life.

Another reason is that sometime during 1947 the Western powers began to reverse their policy of the forcible repatriation of Soviet citizens to which they had so recklessly and tragically committed themselves at Yalta. Even though defectors were not covered by the Yalta agreements, there can be little doubt that many of them were forcibly returned to the USSR, especially in 1945 and 1946 when it was much easier to cross to the Western zones of occupation than later. One may assume that the actual number of defections for the years 1945 and 1946 was much higher than indicated in the KGB Wanted List and could possibly be greater than the figures for 1947 and 1948.

The sharp decrease in the number of defectors from 42 in 1949 to 19, 22, and 11 in the last three full years of Stalin's rule may be attributed to the campaign of intimidation, including the trials of defectors in absentia, which intensified during these years (see Chapter 7).

Stalin's death on March 5, 1953, apparently did not dampen the desire to defect. The number of defections increased from 11 in 1952 to 13 in 1953 and then shot up to 21 in 1954. This sudden increase may be attributed to the fact that the power struggle in the Kremlin in the wake of Stalin's death had a debilitating effect on those charged with preventing defections. The defection of a large group of Soviet sailors from the tanker *Tuapse* in Taiwan certainly pushed the figure for 1954 upward.[4] However, the following year saw only eight defections. The number increased again from 11 in 1956 to 18 in 1957, and then reached the lowest level for the entire 24-year period—5 defectors in 1958. It is quite plausible that just as disillusionment after the Soviet suppression of the Hungarian uprising in 1956 had something to do with the larger crop of defectors in 1957, so the euphoria generated at home and abroad by the first Soviet Sputnik in October 1957 could have served as a deterrent for defections in 1958.

The construction of the Berlin Wall apparently failed to prevent defections to the extent its architects had hoped for. In the pre-Wall year of 1960, there were only 8 defectors. In 1961, when the Wall was constructed, there was a spurt to 14, and in the following three years the level of defection stabilized at about 10 defections each. Even though the Wall dramatically reduced the number of military defections (see Chapter 9), it did not prevent a rise of the annual rate of all other defections (see Chapter 10).

Noteworthy is the increase of annual frequencies from 10 in 1964, the last year of Khrushchev's rule, to 18, 19, and 20 in the first three years of Brezhnev's rule. Apparently, after the ouster of Khrushchev, a few more people lost hope in the ability of the Soviet regime to acquire a human face by reforming itself (see Chapter 10).

COUNTRY OF DEFECTION

There is a total of 33 countries named in the KGB Wanted List as places of defection. (See Appendix 2D for a breakdown by country.) These countries are scattered all across the globe. However, the great majority of defections took place in Western Europe, especially in West Germany. Including 57 defections in West Berlin, West Germany accounts for 201 defections, 44 percent of the 456 registered cases. (In 14 cases KGB clerks apparently failed to establish from their records where the defections had taken place.) A distant second, but still far ahead of the rest, is Austria, with 59 defections. These two German-speaking countries account for 57 percent of all defections.[5] The reason for this is obvious: the division of Germany and Austria into occupation zones after their defeat in World War II brought Soviet citizens into closer proximity to the Western democracies with their powerful allure of freedom. While most of the defections to Austria had taken place before 1955 when the Soviets withdrew their forces following Austria's reunification, most of the defections to West Germany took place before August 1961, the time of the Berlin Wall construction and heavy fortification of the East German borders. Since then, the share of defectors to both countries has sharply diminished (see Chapter 9).

West Germany and Austria are followed by Sweden with 33 defections; Turkey (29); Canada (17); Great Britain (16, which includes 2 defections in Gibraltar); Finland (14); Denmark, Iran, and Taiwan (10 each);[6] Japan (8); Norway (6); France (5); and Switzerland (4). The United States, Spain, and Greece had 3 defections each. Five other countries had two defections each, and twelve countries had one each.

Among the countries that have either a maritime or land border with the USSR, the breakdown is as follows:

Norway	6
Finland	14
Sweden	33
Turkey	29
Iran	10
Afghanistan	2
Japan	8
Total	102

Thus, the share of the border countries of the total of 456 cases amounts to 22.37 percent. However, if we exclude Sweden and Japan, which have only maritime borders, we would have only 61 defectors (13.38 percent) who escaped into neighboring countries—about one out of every seven to eight defectors. The above figures have some significance when compared with each other. Why, for instance, did 33 people defect in Sweden, 29 to Turkey, but only 14 to Finland? The answer lies in the fact that Finland is officially committed to returning Soviet defectors, even though this violates the principles of the 1975 Helsinki Accords. In fact, those 14 defectors must consider themselves extremely lucky for managing to get out of Finland before being caught. Sweden and Turkey, on the other hand, adhere more strictly to a policy of granting political asylum to Soviet defectors.

In addition to the defections to the 33 countries, there were also 9 cases of defection through foreign countries: Czechoslovakia (3); Yugoslavia (2); and Poland, Romania, Hungary, and North Korea, 1 case each. In essence, the defectors used these countries as staging areas for defection in much the same way others used Finland, though, strictly speaking, one does not have to defect from Finland. As an example of using an intermediate country as a staging area for defection, we may cite the case of a Soviet specialist in metallurgy, Ukrainian by nationality. He was a graduate of the Zhukovsky Air Force Academy, a member of the Communist Party, and held the rank of major of engineers. While on an official mission in North Korea, he escaped to South Korea on June 6, 1947.[7]

ZONE OF DEFECTION

As to a breakdown by Western occupation zones, 120 people escaped to the Americans, 66 to the British, and 5 to the French.[8] The combined number is 191. However, since the total number of those who are said to have crossed into Western occupation zones is 229, it must be assumed that in 38 cases the Soviets were not sure precisely where their defectors had gone.[9]

More important than the absolute figures, however, is the breakdown of defectors among the three Western allies. It is clear that almost twice as many defectors escaped through the American occupation zones in Germany and Austria as through the British, while only a few succeeded in escaping through the French. The latter chiefly depends on the fact that the French zone, confined as it was only to the southwest corner of West Germany, had no common border with the Soviet zone. Moreover, France was the least attractive as a host country because defectors knew about procommunist sympathies among large segments of its population and feared that its military and intelligence service might be infiltrated by Soviet agents. But why were the Americans preferred over the British? There seem to be two major reasons. First, America was preferred due to its role as the leader of the free world.

Defectors naturally gravitated toward a country that would stand against the USSR. Moreover, they assumed that the Americans were the least likely to return them to the USSR. Second, especially in the early postwar years, America held the greatest promise of prosperity to those defectors for whom that mattered. We may never learn exactly how many defectors were forcibly returned to the USSR by each of the three Western allies. But we know for sure that the majority of them succeeded in staying in the West by escaping to the American occupation forces in Europe.

METHOD OF DEFECTION

On the basis of information contained in the KGB Wanted List, we can differentiate various methods of defection such as crossing borders, jumping ship, and asking for political asylum while sojourning abroad with the official permission of the Soviet government.[10] For convenience, we shall identify three basic types of defection: a border-crosser (*perebezhchik*) is someone who defected by violating Soviet borders, whether state or zonal; a jumper (*prygun*) is someone who jumped ship; and a nonreturner (*nevozvrashchenets*) is someone who was in a foreign land with official Soviet government permission but chose not to return to the USSR and asked for political asylum.

Although the compilers of the KGB Wanted List did not use the same terminology, they recorded what may be termed "method of defection" in 438 cases. Among them are 312 border-crossers (71.23 percent) who are said to have escaped by illegally crossing the heavily guarded Soviet borders by land, sea, or air. That number includes 229 people who fled to Western zones in Germany and Austria, 60 people who crossed Soviet land borders elsewhere, 18 who escaped by boat, and 5 who flew airplanes.

As to the jumpers, they number 61 people (almost 14 percent). No distinction was made as to whether they defected while ashore in foreign ports or actually jumped off their ships. Nor was there any distinction made between navy men, merchant sailors, or fishermen.

The remaining 65 people (nearly 15 percent) can be classified as non-returners. Among them, 29 people went abroad on tourist visas, 26 were working abroad (the occupations are not specified), 6 were part of cultural and scholarly exchanges, and 4 were on private visits (presumably to relatives).

The KGB Wanted List also shows that 12 people escaped by using various vessels—rowboats, rubber dinghies, or rafts; 11 escaped by swimming; 7 were stowaways; and 6 used cars or trucks to cross the border.[11] Here is a sample of some of the more spectacular escapes registered in the KGB Wanted List:

1. During the night of September 21, 1948, a 24-year-old Russian escaped using a self-made raft from the Soviet-occupied island of Kunashiri to Japan.[12]

2. On August 19–20, 1965, a 26-year-old Russian sportsman, a Master of Sport in pentathlon, escaped to Turkey by swimming across the Soviet-Turkish maritime border from the village of Sarii near Batumi, Adzharia.[13]

3. On March 9, 1966, a 26-year-old member of the biology faculty at Moscow University, while on a tour aboard the turboship *Rus'*, threw himself into the open sea and tried to reach the Philippines with the help of a rubber boat. He was picked up by a Philippine fisherman and delivered to Manila.[14]

4. On July 31, 1966, two Russian brothers, aged 33 and 26, illegally boarded the Soviet turboship *Beshtau* in the port of Ilichevsk. They hid until the ship was in the vicinity of the Greek island of Chios, then they jumped into the sea. They were picked up by a Greek passenger liner.[15]

ORGANIZATION OF DEFECTION

Were defections typically carried out individually or with participation of more than one person? The KGB Wanted List provides an answer to this question. Three hundred sixteen entries of the total 470 contain no reference to anyone who is suspected of accompanying or assisting the defector.[16] That means that two-thirds of the defectors escaped from the USSR entirely on their own. If they confided their plans to anyone, or received help from anyone, it has remained undetected by Soviet authorities.

The remaining 154 entries (32.8 percent) contain references to other persons who are said to have conspired with the defectors. The numerical breakdown is as follows:

Conspired with	Absolute Frequency	Relative Frequency (percentage)
Family member	29	6.2
Lover	60	12.8
Friend	65	13.8
No one	316	67.2
	470	100.0

In most of the cases the co-conspirators fled too, and they were declared fugitives and cross-listed in the KGB Wanted List. A major exception are those women lovers who were not Soviet citizens. In such cases, only their names are noted. Usually they are women of German or Austrian origin who befriended Soviet soldiers in the occupying forces.

The relatively high percentage of lovers as co-conspirators counterpoints the fact that Soviet soldiers in the occupying forces are not allowed to form personal contacts of love or friendship with members of the local population. The inability to establish or maintain such contacts for fear of official persecution has been, no doubt, a contributing factor in defections. Needless to say, the obstacles to normal human contacts that Soviet authorities artificially create in Eastern Europe violate the Helsinki Accords' provisions for human rights.

Only 29 people (6.2 percent) managed to escape in family units, and very few of them with children. This reflects the standard Soviet practice of not allowing all members of a family to go abroad, with rare exceptions for highly trusted officials.[17] This practice amounts, of course, to holding family members hostage for the dual purpose of deterrence and keeping tabs on defectors. This, too, is a gross violation of the Helsinki Accords.

Here are a few examples that will illustrate various forms of "conspiracy":

1. On May 26, 1949, a Russian major, the commander of an artillery battalion and a graduate of the Frunze Military-Political College in Gorky, a Communist Party member, and a Hero of the Soviet Union, abandoned his military unit in Austria, and together with his cohabitant, X, fled to the American sector of Vienna. He took with him a suitcase filled with absolutely secret documents about the Soviet army and passed them on to the Americans. That same year he was sentenced, in absentia, to 25 years of corrective labor by a military tribunal.[18]

2. On July 10, 1957, a Latvian mechanic, 24 years old, while on a fishing trip in neutral waters in the Baltic Sea, entered into a criminal conspiracy with crewmen X and Y. Together they tied up the captain and directed the trawler toward the Swedish coast, where they remained.[19]

3. On September 13, 1965, a Latvian, the deputy captain of the fishing boat *Variag*, conspired with his cousin, X (also wanted), to defect. Together they seized the boat and fled to Sweden, where they asked for political asylum.[20]

WHEREABOUTS AFTER DEFECTION

Consistent with the purposes of the KGB Wanted List, its compilers are careful to note, wherever possible, the country in which a defector is either believed to be living or where he or she was last seen. In 94 entries (20 percent of 470) there is no mention of country of residence. This probably means that the KGB has lost track of every fifth defector and presumes that these people continue to reside in the country of defection. As for the remaining 376 entries where countries of residence are indicated, the following results have emerged. (For a complete list of countries of residence, see Appendix 2E.)[21]

Country	Number of Defectors in Residence	Percentage of 376
United States	107	28.5
West Germany	88	23.4
Canada	42	11.2
Sweden	28	7.4
Great Britain	25	6.6
Australia	19	5.1
All others	67	17.8
	376	100.0

When comparing the above with the list of countries of defection (see Appendix 2D), one notices that whereas the leading countries of defection were Germany and Austria, which together accounted for 57 percent of all defections, the English-speaking countries—the United States, Canada, Great Britain, and Australia—are among the leading countries of residence. Together these four countries host 193 defectors (51.4 percent). Although West Germany is still the second most popular country of residence, it has lost considerably more than half of its defectors. The United States, on the other hand, with 107 defectors in residence, is the most popular country of residence, even though only three defectors actually defected to U.S. territory. Other English-speaking countries are also net-gainers of defectors. Thus, the following tendencies in the resettlement of defectors have emerged.

First, and most salient, there is a tendency to relocate to the United States. This, no doubt, has to do with such factors as the leading role of the United States in the free world, its reputation as the country of immigrants, and its high standard of living. However, even though the United States has the largest share of all defectors at large, 107 people or 28.5 percent, one is surprised that it has not absorbed more. As we recall, 120 people defected into the custody of the American occupation forces in Europe.

Another tendency is to relocate from German-speaking countries to English-speaking countries. This reflects the high status presently enjoyed by the English language in the world community, as well as liberal immigration policies, especially in Canada and Australia. Again, one is surprised that

Britain has not absorbed more than 25 defectors, as at least 66 came under the jurisdiction of the British occupation forces in Europe.

A third tendency is to relocate from countries of defection adjacent to the USSR to such Latin American countries as Argentina, Chile, and Brazil, which have liberal immigration policies. Only Sweden has managed to hold most of its defectors, which is probably due to its liberal immigration policy, its high standard of living, and the fact that its established Baltic communities attract defectors of Baltic origin.

It should be pointed out that Israel has attracted at least eight defectors, which suggests that some defections were motivated by a search for a national homeland.

OCCUPATION AFTER DEFECTION

There are only 128 records (27.2 percent) that indicate defectors' present occupations.[22] As for the remaining 372 cases, it may be presumed that the KGB either lacked the information or did not bother to transfer the data from the individual files to the KGB Wanted List. The latter may be true in some cases, when defectors were deemed unimportant. However, the KGB clerks would be considered remiss in their duties if they failed to take note of a given defector's particularly "treasonous" present occupation, such as working for a foreign intelligence service; working for Radio Liberty/Free Europe, Voice of America, or some other "bourgeois" medium; or entering into a foreign military service.

Still, there are only 44 people, fewer than 10 percent of all defectors on the KGB Wanted List, who are identified as engaging in the above "treasonous" occupations. Among them, 24 are said to be "agents" of foreign intelligence; 9 are called "bourgeois propagandists"; and 11 are said to serve with the "enemy" military. When added to the "crime" of defection, these occupations would no doubt increase defectors' culpability. The remainder of the 128 recorded occupations fall into two broad categories: workers (including drivers, sailors, and fishermen), totaling 43 people; and professionals (including educators, doctors, artists, and businessmen), totaling 41. Thus, the KGB's own records show that the overwhelming majority of defectors, after settling in the free world, engage in nonpolitical occupations, innocuous even by Soviet standards.

In view of the incompleteness and, perhaps, selectivity of the records, a comparison with the figures on occupation prior to defection (see Chapter 5) could hardly yield definitive results. Yet, one can observe a certain increase in the number of those who are said to have links with Western intelligence services, from about 15 to 24 people. The number is still surprisingly low to justify the usual stereotype of a defector as someone engaged in the spooky business of spying. The KGB's own records defy this stereotype that the Soviets like to promote in order to undermine the defectors' credibility in the eyes of the Western public. Otherwise, the only apparent trend is a significant demilitarization of occupations. From among 244 military defectors, including 41 career officers, only 11 chose or were allowed to pursue military careers in the free world.

In sum, our analysis of the KGB's own records on the circumstances of defection and its aftermath shows that the annual frequency of defections peaked during 1947 and 1948 (with 59 and 60 defectors, respectively), bottomed out in 1958 with 5 defectors, then began to climb up again and leveled at about 20 at the end of the period. These fluctuations are apparently influenced by domestic and international politics. (See more about this in Chapters 9 and 10.) The most popular countries of defection were West Germany and Austria, which was obviously due to the presence of a large number of Soviet occupation troops in their vicinity at a time when the borders were not as heavily fortified as they are now. Such neighboring countries as Sweden and Turkey also received a high percentage of defectors, apparently due to the fact that they have adhered more strictly than Finland to a policy of granting asylum or providing safe conduct to defectors. The American zone of occupation attracted nearly twice as many defectors as the British, which was probably due to America's image as the leader of the free world. Although defectors used every opportunity to escape, including jumping ship or failing to return after a sojourn abroad, the vast majority of them, 312 people out of 438 known cases, escaped by illegally crossing the heavily guarded Soviet borders by land, sea, and air, at great risk to their lives. While two-thirds of the total apparently escaped on their own, 154 people are said to have conspired with someone else. Escapes in family units account for only 6.2 percent of the total. Defectors tended to resettle in English-speaking countries, especially the United States. Nearly all former Soviet soldiers abandoned their military occupation in favor of civilian employment. Contrary to the usual stereotype, the KGB's own records show that only about 5 percent of the defectors are suspected of being linked with Western intelligence.

7

CRIMINAL ALLEGATIONS
AND EXPECTED PUNISHMENT

Immediately after the section of an entry in the KGB Wanted List dealing with the circumstances of the defection, there usually follows, in the same paragraph, another section containing allegations about the defector's various crimes and transgressions committed before, during, or after the defection. Below we shall treat them separately.

CRIMES ALLEGEDLY COMMITTED
IN CONJUNCTION WITH DEFECTION

It has been standard practice among Soviet diplomats to publicly accuse new defectors of theft, violence, and debauchery, or in some other way to deprecate their moral character. Yet their own records tell a different story. Below is a summary of the frequency counts for various allegations of crimes committed in conjunction with defection.[1]

As we can see, the highest frequency of allegations in the KGB's own records has to do with so-called state secrets. The KGB Wanted List never specifies the nature of these secrets, and one can presume that at least some of them are innocuous by Western standards. Take, for example, the case of Dr. X, a Russian biology professor and the director of a penicillin research institute. While in England on an official trip (*komandirovka*), he became a nonreturner on August 24, 1948, and, "establishing contact with British intelligence services, passed on to them information about his activities as the head of a commission charged with the purchase of equipment for penicillin

ALLEGED CRIMINAL OFFENSES BY DEFECTORS

Allegations of Crimes	Absolute Frequency	Relative Frequency (percentage)
Theft of money or property	12	2.6
Taking weapons along (pistols, rifles, and hand grenades)	11	2.3
Stealing and revealing secrets	32	6.8
Using force or injuring people	6	1.3
Killing people	5	1.1
Total number of allegations	66[a]	14.1

[a] Since several allegations are often made against a single defector, the total number of people accused of anything in conjunction with the escape must be presumed considerably lower than 66.

factories."[2] By Western standards, his crime seems as innocuous as that of Dr. Dobroumov, whom Aleksandr Solzhenitsyn immortalized in his novel *The First Circle* and for whom our defector may have served as prototype. Yet, on February 26, 1949, the Military Collegium of the Supreme Court of the USSR sentenced him, in absentia, to 25 years in "corrective labor camps."

Surprisingly, there are only 12 cases when a defector is alleged to have stolen money or other state property. That is only 2.6 percent of all defectors on the list, yet it is the most common accusation that the Soviets make when pleading with Western authorities to have a defector returned. Furthermore, considering the fact that soldiers constitute the largest single group of defectors, the number of those who are accused of having taken weapons, 11 people altogether, is also surprisingly small. This is probably due to the fact that Soviet military personnel have virtually no access to weapons in their off-duty hours. The majority of those who escaped with weapons were soldiers on duty at border posts. The alleged killings and violence likewise occurred at border posts, sometimes, apparently, in self defense and always as part of the escape itself. Below is a sample of violent defections, based on the accounts in the KGB Wanted List.

1. On May 7, 1946, a Russian captain and party member, who was serving as adjutant to the commander of reserves of the 8th Guards Army, attempted to cross the zonal boundary with his cohabitant and a group of Germans. When discovered by Soviet border guards, he killed one with a pistol and fled to the American zone.[3]

2. In July 1946, a Ukrainian soldier shot and wounded a sentinel near Zaalfeld, Germany. He fled to the American zone and later, in 1952,

was sentenced to death, in absentia, by a tribunal of the Don Military District.[4]

3. On July 21, 1947, a Ukrainian border guard, while on duty with a border unit, bayoneted and killed his sleeping commander and crossed over to Turkey, taking weapons with him.[5]

4. In July 1948, a demobilized Ukrainian soldier killed his former lieutenant and, using the latter's documents, made his way across the frontier into Austria.[6]

5. On May 20, 1954, a miner sentenced to forced labor for participation in a Ukrainian resistance movement escaped from his place of exile in Siberia, reached the Caucasus, and crossed the border into Turkey. Before reaching Turkish soil, he wounded a watchman in a border village and then shot and wounded a Soviet border guard. A criminal court sentenced him to death.[7]

6. On January 7, 1962, a Russian soldier on patrol at a frontier post in Georgia struck his companion with an axe, took the companion's machine gun and three belts of ammunition, and fled to Turkey.[8]

7. On September 5, 1963, another young soldier serving at a frontier post in Georgia killed his commander with a machine gun and fled to Turkey, taking the weapon with him. While living in Istanbul, he sought to form a band with the aim of destroying the Soviet consulate there.[9]

ALLEGATIONS OF CRIMINAL BACKGROUND

Some people on the KGB Wanted List are accused of committing crimes in the past. Although there is little mention of ordinary crimes such as theft, the compilers spared no effort to trace whatever political deviation they could find in a defector's background. They seem to make special efforts to trace what a defector was doing during the war, that is, whether he was a collaborator with the Germans, a POW, an *Ostarbeiter* (a Soviet citizen forcibly transported from occupied territory to Germany to work in factories), or just a Displaced Person. These efforts were apparently made with a dual purpose in mind. First, war crimes would help to explain away the fact of defection by demonstrating that the defector had long since ceased to be a genuine Soviet patriot. Second, they would increase the defector's culpability if he or she were caught and tried. These efforts yielded the following results: 23 defectors are accused of some kind of collaboration, usually unspecified, with the Germans; 18 were found to be *Ostarbeiters*; 9 were prisoners of war; and 1 was a DP. Thus, the combined number of those who had a "criminal" background—usually the misfortune of having been a POW or a slave laborer in Germany—is 51, whereas 419 defectors (89.1 percent) have clean, unblemished records, even by Soviet standards.[10]

ALLEGATIONS OF POLITICAL CRIMES AFTER DEFECTION

The number of accusations increases sharply after defection. These accusations fall into the following three categories: (1) belonging to, or participating in, the activities of various "anti-Soviet" émigré groups and organizations, Russian or non-Russian; (2) engaging in "anti-Soviet propaganda" by speaking to the "bourgeois" press; appearing on Radio Liberty, Voice of America, and BBC programs; or writing books; (3) having contact with various foreign intelligence agencies.

The respective frequency counts for each of the above categories are 72, 66, and 71—about 15 percent of all defectors.[11] That percentage is not very high, but it is still considerably higher than the number of defectors who are wanted for various "crimes" committed prior to and during defection.

In the first category, 20 defectors were said to belong to NTS; 14 people to various nationalist émigré groups, such as the Ukrainian *Smevor Ukrainy* and the Armenian *Dashnaks*; and 38 people were accused of linking themselves with such nonnationalist groups as TSOPE, SBONR, and the Tolstoy Foundation. (For a complete list of émigré organizations to which KGB records refer, see Appendix 2G.) These figures may not accurately reflect the actual level of defectors' participation in various types of émigré organizations. For one thing, the compilers are more likely to take note of the large émigré organizations than the smaller nationalist groups. Second, KGB knowledge of nationalist activities may be less extensive than their knowledge of Russian-dominated organizations such as NTS, TSOPE, or the Tolstoy Foundation. Nevertheless, these figures suggest a tendency among defectors to associate with larger organizations that do not have specific nationalist programs. Surprisingly, even such nonpolitical émigré organizations as the Tolstoy Foundation seem to worry the KGB.

In the second category—engaging in "anti-Soviet propaganda"—most of the allegations are nonspecific and may include giving an interview to newspapers or being an employee of Radio Liberty. Although on some occasions defectors are accused of having published books, the titles of these books are seldom revealed. In the entries on Khokhlov, Gouzenko, and Kaznacheev, for instance, no books are mentioned at all. Apparently, the KGB editors of the KGB Wanted List do not trust their own agents enough to let them know what defectors have written, much less let them read it.

Although there is no breakdown in the third category of allegations, the most frequent ones refer to the Counter Intelligence Corps of the U.S. Army (CIC), the CIA, and the British Intelligence Service. They also mention Gehlen's intelligence agency in West Germany as well as French and Swedish intelligence. There are a few references to unnamed "foreign agencies." (For a complete list of foreign-sponsored organizations to which KGB records refer, see Appendix 2H.)

According to Soviet laws,[12] defection generally falls into the category of state crimes described as "the betrayal of Fatherland" (*izmena rodine*). As such, it is regarded as the most serious crime, and the prescribed punishment for it has always included death, while the lowest limit has stood at ten years of imprisonment.[13] The KGB Wanted List gives a rare insight into how Soviet laws in regard to defection are put into practice, because it reflects the usual Soviet policy of trying and sentencing the wanted defectors in absentia. The dates of defectors' trials, types of courts involved, and the sentences meted out are meticulously recorded by the compilers of the KGB Wanted List. We shall summarize this information below, beginning with sentencing.

SENTENCE

As can be seen in Appendix 2F, 284 defectors, 60.4 percent of the total on the KGB Wanted List, were tried in absentia in various Soviet courts. Without exception, all were found guilty and given various sentences. "The highest measure of punishment," as the death sentence is called in the Wanted List, was meted out to 224 defectors—47.7 percent of all listed defectors. Comprising 78.9 percent of all sentences, the death penalty was by far the most common form of punishment for the "crime" of defection. The lightest sentence was seven years in labor camps. However, only one defector out of the 287 sentenced was found worthy of it. Another defector was sentenced to a 12-year term. The rest received more standard sentences, in decreasing order: 35 defectors were sentenced to twenty-five-year terms, 15 to fifteen-year terms, and 8 to ten-year terms.[14] One would naturally expect that all those condemned to death are either military personnel[15] or those accused of especially serious crimes like murder or the passing of "secrets." However, the KGB records reflect both the deliberate imprecision of Soviet laws and the arbitrariness of their application. Thus, among those seven defectors who have allegedly used force or committed murder in conjunction with their escapes, only two, the Ukrainian soldier who wounded a sentinel and the exile from Siberia who wounded two people on his way to Turkey, were sentenced to death. The other five, all of them military, were not tried at all, even though they have allegedly killed people. On the other hand, there are many on the

KGB Wanted List who were condemned to death for no other apparent reason than defection itself. Here are a few examples.

1. Russian, born in 1929, elementary education, member of Komsomol. While serving in military unit 15337 in Germany, on October 2, 1956, fled to West Germany with his German cohabitant X. On December 29, 1956, sentenced to death, in absentia, by the military tribunal of military unit 48240.[16]

2. Belorussian, born in 1926, elementary education. While serving in Germany in December 1945, deserted his unit and fled to the American zone. On January 12, 1952, condemned to death, in absentia.[17]

3. Ukrainian, born in 1944, sixth-grade education, former driver. While serving as a private in military unit, field post number 35872, near Mainingen, GDR, on the night of July 24, 1964, fled to the FRG in the company of his fellow soldier X (condemned). Asked for political asylum. On October 9, 1967, sentenced to death, in absentia, by the military tribunal of military unit 75092.[18]

Among those condemned to death are wives whose only crime seems to be that they followed their husbands:

1. Lithuanian, born in 1910. In July 1949, fled to the FRG together with her husband who served in the Soviet army. On July 25, 1951, sentenced to death, in absentia, by the military tribunal of military unit 48240.[19]

2. Russian, born in 1929, former employee of the film studio Mosfilm. In December 1961, fled to Sweden, then to the USA, from Finland where she was living with her husband, a former employee of the organs of State Security. [He defected too and is also wanted—V.K.] In July 1962 she was sentenced to death, in absentia, by the Military Collegium of the Supreme Court of the USSR.[20]

Among those sentenced not to death but to 25-year terms are many who are accused of such serious crimes as stealing secrets or working with foreign intelligence. One of these is the decorated artillery major who defected to the Americans in Vienna with a suitcase of "absolutely secret" documents (see Chapter 6). One can surmise that his life was spared not out of respect for his status as a Hero of the Soviet Union but because he was wanted alive (so that he could tell about how those secrets were handled by the Americans). Similarly, Dr. X, the penicillin specialist, was spared the death sentence not because of his contribution to Soviet science but for what he might be able to tell the authorities if he were caught. Here are two more examples:

1. Ukrainian, born in 1926, while serving in the MGB troops in Austria, on the night of December 23, 1947, escaped to the American zone. During an interrogation by the CIC revealed all the data known to him about his military unit. Together with another traitor of Motherland [blank] drew a sketch of the governmental system of communication and passed it on to the intelligence organ. Later established contact with an anti-Soviet organization, the Guards of the Russian Liberation Movement. On May 12, 1949, was sentenced, in absentia, to 25 years in labor camps by the military tribunal of military unit 28990.[21]

2. Jew, born in 1916, incomplete college education, former member of the Communist Party, and school principal. Working as a civilian employee in military unit, field post number 73518, on April 25, 1949, fled to the American sector of Berlin together with his cohabitant [blank]. Passed on to American intelligence everything he knew about the organization and technical equipment of Soviet troops. In November 1949, was at the American intelligence center in Oberursel. Is suspected of belonging to American intelligence. On December 8, 1949, was sentenced, in absentia, to 25 years in labor camps by the military tribunal of military unit 48240.[22]

Cases like the ones above make it clear that some of the worst culprits are still wanted alive and that their 25-year terms are nothing but suspended death sentences. The categories hardest hit with the death penalty were army personnel (89.1 percent) and civilian employees of Soviet occupation forces (94.1 percent), while only 72.7 percent of persons associated with the KGB were condemned to death. Similarly, the KGB records show that workers and former *kolkhozniki* were among those with the highest percentage of death penalties, 91.1 percent and 89.5 percent, respectively.[23] These figures no doubt reflect the large share of these two groups among military conscripts. Among career officers, on the other hand, the corresponding figure is only 84.4 percent, which again suggests that the more important a defector is, the better chance he has of being wanted alive.

Finally, the cross-tabulations of the variables of sentence and nationality show that Russians, Ukrainians, and Belorussians have the highest rates of death sentences of all Soviet nationalities. All twelve Belorussian defectors were sentenced to death, and the percentages for the Ukrainians and the Russians are 86.8 and 83.5 percent, respectively. By comparison, death penalties are meted out to 72.4 percent of the Jews, 46.7 percent of the Estonians, and 41.7 percent of the Latvians.[24] It appears that a double standard is applied to the imposition of the death penalty. Soviet authorities seem to reserve the harshest punishment for the people who form the ethnic backbone of the USSR while showing more leniency toward the defection of "traitorous" minorities. Again, since the main factor that makes a defector liable to receive the death penalty seems to be membership in the armed forces, the above figure may have been affected by a relative share of various nationalities in them. This, however, is impossible to verify because there are no control figures for the ethnic composition of the Soviet armed forces.

TYPE OF COURT

In 269 of the 284 cases of conviction, the KGB Wanted List indicates the type of court in which a defector was tried. Two hundred people (74.3 percent of all those tried) were tried in military tribunals attached to the military districts in which the defection had taken place. Twenty people (7.4 percent) were tried by the Military Collegium of the Supreme Court of the USSR. This body handles only the most grave cases involving high treason. Forty-nine people (18.2 percent of all trials) were tried in various local courts that could be called civilian. [25]

The three types of courts roughly correspond to the three categories of fugitives. The tribunals handle the cases of soldiers who are charged with desertion and high treason, the Military Collegium handles the special cases of high treason involving the passing of state secrets to foreign governments, and civilian courts are reserved for those who do not fall into either category.

The cross-tabulation of type of court by type of military affiliation shows, for instance, that of the 179 valid cases, 169 were tried by military tribunals, 8 by the Military Collegium (including two pilots and one KGB-related officer of the occupation forces), and only 2 defectors (one a civilian employee) were tried by civilian courts. However, when cross-tabulating with professional background, the role of the Military Collegium becomes more revealing—out of nine security officers, eight were tried by the Military Collegium. As for civilian courts, they tried 50 percent of the fishermen, 63 percent of the sailors, and 66.7 percent of those labeled scientists. Among career officers, on the other hand, 86.7 percent were tried by tribunals and the rest by the Military Collegium. [26]

The general trend seems to be for the military tribunals to handle defecting soldiers and to condemn them to death. The Military Collegium handles security-related cases and passes 25-year sentences. The civilian courts handle nonmilitary personnel and issue a larger percentage of milder sentences. There are, however, many deviations from this trend, and these deviations seem to be rather arbitrary. For one thing, civilian employees of Soviet occupation forces are usually tried by tribunals, and their death-penalty ratio seems to be even higher than that of soldiers. There are also occasions when security-related cases are handled by tribunals. Thus, the case of that Ukrainian who defected from MGB troops and revealed to the Americans the system of Soviet governmental communications was handled by a tribunal, though it gave him a 25-year sentence, which is more typical of the Military Collegium. There are other cases in which a civilian was tried by a tribunal and condemned to death. On November 5, 1945, the Military Tribunal of the Pacific Ocean Basin sentenced to death a stoker from the steamship *Nogin* for having jumped ship in San Francisco earlier that year.[27]

It should also be emphasized that the privilege of being tried by a civilian court is by no means an assurance of receiving a milder sentence. In 1959, the Odessa District Court sentenced to death a Jewish radio operator who had jumped from the turboship *Volga-Don* in 1956 during a port call at Alexandria, Egypt.[28] There is no apparent reason for the harshness of this sentence other than the defector's interrogation by the U.S. Counter Intelligence Corps in Frankfurt-am-Main (he later worked as a dishwasher in an American army kitchen). In another case, the captain of the turboship *Zarnitsa* abandoned his ship at Gibraltar on May 3, 1961, and asked for political asylum. Later that year he was sentenced to death by a criminal division of the Kaliningrad District Court.[29]

Even civilian tourists who defect are not guaranteed more human treatment by a civilian court. As late as November 22, 1962 (about a month after my own defection), the Supreme Court of Lithuania sentenced to death a 32-year-old Lithuanian geologist who had abandoned his "tourist delegation" while in Paris on March 29, 1961, and asked for political asylum.[30] According to his entry, he later moved to the United States and settled in Chicago where he is active in one of "the anti-Soviet émigré organizations and publicly slanders Soviet reality." It is quite possible that his postdefection activities contributed to his death sentence.

Other cases:

1. In 1955, a 20-year-old Estonian student "illegally" crossed the border to Finland, then moved to Sweden, where he asked for political asylum. Although he was not accused of any crime, he was nevertheless condemned to death by the Supreme Court of the Karelian Autonomous Republic.[31]

2. In 1959, a certain sailor was sentenced to death, apparently by a civilian court. He was said to have "vanished" from the steamship *Chuguev* on July 29, 1958, while passing through the Bosporus, and he asked for political asylum in Turkey.[32]

3. On November 16, 1962, the Criminal Division of the Supreme Court of the Adzharian Autonomous Republic sentenced to death a Russian engineer who had escaped to Turkey in the summer of that year.[33]

YEAR OF TRIAL

As a rule, the KGB Wanted List indicates a precise date of trial—day, month, and year. The precise dating makes one thing obvious: the Soviet authorities lose little time either in the preparation of the case—it takes only a few months before the court is summoned—or in its disposal: all cases are settled on the very same day that they are brought before the court.

There is not a single year from 1945 through 1968 (the records for 1969 are incomplete) that did not see the trial of at least one defector. However, the frequency from year to year is very uneven. It peaked during the last years of Stalin's reign: from 8 trials in 1948 to 20 in 1949; 24 in 1950; peaking to 77 in 1952; then down to 17 in 1953, the last year of Stalin's reign. The reader will recall that the peak years for defection were 1947–1949. Thus, the curve of the number of trials generally corresponds to the curve of defection, though with a certain time lag. It seems likely that in 1951 an executive decision was made to speed up defectors' trials as a means of deterring possible future defectors.[34]

Although the years of Khrushchev's and especially Brezhnev's rule show a marked decline in the frequency of trials—from 189 trials under Stalin (1945–1953), to 79 under Khrushchev (1954–1964), to only 3 under Brezhnev (1965–1968)—this dramatic increase is not necessarily a sign of a more lenient attitude toward defectors. As shown above, some of the harshest sentences in the most innocuous cases of civilian defection were meted out by civilian courts during the most liberal Khrushchev years. Likewise, the 1964 defection of a soldier to West Germany was treated no differently in 1967 under Brezhnev: On October 9 of that year he was sentenced to death by the military tribunal of unit 75092.[35] So the decrease in the number of trials and death sentences during these years should be primarily attributed to the decrease in the number of military defectors rather than leniency.

However, as far as the nonmilitary defectors are concerned, it appears that a major shift of official policy took place under Brezhnev but, apparently, before Yuri Andropov became head of the KGB in 1967. That shift manifested itself in two innovations. First, beginning in 1965 the practice of trials in absentia was largely replaced by another type of legal action, namely, the issuance of orders for arrest. To cite an example: a Soviet diplomat and former KGB operative who defected from his UNESCO post in Paris in September 1964 was not tried by the Military Collegium, as one would expect. Instead, on August 21, 1965, the Deputy Procurator General of the USSR "sanctioned his arrest."[36] At least fourteen such orders for arrest were issued under Brezhnev. The second innovation apparently consisted of a massive updating of the files. For instance, the entry of the soldier who defected in 1964 mentions specifically that there is a 1966 photograph on file. There seems to be a disproportionately large number of photographs dated 1966.

This leads us to the question of how the KGB Wanted List helps the KGB to keep tabs on defectors. As already noted, the compilers of the KGB Wanted List recorded not only the availability of photographs and handwriting samples but also whether the defector corresponded with someone in the USSR and whether he or she used pseudonyms. We now turn to the results of our frequency counts for these categories.

CORRESPONDENCE

Of the total of 470 defectors, there are only 95 (20.2 percent) who are explicitly noted to correspond or to have corresponded with someone in the USSR, usually with the relatives listed in the first paragraph of each entry.[37] The actual number of those maintaining correspondence may be somewhat higher. In my case, for instance, there is no mention of correspondence in spite of the fact that I have been regularly corresponding with my relatives since the day of my defection. This should serve to remind us that the KGB is neither omniscient nor very efficient. Thus, we have already noted that the KGB apparently lost track of about 20 percent of all defectors for whom they do not indicate a country of residence (see Chapter 6). Still, the notation of correspondence in the file implies that there are many defectors who do not correspond at all.

The notation of correspondence is a clear indication that the entrant is being watched and that, if need be, a lot more information about that person could be obtained through the KGB office of perlustration.[38] That information may include the defector's whereabouts down to a specific street, a work address, or a city post office number if general delivery is used. In some of the entries, the KGB compilers not only note the fact of correspondence but provide some revealing details. In the entry on a 1948 military defector, we read: "In November 1963, while residing in the USA, entered into correspondence with his mother, concealing his identity under the pseudonym... At the end of 1964, for reasons unknown, ceased to write. A 1964 photograph and a handwriting sample are on file."[39] Since it is very unlikely that the mother denounced her son, one has to conclude that the KGB opened their mail and stole its contents to update the file.

Another entry reads: "In 1964 left [Turkey] for France, from whence twice sent letters to his mother, in September and October of 1965."[40] Yet another entry, on a Finnish miner from Estonia who was allowed to go to Finland "on private business" and became a nonreturner in 1968, reads: "In letters to his wife and son writes that he has no wish to return to the Motherland. From 1969 on he has resided in Sweden."[41] This entry makes clear how the KGB files are being continuously updated.

About a soldier who defected in 1946 with his German cohabitant and who was sentenced to death in 1953, we read that "in 1961, using the false name . . . he began to write letters to his wife from the FRG. A 1961 photograph and a handwriting sample are on file."[42] Again, one has to assume either that his wife (whom he abandoned in 1946) informed on him in 1961 or that the letters that he wrote under an assumed name were routinely intercepted and checked.

Other entries indicate that mail perlustration extends beyond the borders of the USSR. Of a Ukrainian soldier who defected to West Germany in 1945 and was sentenced to death in 1952, we read that he "resides in Canada and corresponds with his brother who lives in Poland."[43] Again, barring collaboration of the brother, one has to assume either that the KGB runs its own perlustration office in Poland or that its Polish counterpart keeps it posted. In another case we read that a defector visited Bulgaria after his defection. It is not clear how the KGB learned about this, nor how the Bulgarian KGB allowed him to slip back out of Bulgaria.[44]

In at least one case there is a notation of persistent attempts to send mail and packages to people other than relatives. A Soviet geologist who defected with his daughter (there is no mention of a wife) to West Berlin in 1956 is noted to have sent a package "with NTS literature" to the head of a geological district administration and "thereafter persistently kept sending his slanderous anti-Soviet letters to official Soviet organs, editors of magazines, etc."[45]

HANDWRITING SAMPLES AND PHOTOGRAPHS

There are 450 (95.7 percent) entries indicating availability of a photograph, and 350 (74.5 percent) entries indicating availability of a handwriting sample.[46] The discrepancy between the two figures is apparently due to the fact that photographs are more readily available to the KGB due to the passport system. However, many of the photographs bear postdefection dates. This shows that such photographs were obtained by opening the entrant's correspondence. Some of the photographs may have been obtained from other sources. In the entry on a Russian soldier who defected in 1954 and was condemned to death in 1959, there is a notation of a 1966 photograph on file, although there is no mention of correspondence. The entry goes on to say that the defector graduated from a seminary and is a priest in San Francisco. It may be assumed that a snapshot of him could have been taken covertly in the streets of that city.[47]

Since there are only 350 notations of handwriting samples, we can assume that at least 120 defectors (about one in four) do not correspond with anyone in the USSR. Perhaps the number of noncorresponders is even higher, because in some cases handwriting samples predate the defections.

USE OF ASSUMED NAMES AND PSEUDONYMS

The compilers of the KGB Wanted List spared no effort to record all the names used by the defectors. Among them are maiden names, pen-names, pseudonyms, and names assumed to conceal identity on an ad hoc basis, especially when a defector would want to establish a correspondence with someone in the USSR without revealing his or her identity or whereabouts. All these names are deleted in the Hoover File. Altogether, there are 90 such deletions. This means that about one-fifth (19.1 percent) of all defectors are known to have used different names at one time or another. Since mention of correspondence often occurs in conjunction with a reference to a different name, we can deduce that the latter was often used in order to re-establish contacts with people in the homeland.

SEARCH STATUS

Eleven entries (2.3 percent) out of 470 bear a rubber-stamp mark indicating that the search for those defectors has been canceled. No reasons for the cancellations are given. The latest such stamp says, "The search is stopped by Update List No. 5, 1971."[48] This means that the stolen copy of the KGB Wanted List was used from the latter half of 1969 (since the latest defection is dated May 5, 1969) through most of 1971, since there are usually no more than five update lists a year. Although no reasons for search cancellations are given, one can assume that the defectors in question either returned to the USSR of their own free will, were abducted or otherwise forced to return, or died. Among those who died was writer Arkady Belinkov, who defected on April 14, 1968, to West Germany and passed away on May 14, 1970, in New Haven, Connecticut.

To sum up our findings concerning criminal allegations against the defectors and the punishment they can expect, the KGB records show very little to substantiate the usual Soviet claim that defectors are deviants deserving neither trust nor mercy. Actually, no more than 66 defectors (14.1 percent) are accused of anything other than defection itself. Almost 90 percent of them are shown to have a clear, unblemished personal background, even by Soviet standards. Nonetheless, 284 defectors (60.4 percent) were tried in absentia and all were found guilty. Of those tried, 224 (47.7 percent) were sentenced to death and the remainder were condemned to long-term imprisonment. One surprising finding is that the death penalty is often meted out to those "less important" defectors, mostly soldier conscripts, who are accused of nothing, while those who are accused of passing "secrets" to foreigners are usually spared a death sentence, apparently because they are wanted alive. It has also been noted that the death penalty is disproportionately meted out to defectors belonging to the Slavic majority of the country. Thus, the KGB's own records show the underlying arbitrariness of Soviet justice. They also show how the KGB, constantly updating its files, keeps tabs on all defectors, often by intercepting their correspondence with relatives in the USSR. Although a direct retribution against defectors' family members in the USSR has apparently stopped since Stalin's death,[49] their harassment continues to the present day. The KGB records show that all defectors are "wanted" by the KGB so that they can be punished in retribution for their "crimes" and as a deterrent to others. However, some of the defectors are "wanted" for other reasons, which we shall discuss in the next chapter.

8

SPY AND FAKE DEFECTORS

One noteworthy finding of the computerized analysis of the KGB Wanted List is the low number of defectors who could be identified as KGB professionals. According to a breakdown by professional training, there are only 15 KGB professionals on the Wanted List, even though a breakdown of those linked with the military shows that there were 17 State Security men who defected while doubling as military officers.[1] Finally, the security variable, which we have not discussed so far and which was introduced for the purpose of distinguishing the different branches of the Soviet State Security system and military intelligence, identifies four defectors as belonging to the KGB, nine to MGB, two to MVD, two to GRU, and one whose membership is not clearly defined. This puts the total number of people who had professionally spied either on their compatriots or on foreign countries at 18, 3.8 percent of all defectors on the KGB Wanted List.[2] Taking into account an inevitable margin of error, we can put their number at around 20. That number is indirectly confirmed by the type-of-court variable, according to which only 20 defectors were tried in absentia by the Military Collegium of the Supreme Court of the USSR. Unlike military tribunals or civilian courts, only the most serious cases, perhaps involving high treason, were referred to the Military Collegium. One would expect that defections of KGB professionals are among them.[3]

As was shown earlier, the number of defectors who are alleged to have taken secrets with them is 32.[4] That number apparently includes some of the secret police officers. However, in the Soviet Union the definition of secrecy is much broader than in the West. Therefore, one can assume that the other secret-carrying defectors were either ordinary soldiers who revealed anything beyond their military unit number or civilians who revealed such things as the level of penicillin production in the USSR.

Finally, there are 71 people who are alleged to have cooperated with foreign intelligence services, presumably beyond the customary postdefection interrogation. These constitute about 15 percent of the 470 cases. Not all of them are suspected of having actually been recruited as agents. It would be realistic to assume that such suspicion exists only in regard to those 35 defectors who were sentenced to 25-year terms. They are wanted alive for intelligence-related reasons. All in all, I am inclined to conclude that no more than one out of ten defectors could conceivably be linked with spying in either direction. Of course, this conclusion contradicts the popular image of defectors as spies. This image has been created by the natural tendency of the news media to accent the more sensational aspects of defection. The KGB, for its part, would like to promote it in order to undermine the credibility of defectors with the Western public.

So far we have dealt with those spy-related defectors who fled the Soviet Union for their own reasons; that is, genuine defectors. The question inevitably arises, however: Don't the Soviets send their agents to the West by faking defection? In other words, don't they use defection as a channel to plant long-term moles in the guise of anticommunist defectors?

My reply to this is yes, they probably do, or at least they try to. Nonetheless, I am inclined to believe that the cover for such possible spies probably does not go so far as placing a false entry in the KGB Wanted List. Consequently, I think it can be assumed that all those included on the KGB Wanted List are bona fide defectors. However, since I am not at liberty to connect the data from the Hoover File to any personal name, I can only refer the curious reader to the *Possev* List, which was compiled from the KGB source (see Appendix 1A). I can also quote and discuss those entries that seem suspicious to me (though again, the names must be deleted). Below is one such entry:

> -------- Armenian, born in 1905 in Istanbul [Turkey], incomplete high-school education, immigrated to the Armenian SSR from Greece in 1947, until 1953 lived in the city of Kirovakan. Wife --------, and sons --------, and -------- live in Kirovakan.
>
> In July 1953 was sent [*perebroshen*] to Turkey on special assignment by the Intelligence Department at the Headquarters [*razvedotdelom shtaba*] of the Transcaucasian Military District. After landing [*posle perebroski*] in Turkey was arrested by Turkish authorities and told them about his belonging to Soviet intelligence and about his assignment. There is a photo on file. [5]

Admittedly, this entry is one of those marginal cases, fortunately few, when it is not quite clear whether the entrant was a genuine defector, that is, one who had prior intent to defect, or an opportunist who chose to switch sides only after an unexpected arrest. In part, this depends on the phrase "after landing." The Russian phrase for it, *posle perebroski*, comes close in meaning to the English "after relocation." Still, it is not clear how this "relocation" was accomplished. The entrant could have crossed the border as a fake defector allegedly escaping political persecution in the USSR. Or, perhaps more likely because the nature of his assignment seems to have been strictly military intelligence, he could have parachuted into Turkish territory unnoticed under orders to merge with the local Armenian population. In any case, I assume that he was a bona fide defector, and I do so mainly on the basis of what happened to many postwar Armenian immigrants to the USSR. Like them, he was probably lured to the USSR by Soviet propaganda but later, having become disillusioned, sought to leave the country. Taking advantage of the interest of Soviet intelligence in him, he accepted their assignment to Turkey with the sole purpose of defecting as soon as he could. It's possible, of course, that my assumption is wrong. But, whether a genuine defector or not, his entry is interesting in that it shows how easily such defectors may become targets for KGB recruitment. Since he was not tried in absentia, it seems that the main reason for keeping him on the KGB Wanted List is to alert KGB agents abroad. If he could be found, he might be targeted for re-recruitment. His family is living in the USSR and could very well be used for blackmail. As an Armenian who had come to Turkey with the help of the KGB, he would not have much credibility with the Turks, and, therefore, it would be difficult for him to resist blackmail.

Here is another entry (with some abbreviations) that sheds more light on the methods of KGB operations in foreign countries:

-------- Mari by nationality, born in 1927 in the village of Staro-Kulchibaevo, Mishkinsky *raion* of the Bashkir Autonomous SSR, seventh-grade education... While serving in Soviet army military unit 46628, on June 19, 1949, deserted, and in August defected to Turkey. Recruited there by Turkish intelligence, underwent special training in Ankara. In May 1950, supplied with the documents of Sr. Lt. of the Soviet Army [name deleted], was landed [*zabroshen*] on the territory of the Georgian SSR, but gave himself up and confessed (*iavilsia s povinnoi*). Was re-recruited [*pereverbovan*] by Soviet intelligence and in June 1950 sent [*napravlen*] to Turkey. On August 29, 1950, Turkish intelligence landed him again in Transcaucasia with a spying assignment. After the interrogation on October 23, 1950, the KGB sent him again to Turkey for intelligence work. In April 1961 he was in the city of Balyksesir [Turkey], where he claimed to be a Crimean Tatar, born in the city of Bakhchisarai and resident of the city of Bursa [Turkey]. There is a 1950 photo and a handwriting sample.[6]

Although a Mari by nationality, the defector apparently grew up speaking the Bashkir language and, possibly, later picked up some other Turkic languages and dialects of the USSR. He certainly also knew Russian. This made him an especially valuable prospect for spying on both sides. Apparently a genuine defector at first, he was probably blackmailed into taking the spying assignment to the USSR. The Turks may have threatened to return him to the USSR unless he went there as a spy. At any rate, he was on the hook and was kicked back and forth like a soccer ball across the Soviet-Turkish border. Either unwilling or unable to spy, he finally managed to evade his Soviet controllers. However, all indications are that the Soviets are still after him. They knew his whereabouts in 1961, and he was still on the KGB Wanted List in 1971, without having been tried. If they find him again, they would try to recruit him. His voluntary confessions did not help in the past, and he will find no forgiveness in the future. If they succeed in recruiting him again, he would be used up, before being done away with.

If the preceding two cases suggest at least a strong possibility that the Soviets use fake defections for planting their agents abroad, the following case would show that they might try to recruit genuine defectors later, after they have settled down in their new lives, if they have something to blackmail them with.

-------- born in 1919 in the village of Lidovka, Arzamas *raion* of Gorky *oblast'*, fourth-grade education, former Soviet army soldier; taken prisoner by the Germans, from August 1941 served as a policeman at the POW camp in Dvinsk. Treated other prisoners cruelly, gave them beatings. From July 1946 worked as a storekeeper [*kladovshchik*] in the army cattle farm No. 439 of the 3rd Shock Army. On June 30, 1947, escaped to the British zone of Germany, where he stayed until 1955; worked at a fertilizer factory in Luneburg. In August 1955, he tipped the German criminal police about one of our agents who had come to him with an assignment. On July 6, 1961, sentenced, in absentia, to death by the Military Tribunal of military unit 48240. There is a pre-WWII photo.[7]

Although no nationality is indicated, this soldier is apparently Russian. It is no accident that the entry emphasizes his "criminal background." Not only was he taken prisoner, which is a crime under Soviet practice, but he also collaborated with the Germans in a POW camp, at which job he is alleged to have been a brute. Yet, despite all criminal allegations, by 1955, a full eight years after his defection, he still had not been tried in absentia and sentenced to death, which was customary for defecting soldiers. Why? The answer suggests itself when we read that in that year he was approached by "one of our agents" who had come to him "with an assignment." Although the nature of this assignment is not disclosed, it is quite clear that the agent came to recruit him, probably by threatening to denounce him as a war criminal unless he cooperated. Apparently the Soviets did not learn about how the attempt failed until 1961, when the defector was deemed unfit for further attempts at recruitment and promptly sentenced to death.

Earlier I referred to a demobilized Ukrainian soldier who had killed his former lieutenant and had used the victim's documents to pass Chop, a Soviet border station, on his way to Austria, where he defected in August 1948 (see Chapter 7). Although his crime was aggravated by his "criminal background"—he too had served as a policeman under the Germans—he was not tried either. But he was watched, even after he moved from Austria to Argentina:

> In 1953 he several times visited the USSR Consulate in Argentina and offered his services to Soviet intelligence. However, he refused to be repatriated. In 1956 he offered his services for setting up a trade firm to be run by displaced persons. According to a 1958 report he lived under the name of -------- in Buenos Aires, and worked as a lathe adjuster at the "Tamini" factory. There is a 1947 photo on file.[8]

There seems to be a mutual attraction, as well as mistrust, between defectors burdened by a "criminal background" and the KGB. In this case the initiative came from the defector. In offering his services to the KGB, he may have been motivated by a desire to make some easy money, or he may have acted on the instructions of the Argentine authorities, who were hoping to entrap Soviet spies. In any case, fearing entrapment, the Soviets decided to play it cool and wait. He, on the other hand, was sensible enough to refuse repatriation. Apparently he was not sure how much they knew about his background, and they certainly did not tell him what they knew. Most likely they wanted to repatriate him not in order to try him on charges of high treason or murder but simply to neutralize him if he were a foreign agent. Then, after blackmailing him with his past crimes, they would have recruited and trained him for missions abroad. His offer to set up a firm run by DPs must have looked especially attractive to them, since DPs have a reputation of being staunchly anticommunist and therefore such a firm would have been an excellent cover for Soviet spying activities. Although they did not accept his offer at the time, they apparently did not give up the hope to recruit him later. That is why he has not been tried and why his moves are still being watched. That is also why there are some other people on the KGB Wanted List who are accused of murders but have not been tried.

Fortunately, there are only a few defectors on the KGB Wanted List who are burdened by crimes in the past and could therefore easily become targets of opportunity for the KGB. Still, the above two cases suggest a strong possibility and even a probability that some bona fide defectors (especially those with criminal records) may be recruited by the Soviets. That inevitably creates an air of suspicion in regard to any defector.

However, the KGB Wanted List contains at least one case that shows that sometimes suspicion goes too far. The entry on a Belorussian driver, born in 1914 on a farm, reads:

> From May 1945 through December 1947, worked as a civilian chauffeur at the military unit field post 62433. On December 20, 1947, escaped to the American zone of Austria, where he was arrested by the CIC, because the Americans suspected that he belonged to Soviet intelligence. He was kept in a jail in the city of Linz under the name of --------. In 1948 he was released from jail and kept in a DP camp. From 1950 through 1953 resided in Buenos Aires [Argentina] under the name --------. In November 1948, he was sentenced to death, in absentia. There is a wartime photo and handwriting sample.[9]

It is clear that the KGB considers him a genuine defector. Otherwise he would not have been sentenced to death only a few months after his defection. Why the Americans suspected him of being a Soviet agent is not spelled out. He may have given them some reason or other to suspect him, but more likely he was simply a victim of the ignorance about the USSR that was so widespread among the Western allies during the early postwar years. He was certainly lucky not to be repatriated to the USSR, as so many other defectors of the time were.

As far as I know, there was only one case when a Soviet defector was caught in the act of spying for the Soviets. Even though this incident belongs to the post-1969 period, a few words about it may be in order here. On January 20, 1977, Ivan Rogalsky, a 34-year-old former Soviet seaman who had absconded from a Soviet ship in October 1970 in Valencia, Spain, and came to the United States in December 1971, was indicted by a federal grand jury in Newark, New Jersey, for conspiring to commit espionage for the USSR. Rogalsky was charged with conspiring with Evgeny Karpov, second secretary to the Soviet U.N. mission. He was arrested on January 7, 1977, after obtaining a copy of a secret space shuttle document from RCA Corporation engineer Paul Nekrasov, who was cooperating with the FBI. Later, Judge Herbert Stern found him incompetent to stand trial, and he was sent to a psychiatric hospital.[10]

It appears unlikely, however, that Rogalsky had been intended as a KGB plant before he defected. Since at the time of his arrest he was unemployed, indigent, and showed signs of insanity, it is more likely that he was a genuine defector who, having encountered difficulties in adjusting to a new country, broke down and decided to obtain Soviet "forgiveness" by spying for the KGB.

In any case, since he defected in 1970, he could not have been entered in our edition of the KGB Wanted List.

To sum up the statistical data extracted from the KGB Wanted List, the following composite profile of the average defector of the 1945–1969 period has emerged:

He is about 28 years old, male, a bachelor at the time of defection, strongly built, with light brown hair and blue or grey eyes. He is neither a ballet dancer nor a KGB agent, but a military conscript. He is likely to have come from a collective farm in Russia or the Ukraine. His education is not much above the elementary level. Prior to defection he knew no foreign languages and had neither a profession nor special skills, except perhaps driving. He probably defected to West Germany in the late 1940s, but now resides in another country of the free world. He may have cut off all connections with his homeland or have changed his name, keeping his correspondence with his immediate family to a minimum. He had an unblemished political background in the USSR, had committed no crime, and is not likely to devote himself to political propaganda or émigré activities abroad. Nonetheless, if he corresponds with someone in the USSR, his correspondence is opened. He is watched by Soviet agents and officials abroad, and his file is constantly updated. The death penalty hangs over his head. Should he ever set foot on Soviet soil again, he is likely to be arrested and executed, for there is no statute of limitations on his "crime."

9

DEFECTIONS BEFORE AND AFTER THE BERLIN WALL

In addition to the aspects of defection discussed in previous chapters, it was deemed necessary to analyze the KGB Wanted List for the purpose of gauging the dynamics of defection within the 24 years covered by the source. We are concerned here with two important considerations. First, how did the construction of the Berlin Wall in 1961 affect the rate of defection, and, second, what changes in the pattern of defections are observable during Stalin's last years and the years in power of Khrushchev and Brezhnev (to 1969)?

The most important single event affecting defections from the USSR during the postwar period was the construction of the Berlin Wall on August 13, 1961, which was followed by mass fortification of the entire length of the East German border with West Germany. First of all, the Wall affected the annual rate of defection. As KGB records show, during the 16.33 years before the Wall, a total of 349 defections were registered. This puts the rate for the 1945–1961 period at 21.37 defections per annum. During the 7.67 years after the Wall—roughly from September 1961 through April 1969, the last month covered by the KGB Wanted List—there were 105 cases of defection, which gives us a rate of about 13.7 defectors per year. This represents a decline in the annual rate of more than one-third[1] (see also Appendix 2I).

However, the Wall's most dramatic effect was not on the number of defectors but on the overall pattern of defection. Before the Wall was built, the overwhelmingly predominant kind of defector was a soldier from the Soviet occupation forces in East Germany who had crossed the zonal lines to freedom. But after the Wall, soldiers were replaced by a number of civilian groups— sailors, fishermen, intellectuals—none of which are as predominant as soldiers were. Thus, before the Wall the total number of military defectors was 232—66.47 percent of the 349 people who were known to defect during that period. After the Wall, their number was reduced to nine. Within this group, defections from the army decreased even more, from 164 to 5, whereas defections of civilian employees of the armed forces were reduced from 35 to zero. No less dramatic was the reduction in the number of defecting Soviet military officers, from 54 before the Wall to just one, a lieutenant, after the Wall.[2]

As to the methods of defection, that pattern changed too. Before the Wall, 227 people, presumably nearly all of them soldiers, were said to have escaped by crossing a zonal line. This constitutes 66.6 percent of all methods used. After the Wall, only one person was said to have used this method. By contrast, before the Wall only 22 people managed to escape by jumping ship (6.5 percent). After the Wall, their number increased to 37. Jumping ship became the most popular method of defection (35.6 percent), followed by crossing borders (21.2 percent, twice the rate of 10.6 percent before the Wall) and not returning from a mission abroad (20.2 percent, while only 1.5 percent before the Wall).[3]

Before the Wall, most defections took place in West Germany: 133 people (38.9 percent) defected there. Together with West Berlin, which received 56 more defectors (16.4 percent), it accounted for 55.3 percent of all defections. After the Wall, only 10 people managed to defect to West Germany, not necessarily across the border, and none to West Berlin. Thus, the total number of defections to West Germany decreased from 189 to 10, and its share dropped to 9.6 percent. The number of defectors to Austria also sharply decreased from 52 to 6, and its share dropped from 15.2 percent to 5.8 percent. However, this decline was mainly caused by the withdrawal of Soviet occupation forces from Austria after that country gained independence in 1955. Still, there are reasons to believe that the construction of the Wall in Berlin was followed not only by a fortification of the East German borders but also by a tightening of the borders of all Warsaw Pact countries, which includes the Austrian–Czechoslovakian border. On the other hand, the number of people defecting to countries other than West Germany and Austria steadily increased after the Wall. For Turkey it increased from 4.4 to 12.5 percent, which made it the most popular country of defection after 1961. For Finland the rate increased from 1.2 to 8.7 percent and for Canada from 1.2 to 11.5 percent, apparently because of the increase in the number of those who jump ship there.[4]

Before the Wall, 249 defectors, about 71.3 percent out of 349, were tried in absentia. Two hundred twelve of them (about 61 percent) were sentenced to death. After the Wall, 13 defectors out of 105 were tried, and 5 of them were sentenced to death.[5] By social and professional background, the share of *kolkhozniki*, from whom conscripts for the Soviet army are mainly drawn, declined from 21.2 percent before the Wall to only 4 percent thereafter. The share of workers also declined from 8.3 to 5 percent, but the share of sailors increased sharply from 3 to 25 percent.[6] Similar increases are registered for intellectual professions. Correspondingly, the level of education among post-Wall defectors rose sharply. If the largest group among the pre-Wall defectors, nearly a third, had elementary education, then the largest group among post-Wall defectors consists of those who had a college-level education—29 people (28.7 percent).[7]

The table below[8] shows that whereas the share of the three Slavic peoples of the USSR among defectors has declined from 68.4 percent before the Wall to 56 percent after the Wall, the share of the Baltic nationalities more than doubled, from 11.8 to 25.5 percent.

Nationality	Number of Pre-Wall Defectors	Percentage of Total	Number of Post-Wall Defectors	Percentage of Total
Armenians	6	1.9	7	7.1
Estonians	16	5.1	13	13.3
Lithuanians	5	1.6	7	7.1
Latvians	16	5.1	5	5.1
Jews	31	9.9	3	3.1
Belorussians	13	4.1	2	2.0
Russians	140	44.6	36	36.7
Ukrainians	62	19.7	17	17.3

The decline in the share of the Slavic peoples cannot be explained solely in terms of the decline of their share of the total population of the USSR, as the share of the Baltic nationalities has also declined in the post-Wall period. A more likely explanation for the decline of the rate of defection among the Slavic peoples has to do with the ethnic composition of Soviet occupation forces in Europe. Apparently, the share of these nationalities among Soviet troops stationed there is higher than their share of the population. If opportunities to defect diminish for the soldiers, they also diminish for the Russians and other Slavs. The same applies to the Jews, or at least applies for the pre-Wall period.

The rise in the share of the Baltic peoples among post-Wall defectors—though it is not uniform, since the share of Latvians remains unchanged—may reflect a growth of centrifugal nationalist tendencies. However, we should also keep in mind that the share of these nationalities is probably higher among fishermen and sailors, the groups that came to displace soldiers as the chief sources of defectors. The increase in the share of Armenians probably reflects an increase of nationalistic sentiments.

In any case, the declining rate of defection among Russians and other Slavic peoples should not necessarily be seen as an indication of their becoming more loyal to the regime. In this respect, the example of the Jews is instructive. Although their share among defectors has decreased dramatically in the post-Wall period, the same years witnessed the rise of their movement for legal exodus from the USSR and their disproportionately high participation in the dissident and human rights movement.

We may conclude that there is a great disparity between defections before and after the Wall was built. In fact, one could speak of two distinctly different periods: the pre-Wall period from 1945 to 1961 and the post-Wall period from 1961 to 1969. Each period produced its own type of defector.

A typical pre-Wall defector (in two out of three cases) is a Russian or Ukrainian conscript who deserted Soviet occupation forces in Germany or Austria and crossed over into the American or British zone. At the time of his defection he was in his early twenties, had elementary education, had no profession, and left his family behind somewhere on a collective farm. After the defection, he was interrogated by American or British intelligence officers but was found not to merit admission to those countries. Now he probably works at odd jobs in West Germany, though many of his fellow defectors found homes in Australia or in Latin America, where they, too, work at odd jobs. He may be the one of four defectors who lives under an assumed name and is unlikely to correspond with anyone in the USSR. He has committed no crime, aside from the defection itself, but is certain to be on the KGB death list.

A typical post-Wall defector was, at the time of defection, a few years older than his predecessor. He is still neither a ballet star nor a KGB agent. Nor is he a soldier. Instead, he is likely to be a sailor, a fisherman, or perhaps a member of some intellectual profession. He is much better educated than his predecessor and is better adjusted to life abroad. He is still likely to be a Russian or Ukrainian, but the chances are increasing for his being a member of a national minority. He defected by jumping ship, by crossing the state border, or by running away from a group of Soviet tourists abroad. He is likely to reside in the United States, Canada, or the European country where he defected. He lives under his own name. He very likely corresponds with his relatives in the USSR. He has not been tried in absentia and does not have a death penalty hanging over his head. Still, an order for his arrest has been issued. His correspondence is carefully checked, and his file is constantly updated. If he ever steps on Soviet soil again, he will probably be sentenced to 10 to 15 years in labor camps, and his future will be permanently ruined.

10

DEFECTIONS UNDER STALIN, KHRUSHCHEV, AND BREZHNEV

As we have already seen (Chapter 6), the annual rate of defection has fluctuated considerably during the 24-year period covered by the KGB Wanted List. We have also observed that the patterns of defection have changed dramatically since the construction of the Berlin Wall in 1961. For the purposes of determining whether the patterns of defection depend on political changes at the top of the Kremlin hierarchy, let us now review the data obtained from our computer-assisted count of defections according to whether they took place during the Stalin, Khrushchev, or Brezhnev eras.

We have divided the entire 24-year span into three periods of rule. Stalin's rule stretches from the end of World War II in May 1945 until his death in March 1953. That gives us roughly seven years and ten months, or 7.8 years. Khrushchev's period was counted as starting in March 1953 and continuing through September 1964 (although he was deposed on October 10), or roughly eleven years, seven months (11.6 years). Brezhnev's period was counted from October 1964 through April 1969, the last full month accounted for in the KGB records. Having obtained absolute frequencies for each period, we divided them by the duration of each period.

The figures in the table "Defections Under Various Rulers" suggest that the curve of the number of defections was at its highest under Stalin, then fell sharply—more than threefold—under Khrushchev and stayed low during his reign, then began to climb again during Brezhnev's first four years in power.

Why such a dramatic decline in the post-Stalin era?

There are several interrelated reasons. One has to do with the personalities of the respective rulers. The high rate of defection under Stalin is

DEFECTIONS UNDER VARIOUS RULERS[1]

Ruler	Duration of Rule in Years	Number of Defections	Annual Rate
Stalin	7.8	263	33.71
Khrushchev	11.6	130	11.21
Brezhnev	4.6	76[a]	16.52
(1945–1969)	24.0	469[a]	19.54

[a] Henceforth we will use these figures because one defection took place in May 1969, which is outside the given period.

consistent with the brutality and arbitrariness of his rule. Another reason can be found in the frustrated expectations of the early postwar years, when it became clear that Stalin was not about to deliver on his promises to grant more liberties to the people once Hitler's Germany was defeated. A third reason may be seen in the escalation of the cold war, which largely coincides with Stalin's years in power. That escalation was followed by a growth of sympathy in the West toward defectors and helped to change the attitude of Western authorities from an initial reluctance to accept defectors to an active interest in them.

However, all of the above would have amounted to little were it not for the simple fact that pre-Wall conditions in East Germany and the city of Berlin (as well as in Austria before it gained independence in 1955) afforded thousands of Soviet soldiers unusual opportunities to see the free world first-hand and then to defect across an unusually—by Soviet standards—porous zone line. In fact, one could argue that pre-Wall conditions were abnormal for the inherently walled-in Soviet society, and therefore the erection of the Berlin Wall in 1961 merely restored the "normalcy" of Soviet existence. In that case, a more accurate picture of the defection would emerge if we exclude those defectors who escaped by taking advantage of the "abnormally lax" pre-Wall conditions.

The above figures show that the entire 24-year period under review was marked by a rising rate of Soviet defection, if we exclude the "abnormal" (zonal) cases. However, if we include them, we are faced with the fact that the average annual rate of defection dropped under Khrushchev as compared to that under Stalin, then rose again under Brezhnev. The question then arises: Why such a drop under Khrushchev? Or conversely: Why did the rate rise under Brezhnev?

One may think, perhaps, that the rate under Khrushchev dipped as a direct consequence of the Berlin Wall, which was in effect for the last three years of Khrushchev's rule. It is quite probable that without the Wall there would have been more defectors under Khrushchev. On the other hand, even though the Berlin Wall had a great impact on the later period, it did not reduce

RATES OF DEFECTION 1945–1969

	Number of Defections	Number of "Abnormal" (Zonal) Defections	Number of "Normal" Defections	Years of Rule Considered	"Normal" Annual Rate
Stalin (1945–1953)	263	206	57	7.8	7.31
Khrushchev (1953–1964)	130	22	108	11.6	9.31
Brezhnev (1964–1969)	76	0	76	4.6	16.52
Entire 24-year period	469	228	241	—	10.04

NOTE: Figures based on Krasnov, Defstudy, p. 190.

the rate of defection under Khrushchev. In fact, in the three full years of his rule after 1961, there were more defectors (29) than in the three years before (22).[2]

The drop in the rate of defection under Khrushchev is all the more remarkable in that these years witnessed the beginnings of Soviet group tourism to "capitalist" countries and a general increase in the number of Soviet citizens traveling abroad (see Chapter 2, Krotkov). Yet, in spite of these new opportunities to defect, relatively few people did.

So, the main reason for the decrease in the rate under Khrushchev should be sought not in the Berlin Wall but in the general change of the political climate inside the USSR for the better after Stalin's death. More particularly, and especially after Khrushchev's speech at the Twentieth Party Congress, hopes and expectations were raised among many Soviet citizens that the USSR would gradually evolve into a society that, though remaining basically communist, would tolerate some forms of ideological heterodoxy and would allow more freedom of expression. True, these hopes were frequently dashed, and expectations were frustrated in the subsequent years of Khrushchev's rule, but, nonetheless, people were more hopeful that the regime would reform itself and the country would become a better place in which to live. More than any other single factor, it was this atmosphere of hope that helped to keep the rate of defection low. It allowed a few more potential defectors to breathe the air of hope, thus preventing them from taking the fatal step of abandoning their country. This happened in spite of the fact that the greatest deterrent to defections, the imprisonment of the defectors' families, was removed under Khrushchev.[3]

Conversely, the rising rate of defection during Brezhnev's first years in power suggests that his coup against Khrushchev in October 1964 signaled to a great number of potential defectors that a regression from the relative letup under Khrushchev was under way. Hopes that the regime would somehow acquire a human face in the foreseeable future drastically diminished.

Although admittedly influenced by other factors—such as the erection of the Berlin Wall, the number of Soviet citizens permitted to travel abroad at any given period of time, and the degree of strictness in the selection of these travelers—the fluctuation in the rate of defection from period to period may nonetheless serve as a barometer of the political climate in the USSR. Its pointer falls when hope for internal evolution of regime rises and goes up when that hope falls.

It is hardly accidental that the rising rate of defection during Brezhnev's first years in power coincides with the emergence of various forms of opposition to the regime, which later came to be known as the dissident and human rights movement. Besides the human rights-oriented organizations, such as the group behind the publication of *The Chronicle of Current Events* (*Khronika tekushchikh sobytii*), which attempted to operate openly and within the confines of Soviet law, there also came into existence a number of underground political organizations that put little trust in the ability of the regime to reform itself. Most remarkable of these was the All-Russian Social Christian Union for the Liberation of the People (Vserossiiskii Sotsial-Khristianskii Soiuz Osvobozhdeniia Naroda), which was set up by a group of Leningrad intellectuals and was led by Igor Ogurtsov, a young Orientalist from Leningrad University. The organization had about 30 active members and perhaps several hundred sympathizers in various parts of the country. However, it was uncovered in 1967, and all of its active members were tried and sentenced to long prison terms. Ogurtsov himself completed his 15-year term in 1982.[4] Another organization was the Union of the Struggle for Political Rights (Soiuz Bor'by za Politicheskie Prava), which was formed in the late 1960s by three Russian naval officers from the Baltic fleet and had connections with dissidents all over the country.[5]

In any case, even the legal-minded organizations had to rely for dissemination of their views on the underground *samizdat* publications, the number of which increased manifold precisely during the 1965–1969 period. It is noteworthy that several *samizdat* authors of the period came out with a favorable appraisal of the role of various Russian émigré organizations, including the NTS, which had absorbed into its ranks at least 20 defectors. As F. J. M. Feldbrugge points out in his book, *Samizdat and Political Dissent in the Soviet Union*, these authors came to argue that "because internal opposition is weak and not very audible abroad, the Russian emigration has the historical task of speaking for Russia and should be strongly supported in the West."[6] This certainly suggests that both the dissident movement inside the USSR and the defectors' exodus abroad have a common origin in the conditions of the USSR and are but two forms of expression of discontent with, and opposition to, the present regime.

Besides the rising rate of defection, our analysis of the KGB Wanted List shows definite shifts in the patterns of defection from Stalin to Khrushchev to Brezhnev. Although to a great extent these shifts are coincidental with the major change in the patterns of defection after the Berlin Wall was built, they also reflect the changes occurring in Soviet society under each ruler.

Educational level changed perhaps most dramatically. Under Stalin, almost 31 percent of all defectors had elementary education. Their share decreased to 22 percent under Khrushchev and 6.8 percent under Brezhnev. Conversely, the share of those defectors with college-level education nearly doubled, to 16.3 percent, under Khrushchev, and then doubled again under Brezhnev. The share of those with postgraduate degrees, though small for all periods, has grown likewise. As to the kind of education, the share of defectors specializing in the humanities rose from 3.6 to 27.6 percent. The same tendency was registered in the sciences. These two categories of defectors grew at the expense of those with elementary education and vocational training. Among other things, these figures suggest a failure of Soviet indoctrination, which is especially evident in humanities at the college level.[7]

By social and professional background, the share of such groups as *kolkhozniki*, drivers, tradesmen, and professional military personnel has steeply declined, which probably has more to do with the decrease in the number of military defectors after the Berlin Wall than with the change of rulers in the Kremlin (see Chapter 9). Conversely, the share of artists, scientists, students, and other intellectuals has steadily increased.[8] The share of workers, sailors, and State Security professionals rose under Khrushchev and then fell somewhat under Brezhnev. Of these, only the sharp increase in both the number and the share of sailors, from 14 (6.2 percent) under Stalin to 32 (27.4 percent) under Khrushchev, seems statistically significant.

Not surprisingly, the share of those who chose to cross zone lines to defect dropped precipitously, from 80.2 percent under Stalin to 17.3 percent under Khrushchev to just 1.3 percent (one person) under Brezhnev.[9] Conversely, the share of "jumpers" rose from 3.1 to 22.8 to 31.6 percent, and the share of "nonreturners" went up from zero to 8.7 to 23.7 percent under the respective rulers. Thus, under Brezhnev, the majority of defectors, 55.3 percent, belonged to these two categories, whereas their number under Stalin was negligible. Under Khrushchev, the largest group of defectors consisted of those who crossed the state border (34 people, or 26.8 percent). Their number is three times higher than under Stalin, but both the number and the share fell under Brezhnev to 15 and 19.7 percent, respectively.[10] This suggests perhaps that just as Khrushchev had ordered the fortification of the East German borders, so Brezhnev may have secretly ordered similar measures elsewhere.

Among other trends that could be extrapolated from our computer-assisted analysis, the following are noteworthy:

1. The share of those defectors who were accused of conspiring with someone else decreased from 38.8 percent under Stalin to 28.5 percent under Khrushchev to 19.7 percent under Brezhnev. Although the trend seems to be toward individual defections, this cannot be considered a sign of diminishing trust among Soviet citizens. Rather, it has to do with the conditions of military life in Soviet occupation forces in Europe, which often necessitated a defection conspiracy. If anything, trust among citizens was at its lowest level under Stalin, which is indirectly confirmed by the growth of the share of those who had conspired with anyone outside their family from 30 percent under Stalin to 64.9 percent under Khrushchev to 66.7 percent under Brezhnev.[11]

2. Contrary to the continuous cant of Soviet diplomatic officials, who love to impugn defectors with all kinds of crimes and sins allegedly committed in the past or during defection, internal KGB records contain very little that could be construed as punishable offenses, even by Soviet standards. Moreover, the trend is away from the already low level of "criminality" under Stalin to almost none under Brezhnev (see Chapter 7). Thus, the number of allegations of theft declined from 11 under Stalin to 1 under Khrushchev to zero under Brezhnev. Even the most frequent and least specific allegation—stealing secrets—declined from 29 under Stalin to 9 under Khrushchev to zero under Brezhnev.[12]

3. As far as the allegations of postdefection "crimes" are concerned, a similar trend can be observed. Thus, the number of allegations of collaboration with foreign intelligence services declined precipitously from 56 (21.3 percent) under Stalin to 13 (13 percent) under Khrushchev to 2 (2.6 percent) under Brezhnev. However, as far as allegations of engaging in anti-Soviet propaganda and émigré politics are concerned, their shares went up sharply under Khrushchev before they fell under Brezhnev to below the level of Stalin.[13] It is impossible to tell whether these figures indicate an actual decline of the defectors' interest in such activities or a diminishing interest of the compilers of the KGB Wanted List in recording such activities.

4. The number of those who had been tried sharply declined from 194 under Stalin to 71 under Khrushchev to just 4 under Brezhnev (see Chapter 7). Respective figures for death sentences are 178, 45, and 1. As

we have already pointed out, these figures do not necessarily reflect a softening of the official attitude toward defectors.[14]

5. The average age of defectors grew from 27.6 years under Stalin to 28.6 under Khrushchev to over 31.7 under Brezhnev.[15] This undoubtedly has to do with the fact that during the earlier period the majority of defectors were young soldier conscripts. During the later period, on the other hand, a substantial number of defectors came from among those traveling abroad. While selecting people for a trip abroad, Soviet authorities consistently give preference to older applicants, on the assumption that they have stronger ties inside the country and therefore are less likely to defect. In any case, the aging of an average defector does not mean that the younger generation is becoming more loyal to the regime.

6. The share of women, though very small for all periods, shows a steady increase.[16] This means not only that women are becoming more disenchanted with the regime but also that they have greater opportunities to defect, as Soviet authorities are anxious to include them in groups traveling abroad to demonstrate to the world the alleged achievements of the feminist cause in the USSR.

7. The share of defectors who left behind their wives or ex-wives steadily increased from 27 to 38 to 47 percent. Even more telling is the fact that, whereas under Stalin the 52.1 percent majority of all spouses left behind were former wives, their share under Brezhnev dwindled to 2.8 percent, while the share of wives went up to 83.3 percent. The share of common-law wives also doubled from 5.6 to 11.1 percent during the same periods.[17] Besides the change in the character of defectors— educationally, professionally, and in terms of age—these figures may also reflect a growing instability of the Soviet family in general as well as an increased reliance on the system of using spouses as hostages.[18]

8. As to the trends in the ethnic composition of defecting groups, the share of Russians, Ukrainians, and Belorussians among defectors has steadily declined over the years. Whereas under Stalin the three Slavic peoples of the USSR made up nearly three-fourths of all defectors, their combined share declined to less than three-fifths under Khrushchev and exactly one-half under Brezhnev (see Appendix 2K). This decline greatly outpaces the decline of their shares in the population of the USSR. The share of the Balts, on the other hand, has just as steadily grown, from 7.3 to 23.4 to 27.9 percent. The same is true of the Armenians. These figures may reflect a growth of centrifugal tendencies among the non-Slavic ethnic minorities and may partly explain the relative decline of the Slavic share. But the main reason for that decline must be seen in the change in the patterns of defection after the Wall (see Chapter 9). The decline of the share of Russians, Ukrainians, and Belorussians among defectors does

not necessarily indicate that these nationalities are becoming more defector-proof than their non-Slavic compatriots. The declining share of the Jews among defectors certainly does not indicate that they were becoming more enthusiastic about the Soviet regime. The mass exodus of Soviet Jews during the 1970s suggests that their share among defectors may have declined precisely because they were more suspect and therefore more carefully watched.

To sum up, the following profiles of typical defectors could be drawn for each of the three periods:

Under Stalin, a typical defector was a military conscript who deserted Soviet occupation forces in Germany and crossed over zonal lines to freedom. In three out of four cases he was a Russian, Ukrainian, or Belorussian. He had grown up on a *kolkhoz*, had little education, and had no professional skills before he was drafted into the Red Army to defend his motherland from Hitler's aggression. He fought bravely and well and had no thought of defection until he saw the occupied lands. Then he became convinced that in every country he saw, even in the ruins of war, people were better off than in his native village, even before the war. After that he stopped believing whatever Soviet propaganda had to say about the Western countries that were, after all, his allies during the war. He defected to Western-occupied zones, hoping to find a welcoming and helpful hand. Instead, he frequently met with a cold shoulder. He was lucky if he managed to avoid repatriation. Now he lives in West Germany, Canada, Australia, or Uruguay, and makes his living working at odd jobs. Using an assumed name, he tries to correspond with whoever is left of his family in the USSR. His father was killed in the war. His mother, sister, and brother have probably perished in Siberia as a consequence of his "treason." He may have been married for a brief time in his village and left behind a wife and children, but during the long years of service in Germany he formed an attachment to a German girl who encouraged him to defect. He fought for his motherland during the war and committed no crime, but even so, a military tribunal sentenced him, in absentia, to death.

Under Khrushchev, a typical defector was likely to be a sailor in the merchant marine (usually a demobilized soldier) who jumped ship while on a port call in Canada, a factory technician who crossed the state border to Turkey, or a young soldier who was lucky enough to escape to West Berlin before the Wall. He was somewhat better educated than his predecessor and had learned to read between the lines of *Pravda*. In two out of five cases, he was a member of a non-Slavic national minority. He lived through the ruthless power struggle in the Kremlin after Stalin's death and heard Khrushchev denounce Stalin's "personality cult" while building up his own. He pondered the meaning of the uprising of German workers in Berlin in July 1953 and of the Hungarian revolution in October 1956. Disillusioned with the Soviet system in general, he defected to the West in order to struggle against communist expansion. However, he came to the West in the midst of its euphoria over Khrushchev's promises of peaceful coexistence, when the convergence theory predicting the end of cold war antagonisms held sway. The best thing he could do under the circumstances was to add his voice to those who warned against believing in Khrushchev's promises and to join like-minded people in various émigré organizations. He may or may not have been on the death roll of the KGB, but he lived in constant awareness of the Soviet death squads that operated in the free world during the 1950s. He knew of their effectiveness through the testimony of Nikolai Khokhlov and Bogdan Stashinsky. The assassinations of Ukrainian émigré leaders Lev Rebet and Stepan Bandera, the abduction of NTS leader Dr. Aleksandr Trushnovich, and the assassination attempts against Georgy Okolovich and Nikolai Khokhlov did not bode well for him.[19]

During Brezhnev's first years in power (from October 1964 through April 1969), a typical defector could have been either a scholar sent to the West as part of a cultural exchange or a distinguished Soviet intellectual who had been rewarded with a tourist visa but had chosen to run away from his group, thus becoming a nonreturner. He was then in his early thirties, married, and had a child. However, his wife was not allowed to go with him on his trip abroad and was left behind as a hostage. In every other case, he was not a Russian, but belonged to a non-Slavic minority. During his student years he read Solzhenitsyn's novel *One Day in the Life of Ivan Denisovich* and probably shared some hopes for a reform of the system under Khrushchev. The ouster of Khrushchev, especially the cowardly and cunning way in which it was carried out, put an end to whatever illusions he may have had about the Soviet system. Neither did he have much faith in the ability of the West to resist Soviet expansionism. He had seen enough of the free world not to expect much of it. He saw how the unity of the West was shattered during the war in Vietnam and how easy it was for the Soviets to crush the reform movement in Czechoslovakia. If he remained in the West, it was not because he had any illusions about it but because he could not stand returning to the USSR. Perhaps he defected to buy himself time to re-evaluate his beliefs. He corresponds with his family in the USSR, but he has little hope of ever seeing his family again. Tending to keep to himself, he has established himself professionally and is better off than his predecessors. Unlike them, he was not threatened with assassination, though he is not completely at peace either. He was not tried in absentia, but an order for his arrest was probably issued. Like those who defected before him, he is lonely. But he is more hopeful than his predecessors, because he hears the stirring of dissidence coming from behind the Wall.

III

DEFECTIONS FROM 1969 TO THE PRESENT

11

DEFECTION AND
LEGAL EMIGRATION

There was an old joke (*anekdot*) circulating in the USSR that I heard before I defected to Sweden in October 1962: "If you happen to be in a border area and suddenly hear Moscow Radio announce that there is no longer an iron curtain, what should you do? You should quickly climb the tallest tree you can find in order to avoid the stampede." Of course, like any such joke, this one grotesquely exaggerates the situation. Still, it reflects the fact that there is an enormous desire among millions of Soviet citizens to go to see foreign lands. When I told this joke to my Swedish friends, they must have thought I was crazy. Then I used a more modest image to make my point. Referring to the multitudes of Cubans lining the streets of Havana in expectation of obtaining exit visas after the swap for American tractors had been arranged in the early 1960s, I told them that, if such a deal could be arranged with the Soviets, the waiting line would stretch from Moscow to Vladivostok.

The post-1969 period has demonstrated to the world that no image is too bold to describe the popular desire to leave the workers' paradise. Since the beginning of the 1970s, when the Soviet government finally allowed, grudgingly, limited emigration, more than 300,000 Soviet citizens have stampeded out of the country, and at least as many more have applied for exit visas, for which they are still waiting.[1] Although the vast majority of the emigrants are Jewish, there are also thousands of Russian Germans and Armenians who have emigrated. Unfortunately, only a tiny number of ethnic Russians and other Soviet nationalities have benefited from this swell of emigration. If all nationalities of the USSR had the same opportunities to leave as the Jews, the number of emigrants would certainly be in the millions.

Whatever the other domestic and international considerations were that may have influenced the decision of the Soviet government to allow Jewish emigration, the increased pressure on the walls from within, through accomplished and attempted defections, was one of the most decisive factors. That pressure manifested itself dramatically by several attempts at hijacking Soviet aircraft in 1969–1970. Most famous among these was the case of the Leningrad *samoletchiki* ("self-fliers").

On June 15, 1970, a group of twelve Soviet citizens, mostly Jewish, made a desperate bid for freedom by attempting to seize an empty domestic airplane, an AN-2, parked at Smolny Airport in Leningrad. They were led by a retired Soviet air force major, Mark Dymshits, and Eduard Kuznetsov, a young dissident. Although they were arrested even before they could board the plane, all twelve—and nine other persons who were not at the airport but were implicated in the conspiracy—were put on trial on December 15. On Christmas Eve, all received harsh sentences, and the leaders, Dymshits and Kuznetsov, were condemned to die. However, thanks to the activities of such dissidents as Vladimir Bukovsky, a friend of Kuznetsov who relayed the verdicts to the Western press, a storm of protest broke out both inside the USSR and abroad. On New Year's Eve, the Soviet government relented, and the death sentences were commuted to fifteen years in labor camps.[2] It was an important victory for human rights in the USSR, and it certainly helped to pry open the doors of Jewish emigration.

Although the case of the Leningrad *samoletchiki* did most to attract world attention to the plight of Soviet Jews and thereby prompt the decision of the Soviet government to allow limited emigration, there were other attempts to defect by hijacking airplanes. Referring to a report published in the *samizdat* magazine *Chronicle of Current Events* in 1970, Professor Albert Parry, a longtime student of Soviet affairs, cites two of them. One involved Lidia Sklyarova, who was sentenced to a 15-year term for a skyjacking attempt made in 1969. Another attempt resulted in a 13-year sentence for Galina Selivonchik. It is known that she was assisted in the attempt by her unnamed husband, who was killed, and her brother, whose fate remains unknown.[3] Other attempts are also known. A third attempt involved several Armenians. Using an old engine discarded by DOSAAF (Association of Volunteers to Assist the Army, Air Force, and Navy, a paramilitary Soviet organization) in the resort city of Azni in Armenia, they tried to assemble their own airplane and fly it to Turkey. They were arrested before the plane was ready, and their fates remain unknown.[4] A little more is known about a fourth attempt, this time in Lithuania. On November 9, 1970, a 34-year-old Lithuanian construction worker, Vitautas Simokaitis, and his pregnant wife, Gratsina Mickute, 21, unsuccessfully attempted to divert a domestic airliner to Sweden from its route from Vilnius to Palanga. On January 14, 1971, the Supreme Court of Lithuania sentenced

Vitautas to death and his wife to three years in jail. However, as in the Leningrad case, the death sentence was later commuted to fifteen years.[5]

Finally, two attempts in the fall of 1970 proved successful. On October 15, a Lithuanian, Pranas Stasio Brazinskas-Koreivo, 46, and his son, Algirdas, 16, succeeded in diverting to Turkey an AN-24 domestic passenger plane from its route from Batumi to Sukhumi. Tragically, in the process they killed stewardess Nadia Kurchenko. Turkish authorities rejected Soviet demands to extradite the hijackers. However, the hijackers spent several years in a Turkish jail for killing the stewardess. On October 27, 1970, two Soviet students, Vitaly Pozdeev, 25, and Nikolay Gilev, 20, succeeded in flying a small aircraft across the Black Sea from the Soviet city of Kerch to Sinop, Turkey. At first the Turkish government stood firm and rejected Soviet demands for the extradition of the two, who had declared that they "could no longer live under the jail-like conditions of the USSR."[6] However, the two were later returned to the USSR, allegedly of their own volition (see Appendix 4). Like the abortive attempt in Leningrad, these two successful hijackings caused considerable embarrassment for the Soviet government, and no doubt influenced its decision to join other countries in supporting a strong antihijacking resolution at the United Nations. (For a complete list of Soviet skyjackings and defections by air, see Appendix 7.)

Besides the hijackings, the Soviet government was embarrassed by a number of other sensational defections that took place in 1969 and 1970. In July 1969, Anatoly Kuznetsov, the author of *Baby Yar* and one of the top writers of the young Soviet generation, defected in Great Britain.[7] In March 1970, Raya Kiselnikova, 30, a commercial attaché with KGB connections, defected in Mexico. Moscow hardly had time to recover from this loss of prestige when it was jolted by new defections in Great Britain and Mexico in September. In Mexico, two dancers of the famed Moiseev Ensemble, Aleksandr Filipov and Gennady Vostrikov, followed in the footsteps of Kiselnikova and asked for political asylum. In Great Britain, Natalia Makarova, the pride of the Kirov Ballet, defected in early September of 1970 and thus proved that Rudolf Nureyev's defection of 1961 was no fluke. Makarova's defection started the exodus of Soviet ballet stars that so stunned the world during the 1970s (see Appendix 3C). Finally, in November 1970, Simas Kudirka, a Lithuanian radio operator aboard a Soviet trawler, made his bid for freedom by jumping to a U.S. Coast Guard ship. Although Kudirka was returned by the Americans to the Soviet ship, his case created a public outcry that attracted more attention to the problem of defection than either the Soviets or the U.S. government wanted during the heyday of détente.

It was under the cumulative impact of these and many other defections, both successful and unsuccessful, widely publicized and completely covered up, that the Soviet government finally relented and decided to allow a limited, restrictive, highly selective, but nonetheless substantial emigration of Jews from the USSR. Why did they restrict it primarily to Jews? Why didn't they extend it to Estonians, Lithuanians, Ukrainians, Russians, and other nationalities who made their dissatisfaction with conditions in the USSR known through numerous defections?

To be sure, the decision to favor the Jews was taken under pressure of the movement for exodus to Israel from inside the USSR and its supporters abroad. For this, organized Jewry deserves full credit. It could be convincingly argued that the government was forced to make concessions to those who had exerted the greatest pressure. However, we should not forget for a moment that this concession was also a tactical move aimed—not very successfully—at diverting world attention from the suppression of human rights in the USSR in general and of the right to choose one's country of residence in particular.

Another objective of this maneuver was to drive a wedge into the ranks of those opposed to the regime by fanning anti-Jewish sentiments. In any case, the decision was not made in the best interests of the Jewish people. By restricting legal emigration to certain ethnic groups, the Soviet government sought to implant the idea that the only people who could conceivably wish to leave the Soviet "brotherhood" of nationalities were a few "treacherous" Jews, some "incorrigible" Germans, and some "unpatriotic" Armenians. Andrei Sakharov saw through the maneuver and warned that

> to reduce this whole problem to one of Jewish emigration is a mistake. Such a concentration would emasculate the social and international significance of the right to leave one's country and return. It would mean that for the people of other ethnic origins the right to emigrate was left undefended; and it would make possible the taking of reprisals. Finally, such exclusivity would enable Soviet authorities to support traditional anti-Semitism and utilize it, in particular, against the democratic movement.[8]

A third objective of this maneuver was to keep world opinion hostage to the expectation that the present, limited emigration was but a first step on the way to genuine free emigration from the USSR. In fact, from the very beginning the maneuver was conceived not as a prelude to an open-door emigration policy but rather as an open-valve policy. That policy was designed to prevent the boiler of dissidence from exploding by letting dissident "steam" out gradually through the valve of Jewish emigration. The fact that the Jews constitute a disproportionately high number among the dissidents was not lost on Soviet leaders.

The decision to allow the first substantial quota of Jewish emigration from the USSR was apparently made in March 1971 during the preparation of the Twenty-fourth Party Congress when the Kremlin felt particularly anxious to avoid any incidents with Jewish protesters in the presence of foreign delegates and journalists in Moscow. In that month alone, more Jews were allowed to leave the USSR than in several previous years. If, during the 22-year span from 1948 to 1970, 7,000 Jews left the USSR, in 1971 alone that number doubled to 14,000; in each of the following two years, the figures approached 30,000; and before the decade was over, about 270,000 Jews had left the promised land of "proletarian internationalism."[9]

Besides the phenomenon of Jewish emigration, the post-1969 period was characterized by a number of important events, both inside the USSR and in the international arena, that had influenced defection during these years. Inside the USSR, this period was characterized by the growth and subsequent gradual suppression of the dissident and human rights movement. It was marked by such events as the award of the Nobel Prize for literature to Aleksandr Solzhenitsyn in 1970 and his expulsion from the USSR in 1974; the award of the Nobel Peace Prize to Andrei Sakharov in 1975 and his banishment to Gorky after the Soviet invasion of Afghanistan; and a series of expulsions from the USSR of the writers Andrei Sinyavsky, Viktor Nekrasov, and Vladimir Maksimov, the cellist Mstislav Rostropovich, and such human rights activists as Valery Chalidze, Andrei Amalrik, General Pyotr Grigorenko, and Vladimir Bukovsky. All these expulsions seem to conform to the general open-valve strategy with which the Kremlin tried to keep the boiler of discontent under control.

In the international arena, this period was chiefly characterized by a shift of the strategic balance of power in favor of the USSR, which was accomplished in the guise of détente. This happened in the wake of the U.S. debacle in Vietnam and its embroilment in the Watergate scandal. These years also witnessed the adoption of the 1974 Jackson-Vanik amendment to encourage free emigration, the signing of the 1975 Helsinki Accords, the revision of U.S. immigration regulations in the wake of the Kudirka incident, and the human rights rhetoric under President Carter. The decade of the 1970s ended with the American defeat in Iran and the Soviet invasion of Afghanistan. However, with the election of President Reagan in November 1980, America again indicated a change of mood in favor of a stronger posture vis-à-vis the USSR.

What impact, if any, did all these events have on defections from the USSR? How is a typical Brezhnev defector of the 1970s different from a typical Brezhnev defector of 1964–1969? Did the annual rate continue to rise? Did the share of Jews among defectors change after legal emigration was allowed? How did it affect other nationalities? What is the current distribution of sexes, ages, and professions? What year yielded the largest crop of defectors?

Unfortunately, these questions cannot be adequately answered without the latest edition of the KGB Wanted List, which we do not have. In the absence of the KGB source for the post-1969 period, this writer had to rely primarily on newspaper accounts of defections and other published reports. However, since relatively few defections are reported, our picture of defections in the post-1969 period must be even more fragmentary and incomplete than that of the pre-1969 period. Moreover, the published reports do not easily lend themselves to statistical analysis because they lack uniformity and provide little data on such variables as nationality, education, party affiliation, civil status, and professional and social background.

In the hope of creating a more reliable public record, I appeal to all defectors from the USSR, and to other concerned people, to send all relevant information to the archives of The Jamestown Foundation, 1708 New Hampshire Avenue, N.W., Washington, D.C. 20009, where it will be collected and preserved for posterity. I believe that such a collection of documents, data, and recollections will help to advance an understanding of the phenomenon of defection in the free world and be in no way injurious to the interests of defectors themselves. For convenience, a questionnaire form is attached at the end of this book to be used by defectors at their discretion.

Meanwhile, deferring the formulation of more definitive answers to the questions of defection during the post-1969 period until we have more information, we shall attempt to outline at least those tendencies that can be gleaned from the available, albeit incomplete, records.

12

TRENDS IN POST-1969 DEFECTION

EMIGRATION WHETS THE APPETITE

The most striking aspect of the post-1969 period—spanning the rules of Brezhnev, Andropov, and Chernenko—is that the massive legal emigration not only failed to stop defection but stimulated it further. Our admittedly incomplete list of defections of the period, based on newspaper accounts, contains about 230 cases. That gives us a rate of about 15 defectors per year, which exceeds the "normal" (see Chapter 10) rate of defection for the entire postwar era and approaches that of Brezhnev's first years in power. For the year 1984 alone I have registered 25 reported cases of defection, with the names of defectors identified. That number does not include abortive defection, re-defection, or cases in which the names of defectors were not reported. Considering the incompleteness of our data, one can assume that the actual rate of defection for the post-1969 period is probably higher than 15.

This assumption seems to be supported by Theodore Gardner, head of the FBI's office in Washington. In the summer of 1981, he took the unusual step of publicly expressing satisfaction with the increasing number of defections from the ranks of Soviet intelligence. He was reported as saying that since 1976 "defections of intelligence agents from the Soviet Union and her Soviet-bloc countries to the USA have increased significantly" and that "in the past five years, fifty people, including highly trained agents of the KGB and spy agencies of other communist countries, have defected to the U.S."[1] Even though his figure lumps together defectors from Soviet-bloc countries with those from the Soviet Union proper, it is still indicative of a rising rate, if we bear in mind that the KGB Wanted List for 24 years contained only about 20 entries on Soviet intelligence-related defectors. As for defectors unconnected with spying, who constitute the overwhelming majority, my interviews with immigration officials in Sweden and France during the summer of 1979 also indicate a rising rate of Soviet defections. Thus, during 1978, there were 13 cases of Soviet defections registered in Sweden alone. Considering the fact that the KGB Wanted List contains only 33 defectors to Sweden for the entire 24-year period, this undoubtedly suggests a rising rate, and not just for Sweden.[2]

More important than the absolute figures, however, is the continuation of the trend toward defection from the most prestigious professions and occupations. Thus, among the 149 cases of defection in which professions were indicated in the reports published prior to 1982, there were 42 intellectuals, including 31 scholars; 32 performing artists (24 musicians and singers and 12 dancers); and 21 diplomats, broadly defined as persons serving in foreign missions. (For separate listings of their professions, see Appendixes 3A, 3B, 3C, and 3G.) Once we group intellectuals, performing artists, and diplomats together, we realize that about two-thirds (99 people) belong to the most privileged stratum of Soviet society. It is they who are supposed to be in the vanguard of the Soviet propaganda effort throughout the world. Yet they lead all other professions in the rate of defection. This underscores the presence of serious weaknesses in the fabric of Soviet society.

What is more, the caliber of defectors from each of the above categories seems to be rising as well. True, the pre-1969 period produced a number of sensational defectors, including Stalin's daughter, Svetlana Alliluyeva. Still, the overwhelming majority consisted of poorly educated soldiers before the Wall was built and sailors and fishermen thereafter. Their defections, barely mentioned in the Western press and completely ignored in the official press of the USSR, were hardly noticed at all beyond their army unit, ship, or fishing village.

The post-1969 period shows a dramatic increase in the number of defectors who belonged to the elite of Soviet society. We shall name just a few:

1. Anatoly Fedoseyev, head of an electronics research institute, winner of the Lenin Prize for science, and a Hero of Socialist Labor, defected in May 1971 during the International Aviation Show near Paris.

2. Mikhail Voslensky, an Academy of Science disarmament specialist and author of several Soviet books on world politics, defected in West Germany in 1972. Since then he has produced a pioneering study of the Soviet *nomenklatura* class.

3. Igor' Glagolev, a senior scholar at the Moscow Institute of World Economy and author of several Soviet books on disarmament, was granted political asylum in the United States in 1976.

4. Viktor Korchnoy, a former chess champion of the USSR, defected in Holland in July 1976. Since then he has been a principal contender for the world chess crown.

5. Arkady Shevchenko, the U.N. Undersecretary General and the highest ranking Soviet diplomat ever to defect, shook the world by asking for political asylum in the United States in April 1978.

6. Kirill Kondrashin, the long-time conductor of the Moscow Philharmonic, defected together with his wife in Holland in December 1978 (died in the United States in March 1981).

7. The famed Soviet ballet stars, Natalia Makarova, Mikhail Baryshnikov, and Aleksandr Godunov, defected in 1970, 1974, and 1979, respectively.

8. Ludmila Belousova and Oleg Protopopov, legendary Soviet figure skaters, defected in Switzerland in 1979.

9. Maxim Shostakovich, son of the world-renowned composer Dmitry Shostakovich and himself the conductor of the Moscow Radio Symphony Orchestra, defected with his son in 1981.

10. The artistic director of the famed Taganka Theater in Moscow, Yury Lyubimov, was kicked out of the party, fired from his job, and finally deprived of Soviet citizenship in July 1984, after he had overstayed his visa abroad and dared to criticize Soviet authorities in interviews with foreign newspapers.

11. During the same month, another Soviet celebrity, the internationally recognized film director Andrey Tarkovsky, decided not to return to the USSR and asked for political asylum.

Each of the above defectors belonged to the very cream of the Soviet establishment. Their names and works were known to millions of Soviet citizens to whom they were held up as models. Each defection dealt a heavy blow to Soviet propaganda at home and abroad. Each contributed to the dilemma that Soviet leaders must now face: they need to improve the Soviet image abroad, but they also realize that those who can best perform the task are also more likely to defect, thereby inflicting further damage to that image. Defections of privileged people suggest that the fabric of Soviet society is beginning to come apart at its seams. As an American scholar correctly observed in reference to one such defector, "If Kondrashin feels like that, it is a fair assumption that many an ordinary Russian is a thousand times more bitter and frustrated." He also drew the right conclusion that the defections are "a sign of the fundamental weakness of Soviet society."[3]

Although we do not have sufficient data to determine what effect, if any, legal emigration in the 1970s had on the ethnic composition of post-1969 defections, it is quite apparent that it failed to stop defections even among its principal beneficiaries: the Jews, Armenians, and Germans. As far as the Jews are concerned, despite the fact that in 1973 about 30,000 of them left the USSR legally, in that same year Leonid Goldgur, a sailor, chose to jump ship in Japan in order to make his way to Israel. In later years, Soviet citizens of Jewish origin continued to defect as if in defiance of legal emigration, which not only involved humiliating "selection" procedures but also turned rejected applicants into the new pariahs of Soviet society—the "refuseniks." Besides Viktor Korchnoy, there were a number of other Soviet citizens of Jewish origin who rejected the emigration option in favor of a direct bid for freedom. In December 1976, Mikhail Rud', a 23-year-old pianist and winner of the international Marguerite Long Competition, defected in Paris. In January 1979, Mikhail Faerman, winner of the Queen Elizabeth Piano Competition, asked the permission of the Belgian authorities to settle in that country "for artistic freedom." In July 1979, the Soviet chess school lost another outstanding player, International Grand Master Lev Al'burt, who defected from a championship match in West Germany. Upon his arrival in the United States on July 27, he explained his defection, saying that he hated the "political system [of the USSR] which in recent years revived a rabid state-supported anti-Semitism."[4] He added that the final impetus for his defection came when he learned that his coach, Mikhail Feinberg, had emigrated. Apparently there are some compelling reasons why many people who are eligible for legal emigration forego it in favor of defection, with all the tragic consequences that inevitably entails for the defector and his or her family.

In August 1979, Aleksandr Jourjin, a 26-year-old nuclear physics graduate of Moscow University, escaped by crossing the heavily guarded Soviet-Finnish border. He then walked across Finland, avoiding the Finnish authorities, until he reached the safety of Sweden. Appearing on Swedish television, he cited lack of freedom as the main reason for his defection. However, he also complained that for him an academic career in the Soviet Union was out of the question because he had quit the ranks of the Komsomol and because it had been discovered that he had Jewish relatives.[5] Apparently he preferred to risk his life by crossing the border rather than to endure the humiliation of applying for an Israeli exit visa, which could still result in his joining the ranks of the "refuseniks."

It was also reported in January 1979 that there was another attempt at collective hijacking, similar to that of the Leningrad *samoletchiki* in 1970. This time the would-be defectors attempted to seize an airplane at Pulkovo Airport in Leningrad with the intent of flying it to Oslo. The conspirators were arrested. There were four of them: Vadim Ehrenberg, his pregnant wife Ludmila Krylova, his brother Aleksei Ehrenberg, and a woman identified only as Lyudmila Listvina. Mikhail Lebed', who did not take part in the attempt but knew of the plans, was arrested for failing to report them to the police.

Unlike their predecessors, the new *samoletchiki* planned to use their escape to publicize their demand for the release from prison of dissidents Aleksandr Ginzburg and Yuri Orlov as well as Jewish exodus activists Slepak and Shcharansky. They were tried in June 1979, and all were sentenced to various terms—from two-and-a-half to thirteen years.[6] Judging by their names, at least some of the would-be defectors were Jewish. Ironically, their quest for freedom ended in tragedy during a year when a record number of Jews—51,300—were allowed to leave the USSR legally.[7]

Armenian emigration on a mass scale began later than that of the Jews. It may have been prompted by the sensational escape to Turkey of Artush Hovanesian, a KGB lieutenant, in September 1972 and the defections of two Armenian scholars, Rafael Akopian and Eduard Oganesian, in Paris in December of the same year. At any rate, by 1976 the legal emigration of Armenians was well under way. Yet, in July 1976, Sogomin Kepekyan, a 17-year-old cyclist who participated in the World Junior Championship in Belgium, chose not to return to the USSR. Apparently, in view of the highly restrictive selection process that gives preference to those Armenians who had emigrated to the USSR after World War II, the young athlete felt it was safer to seize liberty where he found it rather than to ask the Soviet authorities for it.[8]

In July 1973, Viktor Schneider, a 25-year-old bricklayer whose father was a Volga German and whose mother was a Russian, made an attempt to cross the Baltic Sea by rowboat from the Latvian coast to Sweden. He was picked up by a Finnish ship and taken to Helsinki. The Finns were about to deport him to the USSR when he began a hunger strike that attracted international attention. Only the intervention of the West German embassy saved him from the bitter fate of being returned to the USSR. Since then, legal emigration of ethnic Germans has increased drastically, reaching its peak in 1977. In spite of a downward trend after 1977, as many as 6,653 Germans left the USSR in 1980.[9] Yet, in August of the same year, Gidon Kremer, a 23-year-old violinist of German origin, and his pianist wife, Elena, chose to defect rather than take a chance on legal emigration. They were participants in the famous music festival in Salzburg, Austria, when they were ordered by Soviet authorities to return to the USSR. They disobeyed, renounced their Soviet citizenship, and requested West German citizenship.[10]

On Sunday, November 7, 1982, three Soviet citizens of German descent—Arthur Schuller, 30, Vitaly Schmidt, 27, and his brother Boris, 23—commandeered an Aeroflot passenger plane, an AN-25, during a domestic flight from Novorossisk to Odessa and directed it to Sinop, Turkey. Trying to force the pilot to obey their order, they inflicted knife wounds on him. Upon arrival at Sinop, they immediately asked for political asylum and expressed their wish to go to West Germany. Although the Turkish government refused the Soviet demand to extradite them, they were put on trial under Turkish antihijacking laws. After being acquitted in the first trial, they were eventually re-tried and sentenced to up to nine years each. The heavy sentencing was apparently due to the fact that Turkish laws do not differentiate between a terrorist hijacking and a hijacking as the only available means of emigration. Speaking for the defendants, Schuller said: "We want freedom. We want to live in West Germany where our language is spoken."[11]

The above incidents show that the option of defection as a means of getting out of the USSR has not lost its appeal and usefulness, even for those who are eligible to apply for legal emigration. For those who are not, the situation is even more desperate. The most tragic attempt at skyjacking occurred on Friday, November 18, 1983, when a group of young Georgians, pretending to be a wedding party, boarded a domestic airliner in Tbilisi, Georgia, and tried to divert it to Turkey. The attempt failed, but only after several crew members, passengers, and at least one hijacker were killed. According to foreign reports, there were from eight to thirteen people who took part in the tragic attempt.[12] Although the Soviet press was silent at the time, in August 1984 TASS announced that four of the skyjackers—priest Teimuraz Chikhladze, actor Gherman Kobakhidze, and two brothers and medical doctors, Kakha and Paata Iverieli—were sentenced to death, while their female co-conspirator, Tinatin Petriashvili, received a 14-year jail sentence.[13]

WOMEN DEFECT TOO

Whereas changes in types of defectors by ethnic origin during the 1970s cannot be ascertained, there seems to be an unmistakable trend toward a greater number of women among defectors. Thus, there are at least 32 women on my list of post-1969 defectors, whereas there were only 20 women on the KGB Wanted List for the entire previous 24-year period. That represents a growth of their relative share from 4 percent to over 20 percent. About half these women defected with their husbands. Some of them, such as Rasma Leshinskys, were trusted enough to be allowed to travel with their prominent husbands. Others, such as ballerina Valentina Kozlova, figure skater Ludmila Belousova, and pianist Elena Kremer, were sent abroad as performers with their husbands. Still others, such as ballerina Natalia Makarova and pianist Elizaveta Leonskaya, were unmarried women who were sent abroad as performers in their own right and then made the hard decision to defect on their own.

Besides the wives of prominent personalities and those who were sent abroad as performers, there were a number of young professional women among the defectors. Among these were Raya Kiselnikova, a 30-year-old commercial attaché from the Soviet Embassy in Mexico, who defected in March 1970; Maria Vovchok, a 22-year-old interpreter who defected in England in February 1971; Natalia Morozova, a simultaneous interpreter at the International Organization of Civil Aviation in Montreal, who asked for asylum in Canada in November 1977; and Galina Orionova, a 32-year-old researcher of Tatar origin at the prestigious Moscow Institute of the USA and Canada, who defected in London in March 1979.

Whereas all of the above women could be described as nonreturners, the escapes of others were more dramatic. In April 1970, Daina Palena, a 25-year-old Latvian waitress from a Soviet trawler, took an overdose of sleeping pills while onboard ship in order to manifest symptoms of a certain illness that she hoped would alarm the Soviets and cause them to seek medical help from outside. Luckily, the trawler was at the time just outside U.S. territorial waters, and she was airlifted to a New York hospital. Even before she had fully recovered, Ms. Palena declared, in the presence of Soviet officials from the U.N. mission who were visiting her in the hospital, "I do not want to return either to my ship or the Soviet Union. The measures which I had to take in order to get to shore indicate the seriousness of my need."[14]

Mrs. Polina Zelitskaya, aged 26, jumped a Havana-bound Cuban airliner during a refueling stop at Gander Airport, Newfoundland, on May 27, 1971. She did so taking along her two sons, five-year-old Eduard and three-year-old Ernest. She requested political asylum in Canada, but neither her occupation nor the purpose of her trip to Cuba were reported.[15]

Liliana Gasinskaya, an 18-year-old waitress from a Soviet tourist ship, escaped by jumping out of a porthole and swimming for 40 minutes until she reached the shore in Sydney Harbor, Australia. In an interview after her successful escape, she explained that she had been planning to escape from the USSR since she was fourteen. "I understood that communism was built on lies and propaganda and came to hate it." The only possession she took with her to Australia was her red bikini swimsuit. She was granted political asylum.[16]

Gasinskaya was not the youngest defector. That distinction belongs to Walter Polovchak, a 12-year-old Ukrainian boy who became a nonreturner by defying the will of his parents in July 1980. His case is still pending. Generally, the trend seems to be toward a greater range of ages. The oldest defector is Arnosht Kolman, a Soviet citizen of Czechoslovakian origin who was granted political asylum in Sweden in October 1976. At that time he was 84 years old. Kolman also set another record for being a member of the Communist Party, up to the time of his defection, for 58 years, longer than any other defector. He was a prominent Marxist theoretician as well as a professor of cybernetics. After his defection, he wrote a letter to Leonid Brezhnev in which he renounced his party membership. "After Khrushchev's revelation about the blood crimes of Stalin, I began to understand how deeply distorted the party had become," Kolman wrote, explaining his reasons for defection.[17] He died in Sweden in January 1979.

MILITARY DEFECTION

Although there are only a few cases of military defection on the post-1969 list, this does not mean that the Soviet military ranks are becoming less inclined to defect. It rather means that their opportunities for defection have further diminished because of the strengthened Soviet stranglehold in Central Europe, especially after the invasion of Czechoslovakia. The borders with Finland, Norway, Turkey, Iran, and Afghanistan are also more tightly sealed. There are reasons to believe that at present Soviet leaders trust their troops even less than in the past.

Aleksey Myagkov, a KGB captain attached to the Soviet occupation forces, did not challenge the Berlin Wall but rather "slipped the leash" in February 1974 while touring Charlottenburg Palace in West Berlin. (See his story in Chapter 2.) Igor' Alekseychuk, a soldier conscript of Ukrainian nationality, managed to escape across mine fields into West Germany in 1978. Both of them have described the living conditions and morale of Soviet troops in the GDR. Although neither was able to name any recent cases of defection, both agree that Soviet forces have been increasingly plagued by desertions.[18] Of course, such desertions inside the GDR are meaningless unless they are undertaken with the purpose of reaching the West. Alekseychuk estimates, however, that there is only a 5 percent chance for a deserter to succeed in defection.

Besides Myagkov and Alekseychuk, there were at least four other military men who succeeded in defecting to West Germany during the post-1969 period, but their names were not given in press reports.[19] In addition, at least two abortive attempts at defection to West Germany were reported. According to the *Los Angeles Times*, in March 1972 three Soviet soldiers made an apparent attempt to defect to the West. When discovered, they shot and killed two Soviet policemen and an East German guard who tried to prevent their escape. The gun battle ended with the three would-be defectors dead.[20] On June 19, 1978, two Soviet soldiers, believed to be attempting defection, opened fire with submachine guns on pursuing East German police in Berlin. One of the soldiers and three pedestrians, including a West German diplomat, were wounded in the gun battle. Both soldiers were captured. It was reported that the two soldiers were racing down Unter den Linden boulevard toward Checkpoint Charlie in an attempt to break through to West Berlin.[21]

Two successful defections of Soviet soldiers across the border to Norway were also reported, one in August 1970 and the other in July 1979.[22] Neither was identified by name, and it is not clear whether they were allowed to remain in the West. As for the Soviet-Turkish border, it was reported on November 25, 1977, that "recently, two Soviet Army officers defected by swimming across the fast-flowing Arpacay River" and that "they were given asylum over Soviet protests."[23]

In March 1977, *Possev* published an article by an anonymous defector, who apparently managed to escape across the state border between Soviet Azerbaijan and Iran. The article was devoted to the conditions of the border troops in that area. The author claims that there had been very few successful defections there. He quotes a political commissar as saying that those who succeeded in crossing the border are invariably returned by Iran.[24]

As to the post-1969 defections in military aircraft, besides the celebrated case of Viktor Belenko, who flew his super-secret MIG-25 to Japan on September 6, 1976, there were two other cases that did not receive as much attention. In May 1973, Lieutenant Evgeny Vronsky flew his Sukhoi-7 fighter-bomber across the border from East Germany to Brunswick, West Germany, where he bailed out. The wreck of the airplane was returned to the USSR, but Vronsky was granted asylum. Valentin Zasimov, a Soviet air force first lieutenant, also succeeded in crossing Soviet air space to Iran a few weeks after Belenko, but he was returned to the USSR by the late Shah. (For a complete list of defections by air, see Appendix 7.)

Although there were only two cases of defection from the Soviet Navy registered on the post-1969 list—Sergei Kourdakov's in 1971 and Aleksandr P's in 1981 (see Appendix 3F)—this does not mean that navy men are less likely to defect if given the opportunity. In fact, if a 1975 attempt at a collective defection on board a Soviet navy ship had succeeded, the navy would have undoubtedly taken a lead in military defections. I am referring to a mutiny on board the destroyer *Storozhevoy* (Sentinel) of the Baltic fleet on November 8, 1975, during a port call at Riga, where the ship was moored as part of the celebration of the fifty-eighth anniversary of the communist revolution.[25] Although most of the circumstances remain unknown, a number of *samizdat*, émigré, and foreign sources[26] reported that at least part of the crew had mutinied and that their number was large enough to take control of the ship and attempt to run it across the Baltic into Swedish territorial waters. The mutineers had apparently no other objective than expressing their dissatisfaction with the regime by seeking asylum abroad. According to some reports, before reaching the Swedish island of Gotland, the runaway destroyer was first strafed from the air by pursuing Soviet fighter-bombers and then was surrounded by a superior naval task force. Apparently damaged by the air strike, the mutinous ship surrendered without resistance and was towed away to the naval base at Liepaja for repairs.

The most remarkable aspect of the mutiny was that it was organized by no other than the *zampolit* (political commissar) on board, Valery Mikhaylo-vich Sablin. A captain third rank (lieutenant commander), he was the third man in command and quite possibly in charge of the ship after about half of the 250-man crew had gone on a shore leave to mark the revolution festivities. The son of a Soviet colonel, Sablin was a privileged member of Soviet society. Ironically, he was said to be a descendant of Nikolai A. Bestuzhev, who took part in the Decembrist revolt of 1825 against Czar Nicolas I.

As *zampolit*, Sablin had an ample opportunity to get acquainted first-hand with the discontent among the conscripted sailors and officers. However, instead of reporting on the political malcontents to his superiors, he apparently conspired with them to make a dash for freedom at first opportunity. It is estimated that Sablin may have had a following of a dozen petty officers, including a certain Markov, and a number of conscripted sailors. At the start of the mutiny, they locked up some of the more doctrinaire officers. Even if their number was small, they were able to run the ship because the rest of the crew merely followed their orders. They almost made it. Were it not for two unplanned-for incidents, they would have certainly reached Swedish waters. First, one obstinate sailor jumped unnoticed overboard and swam to shore to alert the Riga naval command. His story was disbelieved at first, but then an uncoded message was received—"Mutiny onboard the *Storozhevoy*; we are heading for open sea." That message was apparently sent by one of the locked-up officers. After it had reached naval headquarters in Moscow, the chase was on. Allegedly this message was intercepted by the Swedish armed forces, but the Swedish high command declined either to deny or confirm it. The Swedes conceded, however, that Soviet radio traffic at the time "deviated from the norm."[27]

It was reported that Sablin and perhaps as many as 82 other mutinous crew members were sentenced to death and executed, but the Soviets denied that any disturbance, much less a mutiny, had taken place at all. It is under-standable that they would deny it, for an admission would be too embarrassing for the regime, which prides itself on the revolutionary tradition of the battle-ship *Potemkin*. However, even though it is impossible to prove that a mutiny occurred, overwhelming evidence suggests that it did. First, we know of other defections, mutinies, and attempted mutinies in the Soviet navy (see Appendix 6). Second, it was in the Baltic fleet that the underground Union of the Strug-gle for Political Rights had been formed by three naval officers six years prior to the mutiny (see Chapter 10). Third, several months prior to the mutiny, there appeared in the Soviet armed forces' newspaper *Krasnaia Zvezda* an unusual article in which the *Storozhevoy*'s party organization, including V. Sablin, was severely criticized for shortcomings in ideological work among the sailors.[28] One has to agree with an American student of the *Storozhevoy* incident that "if the Soviet Navy High Command cannot trust the crew of one of its front-line ships, other units are suspect if not of mutiny then possibly of other debilitating problems."[29]

Since the Soviets invaded Afghanistan in December 1979, there have been a number of reports indicating both a strong proclivity of Soviet troops toward defection and great obstacles that minimize that proclivity. According to a UPI report in June 1980, a spokesman from the Islamic Alliance of Afghan freedom fighters declared during a conversation in New Delhi that "suspicious rebels shot dead 45 Soviet soldiers who defected to them to join the Muslim insurgents." The spokesman apparently disagreed with such xenophobic practices of his comrades-in-arms, as he said that he had "saved the lives of three Soviet officers by hiding them from rebels until they gained acceptance."[30] A Russian émigré bulletin, *Vesti iz SSSR* (News from the USSR), published by Kronid Liubarsky, a human rights activist, also reported in its January 1980 issue the defection of 15 to 20 Soviet soldiers to the Muslim insurgents after a battle with them near Badakhshan in early 1980, but it said nothing of their subsequent fate. What it did say was that on January 9, 1980, half a dozen Soviet soldiers were summarily executed for a refusal to open fire against the insurgents. It also pointed out that the execution was in violation of Article 263 of the Criminal Code of the Russian Federation, which stipulates that a death penalty can be imposed only by a court martial.[31]

In September 1980, the world was struck with the news that a 20-year-old Soviet conscript walked into the U.S. Embassy in Kabul and asked for political asylum. Although he was later reported to have changed his mind and voluntarily surrendered to Soviet negotiators sent to the Embassy, there could be no doubt that his was a genuine attempt at defection and that he would not have surrendered were it not for the pressure put on him, and on the American diplomats, by the Soviets, who had menacingly surrounded the Embassy with their troops.

These incidents, occurring as they did in the early stages of the Soviet invasion, were bound to have a chilling effect on would-be defectors. When combined with such factors as the isolation of the country from Western contacts and the inability of small guerrilla units to absorb either prisoners of war or defectors, they certainly helped the Soviet high command to keep the lid on defection. Nonetheless, the reports of Soviet soldiers surrendering, converting to Islam, and seeking safe conduct to other countries abound. On one show of the ABC television program "20/20," shown in February 1982, six Soviet POWs from Afghanistan testified that the fighting spirit of Soviet troops was very low, even though some conscripts had volunteered for duty there because a year of service in Afghanistan counts for two inside the USSR. Of the six POWs, four—Sergey Meshcheriakov, Valery Kiselev, Grisha Suleymanov, and Akram Fuzulaev—called themselves defectors and pleaded not to be returned to the USSR but to be allowed to come to the United States.[32]

According to another report, Anatoly Zakharov, a Soviet soldier of Russian nationality, not only defected to the insurgents but voluntarily converted to Islam.[33] Some of the Soviet soldiers who either defected to the Afghan freedom fighters or were taken as prisoners have sought political asylum in the West. Lord Nicholas Bethell, a member of the European Parliament and a campaigner for human rights, has so far succeeded in the release of four. Unfortunately, Lord Bethell's efforts on behalf of the Soviet defectors in Afghanistan suffered a triple setback. Of the four defecting soldiers he managed to bring to the West, three returned to the USSR. On November 11, 1984, Igor Rykov and Oleg Khlan departed from London to Moscow,[34] and a few weeks later Nikolay Ryzhkov returned to the USSR from the United States.[35] All three seem to have returned voluntarily. The fourth, Aleksandr Voronov, who was brought to the United States, was reported as having difficulties in adjusting to the American way of life. It was reported that among those Soviet POWs who are presently interned in Switzerland through a special arrangement worked out by the International Red Cross with both the Soviets and the insurgents, several have expressed a fear of being forcibly returned to the USSR; one of them, Yury Vashchenko, escaped to West Germany.[36] However, according to later reports, at least two of them were allowed to stay in Switzerland.[37] In June 1983 Russian émigrés in the West formed a special organization to aid Soviet prisoners in Afghanistan, especially those seeking political asylum abroad. Chaired by Count Nikolai Tolstoy, a British scholar and descendant of Lev Tolstoy, Soviet Prisoners in Afghanistan Rescue Committee (SPARC) is headquartered at 78 Beckenham Road, Beckenham, Kent BR34RH, United Kingdom.

Although Soviet leaders seem presently in control of the situation, every incident of military defection and unrest undoubtedly makes them worry.[38] They worry because such incidents undermine the efforts of Soviet propaganda to portray the USSR as a land of unanimity. They worry even more because such incidents call into question the dependability of Soviet troops in a critical situation. They can hardly read without trepidation this prediction by one of their former servants: "If war with the West should break out, Soviet soldiers would surrender by the millions." This prediction was made by one of the latest crop of Soviet military defectors, an officer with a 15-year-long experience in the Soviet army, graduate of the Frunze Military Academy, and commander of a motor rifle company during the invasion of Czechoslovakia. Writing under the suggestive pseudonym of Viktor Suvorov, he made the prediction in his highly revealing book, *Inside the Soviet Army.*[39] Suvorov's low assessment of the morale of Soviet troops, as well as the tenor of his book on the whole, remarkably coincide with the predominant opinion of the State Department interviewees of the 1950s. Also remarkable is the fact that he dedicates his book to the memory of Andrei Vlasov, a former Soviet general who during World War II led the Russian Liberation Army, the largest anticommunist force that Hitler allowed to be formed after the fortunes of the war turned against him.

Suvorov seems to predicate his prophecy of mass defection of Soviet soldiers on one condition: that the momentum of an initial Soviet push at the outbreak of war is slowed down. In other words, only when and if the initial Soviet push is thwarted would the Soviet armed forces be put under pressure and begin to disintegrate. According to Suvorov, Soviet leaders have no illusions about the dependability of their troops; therefore, their whole strategy is based on achieving a quick nuclear victory before the West could respond. "What alternative could there be?" argues Suvorov. He writes:

> In peacetime Soviet soldiers desert to the West by the hundreds, their sailors jump off ships in Western ports, their pilots try to break through the West's anti-aircraft defences in their aircraft. Even in peacetime, the problems involved in keeping the population in chains are almost insoluble. The problems are already as acute as this when no more than a few thousand of the most trusted Soviet citizens have even a theoretical chance of escaping. In wartime tens of millions of soldiers would have an opportunity to desert—and they would take it. In order to prevent this, [Soviet leaders make sure that] every soldier must realize quite clearly that, from the first moment of a war, there is no sanctuary for him at the other side of the nuclear desert. Otherwise the whole Communist house of cards will collapse.[40]

While it is hoped that such speculations about an all-out nuclear or even conventional war in Europe may remain academic, it is reasonable to assume that the fear of defection has been a constraining factor in the use of Soviet troops as a primary instrument of Soviet foreign policy, especially in environments conducive to defection.[41] It has been also observed that whenever Soviet troops are used, as presently in Afghanistan, their effectiveness is greatly reduced by the same fear.[42] The phenomenon of defection should be viewed therefore as an important and potentially decisive factor in the total correlation of forces in the world.

DEFECTION AS A FORM OF DISSIDENCE

Another feature of the post-1969 period is a blurring of the distinction between defectors and dissidents on the part of the Soviet authorities. The *Chronicle of Current Events* has been reporting cases of persecution against defectors as if they were just another group of prisoners of conscience, which, in my opinion, they are. A number of *samizdat* documents register both successful and failed attempts to defect. In his memoirs of imprisonment in the

USSR, Mikhail Kheifets, a dissident who later emigrated to the West, favorably portrays Aleksandr Zagirnyak, who failed in his skyjacking attempt in 1977, and Maigonis Ravinsh, a 23-year-old Latvian who was caught during his attempt to cross the Finnish border.[43] At least one former prisoner, Lithuanian dissident Vladas Sakalys, succeeded in defecting across the Finnish border and now lives in the United States.[44] The late Andrei Amalrik came to the defense of Yuri Vlasenko, whose attempt to defect through the U.S. Embassy in Moscow ended in his death[45] (see next chapter). Mahmet Kulmagambetov, a dissident from Kazakhstan who had served a 10-year term in labor camps in Mordovia, devoted a series of articles to those defectors who returned to the USSR but wound up in the same camps.[46]

Here is how Vladimir Bukovsky, an outstanding human rights activist who in 1976 was released from prison, and from the USSR, in exchange for the Chilean communist leader Luis Corvalan, describes his encounter with would-be defectors in a Soviet insane asylum:

> Section Ten had more politicals in it than any other—about thirty-five or forty men out of fifty-five. The majority consisted of "fugitives," people who had tried to skip over the Soviet border: by water—in rubber dinghies; underwater—with aqualungs; by air—in homemade helicopters, gliders, and rockets; on foot; in ships' holds; and under railroad cars.
>
> And every one of them was, of course, demented, for what normal person would want to flee at a time, when, after all the mistakes, the contours of true communism were at last beginning to grow visible? A few of them had crossed the border successfully and been handed back—one by the Finns, another by the Poles, a third by the Rumanians.
>
> Another large group consisted of men who had tried to enter a foreign embassy.[47]

Bukovsky's reference to foreign embassies is symptomatic, for legal emigration not only failed to stop defections but apparently had a stimulating effect on the efforts of Soviet citizens to obtain their freedom by other means. In the wake of the Helsinki Accords and spurred by President Carter's position on human rights, an increasing number of Soviet citizens began to defy Soviet authorities by sneaking around Soviet guards at the gates of foreign embassies in order to find refuge there. Thus was created a new form of defection.

CRASHING THROUGH EMBASSY GATES

The first few attempts at breaching Embassy gates were decidedly unsuccessful. On August 22, 1976, an unidentified man ran past Soviet guards into the residence of the U.S. ambassador, Walter Stoessel, Jr., and asked for political asylum. The ambassador was out of town at the time, but the request was denied and the man agreed to leave ten hours later. He was immediately arrested by plainclothes police. It was reported at the time that that incident had been preceded by a similar incident in November 1975, when a young man was arrested after being denied asylum.[48] On Friday, November 25, 1977, several Soviet citizens, including a man, his wife, their two small children, and another woman, tried to enter the U.S. Embassy's Commercial Office but were prevented by plainclothes police. The man was severely beaten and then forced into an unmarked car.[49]

On June 27, 1978, another group of Soviet citizens finally succeeded in penetrating the gates of the Embassy. Led by Pyotr Vashchenko, who was 51 at the time, seven Pentecostalists from the Siberian town of Chernogorsk stormed past Soviet guards into the Embassy and requested the assistance of the U.S. government in securing their emigration from the USSR. Unwilling to go back to Siberia and unable to leave the USSR, the "Siberian Seven" stayed on the Embassy's premises for nearly five years. The Soviets were particularly stubborn in this case because they were afraid to create a precedent for emigration on the grounds of religious persecution. They feared that such a precedent would open a Pandora's box, for it would encourage thousands of others— Catholics, Orthodox Christians, Moslems, and Buddhists—to seek emigration, possibly by forcing their way past Soviet guards at foreign embassies.[50] In April 1983, the Soviets finally yielded to the pressure of world public opinion and allowed the Vashchenko group to emigrate. This was a significant victory for human rights.[51] It indeed created a precedent[52] that defection through the gates of an Embassy is possible, if only free world governments show determination in reminding the Soviets of their duty to observe the Helsinki Accords and other international guarantees of human rights.

It did not take long before this new form of defection, through the gates of the U.S. Embassy, produced its first martyr. On March 28, 1979, Yuri Vlasenko, 27, a merchant seaman of Ukrainian nationality, arranged to enter the U.S. Embassy in company with Robert W. Pringle, a consular officer. Once inside the Embassy, he demanded that it assist him in securing his right to emigrate. He is reported to have said that he was a dissident and "hated" Brezhnev. When told that he could not be helped, he exposed an explosive device strapped to his waist and threatened to blow himself up unless the embassy complied with his request. Ambassador Malcolm Toon decided to call in the Soviet police. After the Soviets entered the compound and fired four rounds of tear gas, two popping sounds were heard and then were followed by an explosion. Badly burned by the explosion, Vlasenko was taken away in a Soviet ambulance and pronounced dead on arrival at an emergency clinic. *Izvestiia*, claiming that Vlasenko had a history of mental illness, upbraided the U.S. Embassy for escorting him past the Soviet guards. Later, Ambassador

Toon took responsibility for the embassy's handling of the case. "Since it was apparent that the man was unbalanced, and since he appeared in our view to represent a threat to the safety of American personnel and property, and since he was a Soviet citizen, we called upon the Soviet authorities for help," explained Toon. "Frankly, if I had to do it again," he added, "I would do it exactly the same way."[53] Responding to charges by Soviet dissidents that the embassy's handling of Vlasenko was "dishonorable beyond words" and should be subject to investigation,[54] Marshall D. Shulman, then adviser to the Secretary of State on Soviet Affairs, expressed the State Department's full support of Ambassador Toon's actions.[55]

Yet, in the absence of a detailed report, I am inclined to believe that the case was handled improperly. Above all, it was handled in discord with the Carter Administration's human rights stance. What Ambassador Toon particularly failed to take into account was the fact that Vlasenko's was not the terrorist act of a malicious man, but the self-sacrificial act of a desperate man. Desperate at not being able to emigrate legally, as thousands of others had, he tried to obtain his freedom by staking his life on it at the Embassy of a country that, he must have heard, has a high regard for human life. As Toon himself admitted, the two shots that preceded the explosion might have been fired by the Soviets; if so, Vlasenko's death appears more like a killing than an accident. At the very least, the ambassador should have taken exception to the brutality of the Soviet action and demanded an autopsy to determine the cause of Vlasenko's death.

Vlasenko was not the last to try to defect by forcing his way through the U.S. Embassy gates.[56] Nor was he the last to be accused of insanity.[57] Soviet citizens of different nationalities, religions, and, arguably, of varying degrees of sanity, continue to assail the gates of Western embassies because they expect the West to insist on Soviet adherence to the Helsinki Accords. If the Soviets honored their international obligations, only a truly insane person would try to crash through an open gate.

13

DEFECTION AND DÉTENTE

THE DAY OF SHAME

The decade of the 1970s began with the "day of shame," November 23, 1970. On that day, Simas Kudirka, a Lithuanian radio operator from the Soviet trawler *Sovetskaia Litva*, jumped to a U.S. Coast Guard cutter, the *Vigilant*, and asked for political asylum. This happened in U.S. territorial waters, off Martha's Vineyard, during official fishing rights negotiations between the United States and the USSR, when the two ships were moored alongside each other. What happened later is well documented in Algis Ruksenas's book, *Day of Shame*, and in Kudirka's own account, *For Those Still at Sea*, coauthored with Larry Eichel.[1] On orders from a Coast Guard admiral, the captain of the *Vigilant* gave permission for a Soviet detachment to board the cutter, locate the hapless defector, savagely beat him into submission, bind him with cord, and haul him back to the Soviet trawler on a lifeboat readily provided by the American side. Later, Kudirka was charged with treason and sentenced to labor camps in Siberia. However, under pressure of world public opinion, he was released from the camps four years later, and on November 5, 1974, flew to the United States with his family. The irony was that at the time of his futile attempt, Kudirka was unaware that he was entitled to U.S. citizenship because his mother had been born in Brooklyn.

The denial of political refuge to Kudirka and his shameful return to the USSR were blatant violations of long-established U.S. policy. The incident instantly produced public outrage. President Nixon ordered the State Department to issue new guidelines to regulate requests for political asylum. At the beginning of January 1972, the new regulations were made public. In an apparent reference to the Kudirka incident, they authorize "the use of force against attempts at forcible repatriation." Under the new rules, the State Department's Special Operations Center, as well as the White House, are to be immediately notified of any request for political asylum made on U.S. territory. Outside the United States, requests for asylum are also to be reported, even though "it is the policy of the United States not to grant asylum at its units or installations within the territorial jurisdiction of a foreign state." However, the limitations on granting asylum at American installations abroad do not apply to defectors that have intelligence information. Their requests for asylum are handled under separate rules. Moreover, "temporary refuge for humanitarian reasons" may be granted "in extreme or exceptional circumstances,"[2] as was the case with the Siberian Pentacostalists.

In spite of the new guidelines, Smith Simpson, a retired U.S. diplomat, convincingly argued that even as late as 1979 the State Department's readiness to handle similar cases has not improved.[3] "Kudirka and his unhappy experience, which should have taught so much," says Simpson, "wound up teaching nothing at all." He puts the blame squarely at the doorstep of the State Department. Detailing the twelve "slips" committed by the department's officials on that fateful day, Simpson lambasts the department for its failure to analyze its slipshod performance.

According to Simpson, Kudirka's case was mishandled not just because of individual failures but because of "systemic weaknesses" in the process of selection, training, staffing, and promotion of foreign service officers. During selection, for instance, candidates are examined "as though they were simply entering a bureaucracy, without reference to political aptitudes and action mentality... Do such systemic factors seal the United States into an excessively cautious and essentially reactive attitude in international politics?" wonders Simpson. If so, how would the United States be able to meet the challenge of the USSR "whose dynamic diplomacy exploits every vacuum, every weakness, every mistake" of ours?[4]

Simpson suggests that, in spite of the host of new regulations, the staffing situation at the State Department has actually deteriorated since 1970. If, in the past, candidates for foreign service were introduced to the general outline of U.S. foreign policy during their basic training, now a number of "important areas have been omitted such as those relating to defection and asylum, basic though these are to what the United States stands for in the world." Concluding that "attitudes, not the lack of organizational devices... are at the root of many of our serious problems," Simpson pleads for an approach to foreign policy that would view all international incidents, including defections, as "a political process of international maneuver to obtain certain strategic goals."[5]

That kind of approach, in my opinion, has been sorely missing in the U.S. handling of defectors.

NEW RULES BUT OLD WAYS

Even though Simpson did not go beyond Kudirka's case, there are other cases of failed defections that bear out his assertion that the State Department was no better prepared to handle defections after 1970 than it had been before. In each of them the U.S. response seemed improper, inadequate, or simply inept.

At the beginning of October 1971, Anatoly K. Chebotarev, a member of the Soviet Trade Mission in Belgium, defected and asked for political asylum in the United States. As it became clear that he had actually been a GRU major, Chebotarev was brought to the United States and interrogated. It was reported that he "had exposed a Soviet spy network that had been eavesdropping on telephone conversations at NATO Headquarters."[6] On December 21, at the request of the Soviet embassy in Washington, a meeting between Chebotarev and Yuli Vorontsov, the Soviet chargé d'affaires, was arranged at the State Department. This meeting was also attended by two State Department officials. According to Charles W. Bray, a department spokesman, Chebotarev told Vorontsov that he "had come to the United States of his own free will and had no desire to return to the Soviet Union." However, two days later, on December 23, Chebotarev left his Washington area hiding place, where he was living with an American escort officer, and the next day Vorontsov phoned the State Department to tell them that Chebotarev was in their custody and that the embassy was requesting the cooperation of the U.S. government in the return of Chebotarev to the USSR. On December 26, after an Immigration and Naturalization Service officer interrogated him at Kennedy Airport and was satisfied of his willingness to return to the USSR, Chebotarev was flown by Aeroflot plane to Moscow. "We are convinced he returned of his own free will," Mr. Bray was reported as saying. "We think he was a genuine defector who changed his mind."[7]

Without going into details, three questions must be asked in regard to the Chebotarev affair. First, was Chebotarev a genuine defector or a KGB plant who was ordered to fake a defection for some unknown purpose? Second, if he was a genuine defector, did he really return to the Soviet Embassy voluntarily or was he abducted while on a walk near his hiding place? Third, even if he, being a genuine defector, indeed "changed his mind," wasn't his decision taken in a state of depression from which all defectors suffer to various degrees, as has been described by Oksana Kasenkina (see Chapter 2) and, more recently, by

John Barron in regard to MIG pilot Viktor Belenko? It was not for nothing that during the meeting at the State Department, Vorontsov gave Chebotarev, a 38-year-old man whose wife and children had been left behind in Moscow, "a number of pieces of correspondence from his family." (The Soviets do know how to exert psychological pressure on their subjects, but does the State Department know how to counteract these pressures?) The State Department obviously failed to provide Chebotarev with an adequate escort, just as it failed to provide him with the time, security, and sympathy that are needed to make a truly independent choice. One can see very well why the Soviets were in such a hurry to get Chebotarev out of the country. From their point of view, it was crucial to downplay the whole incident. But why the U.S. government had to cooperate with the Soviets in saving them further embarrassment is not clear.

A couple of weeks after the "re-defection" of Chebotarev, at the time when the new regulations on political asylum were being issued, there occurred another incident that looked very much like an attempt at defection. During the first week of January 1972, two Soviet exchange students, Merab Kurashvili and Grigory Smely, were accused of shoplifting at a supermarket in Berkeley, California. Although the State Department worked out an agreement not to press charges and thus save the Soviets embarrassment, the Soviet embassy recalled the two men and ordered them to pack for home. On Sunday, January 9, while the two men were being driven in a Soviet car to Kennedy Airport in New York, Merab Kurashvili, a 36-year-old Georgian, slashed his wrists and throat and jumped out of the car about six miles from the airport. Since there were four or five Soviet officials in the car, it is not quite clear how he managed to do it. Anyhow, he was forced back into the car and delivered to the airport. Upon learning of the incident, airport officials arranged for Kurashvili to be taken to a New York hospital.

According to Mr. Bray, even though Kurashvili made "no request for asylum," he was interviewed just the same in order "to ascertain his desires." During his interview with the New York police, Kurashvili explained that he had slashed himself "because I didn't like myself at the time." He confirmed that he was not seeking asylum. The State Department immediately allowed the Soviets to transfer Kurashvili to the Soviet U.N. mission in New York and whisk him out of the country.[8] Again, one is surprised at the speed with which the State Department accepted the "no defection" explanation from a man who was hardly in a position to decide for himself. Since he was forced by the Soviet officials back into the car from which he had escaped, there were sufficient legal grounds to suspect coercion. At the very least, the incident should have been investigated by American authorities.

On December 20, 1975, Nikolay Artamonov, a former commander of a Soviet destroyer who had defected to the United States in 1959, disappeared from a church in Vienna, Austria, where he had a prearranged meeting with two KGB officers. Artamonov was a double agent working for the U.S. government. He is believed to have been kidnapped by Soviet agents and taken back to the USSR. The news of the disappearance of Artamonov, better known under his assumed name of Nicholas Shadrin, was not made public until the summer of 1977. The alleged reason for the delay was to avoid jeopardizing the U.S. government's "quiet efforts" to obtain his release from the USSR. However, in August 1977, columnist Jack Anderson broke a story on Shadrin's mysterious disappearance.[9] Later the macabre incident became the subject of Henry Hurt's book, *Shadrin: The Spy Who Never Came Back*.[10] Hurt alleges that, in spite of Artamonov's outstanding contribution to the national security of the United States—first as a defector who provided critical information about the Soviet navy, second as a research analyst for the Pentagon's Defense Intelligence Agency, and finally as a double agent—government officials were neither imaginative nor persistent in their efforts to obtain his release from the USSR. Nor were they cooperative with Hurt's efforts to get the true story of Artamonov's fate. Artamonov's wife, Eva Shadrin, a Polish woman who defected with him in 1959, has complained that she was stonewalled by official Washington. This was apparently done not so much for security reasons, but to cover up the incompetence of those who first pressed Artamonov into service and then failed to protect him during his fatal visit to the church in Vienna. One has the disquieting feeling that U.S. officials have written off Artamonov as a case of re-defection. On their part, the Soviets not only denied that they kidnapped Artamonov, but they also insinuated that he was done away with by the Americans. As any other American citizen, Artamonov deserves no less than the full protection of the U.S. government, and a high-level inquiry into the matter of his disappearance must be made.

On September 23, 1976, only a few weeks after Viktor Belenko flew his MIG-25 to Japan, Valentin Ivanovich Zasimov, a first lieutenant in the Soviet air force, flew his Antonov-2 plane to Iran. Although the Iranian government made it clear that Zasimov had immediately asked for asylum in the United States, a U.S. Embassy spokesman in Teheran was reported as saying that no official request for asylum had been received. At any rate, on the orders of the late Shah, Zasimov was returned in November to the USSR, where he was sentenced to twelve years at hard labor. Although the U.S. government was not directly involved in the incident, it nevertheless bears responsibility for failing to exert necessary pressure on Iran, then a staunch U.S. ally, to prevent Zasimov from being returned to the USSR. One cannot help thinking that, unlike Belenko's, Zasimov's defection ended in tragedy because he had not escaped in a MIG but in an old single-engine crop duster, and therefore he was of no interest to U.S. intelligence.

In August 1979, Vladas Cesiunas, a Lithuanian canoeist and a gold medal winner in the 1972 Olympics, defected from the Soviet team at the World

Canoe Championship in Duisburg, West Germany. He was granted political asylum in West Germany, began to study German, and made known his plans to write a book on how Soviet athletes are given drugs in order to make them excel in international competition. However, in mid-October he disappeared from outside a school in a suburb of Dortmund where he was studying German. The news of his disappearance was announced by Kurt Rebmann, West Germany's chief federal public prosecutor. Rebmann said that "there are definite indications that [Cesiunas] was abducted by the Soviet secret service and forced to leave the country against his will."[11] A few days later, the West German Embassy in Moscow received an anonymous phone call from a Russian who claimed that Cesiunas was being held in a Soviet prison hospital and was suffering from severe injuries, including a cracked skull.

According to John Barron, "in late 1962 or early 1963, the leadership [in the Kremlin] did drastically curtail the practice of assassinations and told the KGB that henceforth people would be liquidated in peacetime only in special circumstances."[12] The terrorist act that was apparently carried out against Cesiunas suggests that the policy of KGB restraint, if it was ever adhered to, was abandoned around 1978. In September of that year, Georgi Markov, a prominent Bulgarian defector who worked for the BBC's Bulgarian-language broadcasts, was assassinated in London.[13] Even if the Soviet KGB was not directly involved in the assassination, the Bulgarian KGB could hardly have undertaken the task without the blessing of Moscow. The mysteries of the Bulgarian's death and of Cesiunas' abduction were never solved. Moscow kept silent on the Bulgarian. As to Cesiunas, Moscow maintained that he had managed to reach the Soviet Embassy in Bonn on his own, and then left for Moscow "with the help of Soviet officials." It also insinuated that his defection was the result of an anti-Soviet provocation and that "his will and intellect were impaired" by means of a poisonous substance that had been added to a drink.

The fact that Moscow has not been caught in a terrorist act[14] since Bogdan Stashinsky, a defecting Soviet assassin, made his revelations in a courtroom in Karlsruhe in October 1962 gives credence to John Barron's supposition that since 1962 KGB policy has required that "future assassinations should be entrusted not to Soviet personnel such as Khokhlov and Stashinsky but to hired foreign criminals and illegal agents of other nationalities who could not be easily linked to the Soviet Union."[15]

The decade of unhappy defections that began on the shameful day in November 1970 when Simas Kudirka was dragged, in the presence of the U.S. Coast Guard, from U.S. territory to that of the USSR, ended in a no less tragic incident ten years later. On Monday, September 15, 1980, Aleksandr Kruglov, a 21-year-old conscript in the Soviet invasion forces in Afghanistan, armed with a Kalashnikov-47 assault rifle, entered the U.S. Embassy in Kabul to ask for political asylum in the United States. He must have been utterly astonished to find that no one at the embassy spoke Russian. Learning of Kruglov's defection, the Soviets immediately demanded his extradition. They insinuated Kruglov's criminality by telling the Americans that he had pointed a weapon at his superior. To make the demands stick, they ordered Afghan security forces to surround the Embassy, while Soviet helicopters buzzed over it. For several days official Washington maintained silence, trying to find an interpreter who could make sense of the whole affair. It was not until Friday, September 19, that an interpreter was found in the person of Robert F. Ober, Jr., a Russian-speaking diplomat from the U.S. Embassy in Moscow, who was flown into Kabul. After meeting with the Soviet Ambassador, Fikryat Tabeyev, at the U.S. Embassy on Sunday morning, September 21, Kruglov was reported to have freely chosen to return to the USSR. In any case, he left with the Soviet visitors and has not been heard of since.

All this happened nine months after President Carter had denounced the Soviet invasion of Afghanistan as the most serious threat to peace since World War II and announced a number of steps to counter Soviet expansion in the region. Posting a single Russian-speaking diplomat in a country invaded by the Soviets evidently was not one of these steps. This fact in itself is a glowing vindication of Smith Simpson's assessment of U.S. conduct of foreign affairs as "a resounding hosannah to superficiality and amateurism."[16]

However, since this also happened in the midst of the presidential election campaign, the Carter Administration was careful enough to present the surrender of Kruglov to the Soviets as totally voluntary. The whole affair was touted, if not as a victory for American diplomacy, then as an example of restraint and statesmanship on both sides. The State Department was instructed to issue a detailed report on the meeting at the Embassy to prove that Kruglov had the option "to remain at the embassy while efforts were made to arrange for travel to the United States or to a third country." Still, it could not be concealed that the Americans were relieved that Kruglov did not choose that option. But then, how could he? The young soldier was sensible enough to understand, even without an interpreter, but simply by looking into the eyes of the American diplomats, how worried they were that his selfish insistence would aggravate their situation in the besieged Embassy (think of our colleagues in Teheran!) and might even precipitate World War III. Anyhow, from the moment he found out that the Americans did not have a single Russian-speaking person in the country that their president had proclaimed the most crucial point in the world, he could not take them seriously, and gave up all hope.

The State Department quoted Ambassador Tabeyev as promising Kruglov that "he would be able to leave the Soviet Army immediately and return to his technical education with no charges or penalties against him for

having come to the American Embassy." One wonders if the State Department
made any effort to hold the Soviet Ambassador to his word.

DEFECTION DURING THE DECADE OF DÉTENTE

There are reasons to suspect that the U.S. handling of defectors during
the 1970s was worse than at any previous time associated with the so-called
cold war. The 1970s were known as years of détente, a decade during which the
prevailing opinion in Washington was antithetical to the cold war. In a commentary in the *New Republic* on the defection of Arkady Shevchenko in April
1978, Charles Fenyvesi, a Washington writer, explains how the change of the
predominant mood in favor of détente affected the U.S. approach to defectors:

> During the days of the cold war, a refugee from Eastern Europe was
> welcome in the West as live ammunition in the great propaganda battle—as
> proof of tyranny on the Other Side, and of freedom on ours. In these days
> of détente, he is viewed as an embarrassment, a liability, a factor that can
> adversely affect the precious balance of U.S.–Soviet negotiations over a
> wide range of issues. *U.S. officials no longer keep a tally of defectors;
> guidelines call for minimizing their importance, avoiding publicity.*[17]

Mr. Fenyvesi, who claims to have access to U.S. officials, thus reveals,
perhaps inadvertently, a fact that those officials kept secret, namely, that in the
handling of defectors they were guided by two contradictory sets of guidelines.
One, issued after the Kudirka incident, had the ostensible purpose of assuring
defectors' rights; the other was designed to deprive them of the publicity that is
the only effective means of protecting those rights. Lest one suspect him of
loose speculation, Fenyvesi elaborates:

> State Department instructions call for talking to potential defectors like a
> Dutch uncle: the preference is that an East European ask not for asylum
> but rather return to work within the system, or apply for emigration if
> feasible. The fallback position is settlement in the West without the
> theatrics of denouncing The System.

The bottom line of the official U.S. attitude toward defectors was this:
"Ideally, U.S. diplomats in these days of bridge building would like to have no
defectors from the Communist bloc." If Fenyvesi described the mood of the
State Department correctly, and I believe he was certainly right with respect to
the Carter Administration that warned against an "excessive fear of communism," one may well conclude that the decade of détente was bought at the
expense of defectors.

However, we should not make the mistake of thinking, by reverse reasoning, that during the cold war period the U.S. just fed milk and honey to defectors. According to a CIA report released by a U.S. Senate subcommittee in September 1977, they were also fed "speech-inducing drugs." The report says that in August 1952, the Navy told the CIA that it "had developed drugs that might have the desired [speech-inducing] characteristics and was about to test them on human subjects who would be unaware of the test." A month later, the report went on, "the drugs were administered to about eight subjects, each of whom was a Soviet defector and each test was done in Europe." After September 1952 the tests were discontinued, not because the American interrogators began to feel pangs of conscience, but "because the drugs used had such a bitter taste that it was not possible to keep the human subjects from knowing about the test."[18] So much for the use of defectors as guinea pigs.

A bitter taste was left in the mouths of more than just those eight subjects. The mistrust and misunderstanding that were routinely shown toward defectors, even during the height of the cold war, may have something to do with the fact that in the last few years of Stalin's rule, particularly in 1952, the number of defectors who are listed in the KGB Wanted List sharply declined. Still, for all the unhappy incidents that occurred during the 1970s, that decade has shown an improvement at least in one respect: the mistreatment of defectors in the past was officially acknowledged.

IN OTHER COUNTRIES

The United States is by no means the only country that at times has been less than hospitable to defectors. We have already mentioned Iran in conjunction with its return to the USSR of the defecting pilot Valentin Zasimov. Moreover, in the last few years reports have surfaced that Finland, a free country where the Helsinki Accords on Security and Cooperation in Europe were signed in 1975, has repeatedly compromised the accords by yielding to Soviet pressure to "cooperate" in catching defectors. As Chris Mosey of London's *The Observer* reported in November 1980, "Finland has tightened security along its borders with the Soviet Union to stop Russian dissidents entering the country to seek exile in the West."[19] Referring to a Finnish security police source, Mosey says that "there are around 50 illegal border crossings annually" and that Soviet defectors to Finland "are usually sent straight back to the Soviet Union." Mosey cites one case that occurred in October 1980 when a Soviet defector was returned to the USSR without a public hearing. That case was made public only because a member of the Finnish Parliament had drawn attention to it by asking the government why the Russian was not given a residence permit under the terms of the Helsinki Accords.

Fortunately, not all defectors to Finland are caught. Some of them manage to cross the country safely to Sweden. Sometimes they rely on the help of private Finnish citizens who know better than to inform on them to the police. Once in Sweden, they are usually out of danger, because the Swedish government has been generally respectful of the principle of political asylum. However, even in a country whose government and citizens show hospitality, defectors can never feel completely safe in the hands of bureaucrats, unless their plight is widely publicized. This is because the KGB would not miss a chance to infiltrate precisely those services that deal with the incoming defectors. Thus, in May 1979, a court in Stockholm sentenced Hans Melin, a high-ranking official of the Swedish Criminal Police, to four years in prison. He had access to the official files on defectors to Sweden, and he was found guilty of spying for the Soviet Union. Among the documents that he was about to pass over to the Soviets were copies of Swedish defense plans as well as a transcript of the interrogation of a Soviet citizen who sought asylum in Sweden.[20]

UNDER THE REAGAN ADMINISTRATION

One would expect that the U.S. attitude toward Soviet defectors would have changed considerably under President Reagan, who has called the USSR "an evil empire" and dismissed the entire communist experiment as a "bizarre chapter" in Russia's history. However, there are a number of incidents that make one ponder whether any significant change has occurred.

In January 1982, the *Washington Post* carried an article by Robert G. Kaiser and Bob Woodward about an incident that had taken place a few months earlier. On September 25, 1981, Irina Mamedova, wife of Georgy Mamedov, who served as second secretary at the Soviet Embassy in Washington and was known as a KGB operative, took their five-year-old daughter, Tatyana, and entered an FBI office to ask for asylum.[21] A few days later her KGB husband was put on a plane by Soviet security agents and flown to Moscow. Meanwhile, in the course of twelve days, Mrs. Mamedova was staying in American custody. At first, she declared that she had no intention of ever meeting with officials from the Soviet Embassy. She is said to have told her American friends that she defected because of her marital difficulties and for the sake of her daughter. However, Mrs. Mamedova's initial certainty about her defection gradually evaporated. Finally she agreed to meet with Soviet officials. During the meeting, which took place on October 7, 1981, they told her that they knew about her marital difficulties, appreciated the emotional stress caused by them, and promised that there would be no reprisals if she returned to the USSR. "At the end of the meeting she decided to return to her homeland. She left the State Department in the custody of the two Soviet officials," report Kaiser and Woodward.

To explain Mrs. Mamedova's "abrupt change of heart" they quoted an unnamed counterintelligence officer who said that she had defected "not for any political reason, but because she wanted to get away from a husband who regularly got drunk and beat her."[22] What the officer did not say was that her attempt at defection would be treated in the USSR as a grave political crime *regardless* of her motives. Even if she indeed experienced a "change of heart" and believed in the promise of Soviet officials, the State Department professionals should have known better. At the very least they should have allowed her a couple of days to remain in their custody so that she could sort out her feelings. They also could have assigned her a lawyer and put her in contact with the Russian émigré community. Nothing of that sort was done. What is worse, the incident was not even reported until it was too late.

On July 4, 1981, Galina Chursina, a 26-year-old Bolshoi Ballet dancer, entered the U.S. Consulate in Istanbul, Turkey, and made it clear that she wanted political asylum. An officer on duty gave her a typically bureaucratic answer: "Go back to your hotel, wait three days, and we'll call you." Fortunately, after the terror-stricken ballerina, who knew neither Turkish nor English, began crying in front of the officer, he relented and arranged to put her outside the grasp of the Soviets.[23] This case clearly indicates that the U.S. foreign service continues to be plagued by problems of poor staffing, as described by Smith Simpson.

More recently, in August 1983, the case of Andrey Berezhkov, the 16-year-old son of a Soviet diplomat who ran away from his parents' home in a Washington suburb and allegedly wrote letters to President Reagan and the *New York Times*, was also handled in a way that leaves much to be desired. To be sure, this case was not as clear-cut as those of Mamedova and Chursina, and it was further complicated by Berezhkov's young age and the fact that he never was in American custody. Nonetheless, the U.S. government failed to do its utmost to obtain the full truth of the matter. After initially insisting on guaranteeing Berezhkov "an opportunity to clarify his own wishes in a setting that permitted him to do so freely," the government stood up to the Soviets for less than a week before it beat a retreat and settled for a couple of interviews that took place under circumstances that fell far short of guaranteeing a free choice. Wishing to save face, the State Department declared that it took the boy's statements during the interviews at face value and therefore decided to let him go.[24]

The *Times*, on the other hand, was not so convinced. In an editorial that appeared after the boy vanished back into the cold, the *Times* applauded the U.S. government for the way it handled the case. Nonetheless, it admitted that most crucial questions remain unanswered: "Did young Berezhkov in fact write to the President and the *Times* asking for help in staying in this country?" and "Was he telling the truth when he said, on departure, that he really wanted to go home to the Soviet Union?" The *Times'* own answer to these questions is both paradoxical and cynical. According to the *Times*, it does not really matter how one answers them: "One need not accept his [Berezhkov's] answers or those of the Soviet Government to realize that there are times when fig leaves are in everyone's interest."[25] Although I am far from convinced of the latter proposition, I must give credit to the *Times* for being more candid than the government. The *Times* may not have spoken for the public at large, but I cannot help thinking that those in the government who influenced the decision were guided by the same kind of reasoning. Whether they are grateful to the *Times* for its back-handed compliment is another matter.

All the above cases in which the handling of defections can be at least questioned—from Simas Kudirka, Anatoly Chebotarev, Nikolay Artamonov, and Valentin Zasimov to Vladas Cesiunas, Aleksandr Kruglov, Irina Mamedova, and Andrey Berezhkov—occurred in the span of the past 13 years.[26] They took place under four different administrations, both Democrat and Republican. They all exhibited, in varying degrees, the same pattern of negligence; ineptitude; incompetence; and lack of sensitivity, compassion, and political will that characterized Kudirka's case. Even when they occurred in other countries, the United States can be charged with abdicating its responsibility. As the leader of the free world, the United States has failed to do battle for the lives of individual defectors, who defied the regime that presents the principal threat to the United States.

It is dangerous self-delusion to think that the fate of a few defectors is of no consequence for the security of the United States and the rest of the free world. "Like medicine," observes Smith Simpson, "diplomacy concerns people's lives, not only those of individuals, as in the Kudirka case, but, again, on a very large scale, with successes and failures affecting the lives, health, and fortunes of whole populations."[27] By failing to properly administer the "medicine" of diplomacy in order to protect human rights and save the lives of individual defectors, the U.S. government put in doubt its ability to protect human rights and all our lives. Such failures have tragic consequences for defectors. They have a chilling effect on many *prospective* defectors, including those with intelligence information critical for the United States. They have damaged the reputation of the United States as a beacon for the persecuted and oppressed. Conversely, they have saved our principal adversary embarrassment and loss of prestige.

All these facts considered, one has to conclude that the free world, including the United States, has failed to implement fully and consistently the principle of political asylum in respect to defectors from the USSR, and that the last decade has shown few signs of improvement. Too often in the past, basic human rights of defectors have been unnecessarily compromised and their lives endangered, ruined, or destroyed when Western officials have yielded, for the sake of political expediency, to the Soviets' bullying pressure.

CONCLUSION

Brothers [she was speaking]—brothers! There, in the city within the Wall, they are building the Integral. And you know that the day has come for us to raze this Wall—all Walls—so that the green wind may blow over all the earth, from one end of it to the other.

Evgeny Zamyatin, *We*

Defection is best understood as a uniquely twentieth-century phenomenon inherent in totalitarian communist regimes. Indeed, defection is an integral consequence of these regimes. It cannot be explained away by equating defectors with traitors and turncoats, who have existed and will exist as long as there are human failings, vices, and frailties. Defectors are something else. The word "defector" came into common use only after World War II. It was used to distinguish Soviet soldiers who went over to the West from the millions of refugees who just happened to be in the West. Those who coined the word apparently sought to suggest that if these soldiers were not quite traitors, there was still something defective about them. As one contemporary author explains, "Defection is such an ugly word—its sound and etymology imply a defect, a flaw, a regrettable lack of something. Refugee on the other hand invites sympathy and compassion—there is courage in the word and an intimation of character."[1] He reminds us, perhaps unwittingly, that the battle of ideas starts with word definitions. Although a large segment of American opinion makers seems to accept the above definition of defectors, I do not think they have read the coin right. This is because they have read just one side of it.

But the other side of the coin clearly reads "Made in the USSR," so that whatever negative qualities defectors might have, they reflect poorly on the minter-state, which has openly and loudly proclaimed its goal of remolding mankind into *Homo soveticus*. This "new species" of humankind is an utterly artificial creature. It is artificial because it cannot live under the open sky, cannot breathe the fresh air of its winds. It can exist only in a laboratory environment, more precisely, in the hothouse conditions of the USSR. That is why the Wall is needed, and—to maintain the illusion of domestic success—it must be defector-proof. But defector-proof it is not. Far from it; defection seems to afflict the country as an unshakable malaise. In the words of an American Sovietologist, "When a country reaches a point where, despite its enormous size, natural wealth and untold other possibilities, large numbers of its citizens are willing to risk starting a new life under difficult conditions in strange lands whose language they do not understand, we have every reason to question whether that country is in a state of health."[2]

In *Notes from Underground*, Dostoevsky sought to denigrate a future communist society by comparing it to an ant hill. Actually, his comparison is unfair to ants, for they do not surround their hills with walls. The ant hill has a natural attraction for the ants that live there. The USSR does not have, never has had, and never will have, such an attraction. Evgeny Zamyatin, a Russian writer and former Bolshevik, was horrified when he saw the Wall rising around the Soviet state right after the revolution. In the novel *We*, he warned mankind against allowing the Wall to divide it against itself. He realized that for the One State to exist, the Wall is a must, for it helps to isolate its citizens, the "numbers," from the outside world and from their own past. The Wall renders the "numbers" powerless before the demands of the One State. Zamyatin also understood that the Wall is an important precondition that enables the One State to expand its power abroad. The spaceship *Integral* built by the "numbers" can be successful in carrying out its mission of "integrating" the outside world with the One State only as long as the outsiders remain unaware of, or confused about, what is going on inside the Wall. That is why when the "numbers" of the One State rebel against their self-appointed Benefactor, they want to raze the Wall first of all.

Zamyatin was the first to warn mankind against succumbing to the temptation of walled-in communist existence, and he was the first to predict the degeneration of the young Soviet state into an Orwellian 1984 society. He cried out against the Wall, but his voice was choked by Soviet censors. Even though his book eventually reached the West, his warning was little understood, much less heeded. Only after World War II did the wise men of the West begin to notice—not without the help of such defectors as Kravchenko and Gouzenko—the ominous contours of the Wall. They came to fear the rustle of the Iron Curtain, behind which the Wall was steadily expanding in Eastern Europe. But it was not until August 1961 that Zamyatin's fictional Wall became embodied in fact, in the Berlin Wall, an eyesore of the world, which only the blind do not see. Unfortunately, many influential people in the West are blind. Even in the shadow of the Wall, they argue that the Wall is there for a defensive purpose. Apparently it does not matter to them that the Wall offends the human spirit itself. Perhaps the following observation made by Prince Philip in 1981 may prove more convincing to them than the testimony of the defectors: "It is interesting," said he, "that all the great walls of history were built to keep enemies out; the Soviet empire is the first to build walls to keep their own people in."[3]

In order to realize how inhumane and uncivilized a modern walled-in society is, one has to recall that, in ancient Greece, ostracism, or banishment of a person from his native land, was considered one of the cruelest punishments next to death. Yet many a Soviet citizen can only dream of being so punished, and hundreds of them have risked their lives in quest of voluntary ostracism, knowing full well that they would never again be able to set foot on the land of their fathers. The Soviet Union thus represents a gigantic step backward, past the slave-owning society of ancient Greece, as far as respect for basic human rights is concerned. Why such a regression? The answer is that whereas in ancient Greece human rights were respected at least for citizens, if not for slaves, in a modern communist state all citizens are considered state property and therefore their legal status is virtually indistinguishable from that of the slaves. What would you do if your property, a cow or other livestock, jumped over your fence? Wouldn't you try to stop it by any means, rather than allow it to run away to be used by others? In this sense, defection seems indeed inherent in a communist state that claims property rights over all its citizens.

In terms of Russia's own history, the communist walled-in society is a throwback to the time of the Mongol yoke, when Russia's foreign masters sought to perpetuate their rule by keeping her isolated from the Western and Byzantine sources of her cultural and religious heritage. That period of foreign domination was followed by centuries of self-imposed isolation that lasted until Peter the Great opened Russia's "window" to the West in the eighteenth century. The Russian educated class has never accepted the state of isolation as a norm. It gave birth to a number of outstanding "defectors," most notably Prince Andrey Kurbsky, who escaped from under the despotic rule of Ivan the Terrible to Poland, and Grigory Kotoshikhin, a foreign service clerk, who escaped to Sweden during the reign of Czar Aleksey, Peter's father. While abroad, both produced writings that have become important testimonials for their respective periods of Russia's history.

Another antecedent to defection in Russian history may be seen in the tradition of the Cossacks, those peasant serfs who fled from the arbitrariness and despotism of their landlords to the freedom of Russia's southern frontiers. There, under the most dangerous and exacting conditions of the steppe, they proved their fitness for a free, democratic, and dignified existence as they proved their loyalty and devotion to traditional Russian values and customs. Like the Cossacks, the defectors of today defy the masters of the USSR, but they do not necessarily abandon their national heritage nor do they renounce their duties to the land of their birth.

In terms of ancient history, the only remote parallel to defectors that comes to mind are those citizens of the Roman empire who, led by Emperor Julian, committed an act of apostasy—they renounced the beliefs they had embraced when Christianity became the state religion and reverted to the gods of the past. Like them, defectors have renounced the official state ideology of Marxism-Leninism, and many have turned back to precommunist beliefs and values. However, unlike the ancient apostates, defectors have no emperor to lead them in their assault on the Wall of their imprisonment. Moreover, the apostasy of the ancients led them into isolation in their own land. The apostasy of the defectors, on the other hand, leads them across the Wall to rejoin the mainstream of humanity, where precommunist and noncommunist beliefs and values fortunately still hold sway.

The state of isolation imposed on Russia by the communist rulers recalls, finally, the Tokugawa period of self-imposed isolation in the history of Japan. Until Commodore Perry and—ironically—the Russian Admiral Putyatin opened that country to the outside world in 1854, no Japanese had been allowed to travel abroad without risking punishment by death. However, the present isolation of the USSR is all the more anomalous because it is being maintained in a modern world of instant communication and mass information. It is an isolation that is especially hard to bear because it is imposed upon the bulk of the population, while the leaders of the USSR seek to expand their power all over the world. They do so under the slogan of proletarian internationalism—"Proletarians of the world, unite!"—and yet their working class was never more isolated than now, not only from its "class comrades" in the capitalist countries but also from the "liberated" workers in the communist countries, from Yugoslavia to China, from Cuba to North Korea.

Although Western legal terminology (political asylum, political refugee, and so on) often makes one think of defection as a strictly political matter, it is not exactly so. The decision to defect usually involves a number of reasons: ideological and political, religious and moral, ethical and aesthetic, national and personal, noble and petty, altruistic and egotistical, reasons of ambition and vanity, curiosity and adventure. Each defector has his or her own set of reasons. The majority of defectors are ideologically and politically motivated.

But I would not be surprised if some would object to being thus described. Yet there is a common denominator for all, and it has to do with the matter of conscience. The individual defector—whether an intellectual or an artist, a soldier or a sailor, an engineer or a dancer—must have asked himself before his defection: If I do not believe in the System, can I live in the USSR in good conscience and work for its government? Just as the term "prisoner of conscience" is best suited to those imprisoned in the USSR for their moral, religious, and ideological deviations from the official Soviet norms rather than for purely political offenses, so defectors can be best described as escapees of conscience.

Under present conditions, any Soviet citizen who disagrees with the state monopoly on truth has basically two choices. The first is to suppress all thoughts and feelings and to obliterate any personality, becoming a human robot. Among those who choose that option only a few succeed, while the majority drown themselves in alcohol or wind up in an insane asylum. The second option is to join the few heroes and martyrs who dare to oppose the regime openly or clandestinely. These attempts are usually short-lived, and the dissidents are either imprisoned or locked up in an insane asylum. There is no way to work for one's convictions within the system, even if one is a Marxist and a Communist. Nor can one simply drop out of the system and be left alone.

Hence, the third choice: defection. However, this option is available only for the privileged ones who are allowed to travel abroad and for the daring few who succeed in crossing the border against overwhelming odds. By choosing defection, both categories choose eternal damnation in the eyes of the Soviets, whether they succeed or fail. Even when they succeed, they live under a Damoclean sword of retribution hovering over them or their relatives. Still, the number of those who have chosen this third option has continued to grow steadily in the postwar period. Faced with the insane asylum at home, they stake their lives on obtaining political asylum abroad.

The United States has traditionally offered refuge to the homeless, the persecuted, and those seeking freedom. It has led the world in extending hospitality to large numbers of postwar defectors. For this it deserves their gratitude. However, the U.S. government has been neither consistent nor steadfast in the implementation of the principle of political asylum. Often it has played along with Soviet efforts to silence defectors. At times it has needlessly yielded to Soviet pressure and has actually returned escapees to their jailors. Most of the time, it has failed to approach defections as part of the global battle for human rights. Warren Christopher, deputy secretary of state under President Carter, described the dilemma that the U.S. government faces in respect to new defections:

> For us in the United States, these requests for refuge may create temporary abrasions and difficulties. But they are a tribute to our way of life—and to

the values we represent in the world. They are also a recurrent challenge to our support for human rights.[4]

Unfortunately, the United States has been late in recognizing the human rights aspect of defection. This was due in part to a skewed perception of defectors as persons with dubious pasts and murky futures. For all the spy and counterspy publicity that they have received, the overwhelming majority of defectors are neither. True, some of them have provided the United States with vital national security information and have thus saved American taxpayers billions of dollars that would have been otherwise needed to maintain the present level of security. Yet, the defectors' chief contribution to this country and the free world lies in exposing the essence of Soviet communism, thus strengthening our psychological defenses. Before Boris Pasternak and Aleksandr Solzhenitsyn, Andrei Sinyavsky and Yuli Daniel, Andrei Sakharov and *samizdat*, and even before the human rights movement, the defectors gave early warning signals to the free world about the designs hatched inside the Wall. They had a hard time trying to overcome the incredulity and resentment of the intellectual establishment of the West, which stubbornly clung to its wartime illusions. "It has been a hard lesson to learn," admits Susan Sontag, one of the pillars of that establishment, "and I am struck by how long it has taken us to learn it."[5] Hopefully, the lesson has been learned well, and defectors can now count on a better reception than in the past.

As the leader of the free world, the United States bears the primary responsibility for offering refuge and protection to those who seek freedom from persecution by that very government that threatens U.S. security on a global scale. The United States should bear that responsibility in good conscience and with pride. After all, the U.N. Declaration on Human Rights was signed by both the U.S. and the Soviet governments, and it stipulates that "everyone has the right to leave any country . . . and seek and enjoy in other countries asylum from persecution." Moreover, as a country of immigrants, the United States has been traditionally looked upon as a beacon of hope for all persecuted people. To abdicate that role would mean to undermine the very reason for the existence of this country.

If we, as a nation, have both a moral and international obligation to offer a refuge and protection to defectors and have greatly benefited from their defection, politically and otherwise, one would expect that the matter of defection would have high priority in our foreign policy. However, this is not the case. Throughout the entire postwar period, from 1945 to the present, U.S. policy toward Soviet defectors has been as inconsistent and contradictory as our overall strategy vis-à-vis the Soviet Union. The U.S. attitude toward defectors has ranged from handing them over to the Soviets (in the years 1945–1947) to attempting to induce defections in the early 1950s. In later years, the United

States alternated between indifference and benign neglect, pretended friend-liness, and expressed actual annoyance and contempt. During the entire period, our handling of defectors has been characterized by political inepti-tude, failure to understand defectors' motives, and insensitivity to their needs and problems.

The United States has yet to formulate and implement a policy toward Soviet defectors that would both assure their human rights and maximally satisfy U.S. national security needs and political interests in every aspect of our global competition with the Soviet Union. It is the view of this writer that the first step must be a recognition of the fact that defection has been, is, and will be, first and foremost, a human rights issue. Second, defections should always be viewed in the context of the global competition between the United States and the USSR for the hearts and minds of people around the world. Third, we should never lose sight of the possibility that defections of hundreds of people in peacetime might very well turn into desertion of thousands during a war. Whether these deserters would become our comrades-in-arms or be consigned to the sad role they played during World War II would depend on the United States. A failure to establish better U.S. rapport with Soviet defectors in peacetime might not only tempt the USSR to start a war, but it could also spell disaster for the United States during a war. Conversely, if the Soviet govern-ment is made to understand now that it might lose half of its troops through defection to our side, this might very well deter it from ever resorting to war as a means of solving international problems.

More specifically, the United States should consider the following actions:

1. proclaim and implement a genuine open-door policy by issuing an official promise to the effect that any person defecting from the USSR would be exempt from regular immigration procedures and allowed an immediate entry, residence, and work permit in the United States;

2. encourage our allies to do the same;

3. champion defectors' rights in the U.N. Human Rights Commis-sion and other international organizations;

4. make sure that every defection is publicized, whenever a defector does not have serious objections to that;

5. provide free legal counsel to any would-be defector;

6. encourage and facilitate contacts between a new defector and local émigré communities;

7. encourage and stimulate the creation of a public agency with the aim of facilitating practical details of resettlement and adjustment (such as job referral, language training, and loans for re-education) as soon as all national security precautions had been taken.[6]

Such steps would greatly benefit both defectors and the United States. They should be undertaken not to induce defections but to eliminate many bureaucratic practices and unnecessary strains on defectors that prevent the United States from implementing fully and effectively its time-honored policy of offering refuge and protection to those seeking freedom. For the Soviet regime, a defection is like a hemorrhage to a hemophiliac. For the United States, on the other hand, it is like an injection of antibiotics that provide it with greater resistance, if not total immunity, to Soviet propaganda. I hope that one day Soviet leaders may decide that the contributions that defectors make to the outside world, as well as the damage they cause to the prestige of the USSR, outweigh the risks of allowing a modicum of legal opposition inside the USSR. Only when they begin to reform the system in the direction of greater freedom of expression will the flow of defectors abate. Only then will the need to maintain the Wall diminish.

Until then, defectors will remain a living monument to a fundamentally defective system, which is so unsure of itself that it cannot tolerate even token opposition. Defectors will also remain living proof that the human spirit has great capacity to resist attempts to mold it into *Homo soveticus*. Of course, defectors have flaws and defects like everyone else. They certainly lack the quality that would allow the state to use them at will and whim. But their supreme fault is that they exist at all, because Soviet indoctrination is not supposed to produce defective products. To the consternation of Soviet quality controllers, they cannot even tell the rejects from exemplary citizens until after defection.

If one believes that *Homo soveticus* is the future of mankind, one will see defectors as traitors and turncoats just as they are described in the KGB Wanted List. However, if one still clings to the image of man as *Homo sapiens*, with all his flaws and failures and also his strengths and virtues, one will not fail to recognize in defectors fellow human beings who, though they might be maimed and disfigured in the cogs of the communist mint, nonetheless have managed to retain their essential humanity. One will see defectors as proof of the resilience of human nature against any attempt to "integrate" it into an artificial monster. One will not fail to hear those brothers and sisters still within the Wall, who, like the rebellious heroine of Zamyatin's novel, call upon free men to "raze this Wall—all walls—so that the green wind may blow over all the earth, from one end of it to the other."

APPENDIXES

LIST OF ABBREVIATIONS USED IN APPENDIXES

COUNTRIES

AL	Algeria	IT	Italy
AR	Argentina	JA	Japan
AS	Australia	KU	Kuwait
AU	Austria	LE	Lebanon
BE	Belgium	MX	Mexico
BR	Brazil	NO	Norway
CA	Canada	PH	Philippines
DE	Denmark	SW	Sweden
EG	Egypt	SZ	Switzerland
FI	Finland	TU	Turkey
FR	France	UG	Uganda
GR	Greece	UK	United Kingdom
HO	Holland	US	United States
IC	Iceland	VE	Venezuela
IN	India	WB	West Berlin
IS	Israel	WG	West Germany

OTHER

Actr	Actor/Actress	Sail	Sailor
Art	Artist	Scho	Scholar
Asyl	Political Asylum	Sci	Scientist
Cell	Cello, cellist	Sea	Seaman
Ches	Chess player	Secr	Secretary
Cond	Conductor	Sing	Singer
Danc	Dancer	Sold	Soldier
Edit	Editor	Sprt	Sport
Empl	Employee	Stew	Steward/Stewardess
Engi	Engineer	Teac	Teacher
Fish	Fisherman	Tour	Tourist
Jour	Journalist	Tran	Translator/Interpreter
Ofcl	Official	Work	Worker
Pian	Piano, pianist	Writ	Writer
Prof	Professor		

1A

Possev List (May 1945–April 1969)

Abaykhanov, Akhmat Akhlavovich
Abramenko, Anatoly Nikolaevich
Abrosin, Nikita Ivanovich
Adigamov, Sabikh Nurullovich
Adomavichyus, Prantsishkus syn
    Prantsishkusa
Adrik, Evgeny Simeonovich
Ageev, Aleksandr Trofimovich
Akhmedov, Izmail Gusseynovich
Akimov, Aleksey Parfenovich
Akimov, Vladimir Borisovich
Akperov, Yusif Akper Ogly
Aksarin, Mikhail Ivanovich
Aleksandro, Georg
Alekseev, Aleksandr Konstantinovich
Alekseev, Nikolay Sergeevich
Alendorf, Vladimir Vladimirovich
Alt, Yury Iohannesovich
Amelin, Semen Nikolaevich
Anakyan, Karapet Arutyunovich
Andreeva, Evgenia Petrovna
Andreev, Nikolay Aristarkhovich
Andreev, Pyotr Ivanovich
Andrianov, Ivan Fedorovich

Anfilatov, Vasily Filippovich
Anisimov, Ivan Ivanovich
Antonov, Georgy Semenovich
Antonov, Rostislav Lvovich
Anurkin, Pyotr Ivanovich
Arabadzhev, Gisak Artemovich
Arays, Viktor-Bernhard Teodorovich
Arayums, Ilmars Ansovich
Ardin, Leo
Arshansky, Boris Meerovich
Artamonov, Nikolay
Astamenko, Valentin Vasilyevich
Atayunas, Aleksandras
Atakhanov, Zulfikar
Atamanchuk, Stepan Nikolaevich
Averchenko, Lyudmila Konstantinovna
Averchenko, Nikolay Afanasievich
Ayzenman, Anatoly Yudovich
Baev, Anatoly Vasilievich
Baev, Mikhail
Balalaev, Ivan Petrovich
Baranchuk, Mikhail Petrovich
Baranov, Ivan Iosifovich
Barashkov, Vladimir Fedorovich

Baryshev, Igor Nikanorovich
Batis, Nikolay Grigorievich
Batrak, Ivan Efimovich
Bayukhin, Vadim Demidovich
Bazarov, Ivan Ivanovich
Bedarfars, Balis syn Stasisa
Belinkov, Arkady
Belinkova, Natalia Aleksandrovna
Belinsky, Leonid Petrovich
Belousov, Aleksey Nikolaevich
Belov, Aleksandr Afanasievich
Belyachenok, Ivan Andreevich
Belyaev, Ivan Petrovich
Belyakov, Nikolay Alekseevich
Belyakov, Pyotr Afanasievich
Bendlin, Gugo Adolfovich
Bentsler, Grigory Ivanovich
Berezenko, Timofey Mitrofanovich
Beridze, Khuseyn Ismailovich
Berngart, Walter
Bertkhold, Vilnis Arvidovich
Berukshtis, Igor Sergeevich
Betts, Genrikh Ioganovich
Bikhler, Ivan Ivanovich
Bilevichute, Kazimira Birute doch
    Anastasa
Blizhenok, Maksim Fedotovich
Bocharov, Igor Vladimirovich
Boev, Valentin Georgievich
Bogachev, Nikolay Matveevich
Bogdanov, Sergey Ivanovich
Bogdanov, Stepan Ivanovich
Boguslavsky, Igor
Bondarenko, Pyotr Fridrikhovich
Bondarenko, Vladimir Alekseevich
Bondarev, Nikolay Ivanovich
Bondarev, Vasily Andreevich
Borisov, Pavel Nikolaevich
Borodin, Nikolay Mikhaylovich
Borozdin, Nikolay Zakharovich
Borsuk, Nikolay Fedorovich
Bort, Valentin Kondratievich

Boyko, Grigory Aleksandrovich
Brandt, Nikolay Gustavovich
Bratusevichus, Antanas Algirdas
Braumshtayf, Iozef
Brekht, Anatoly Grigorievich
Bruzhas, Iozas Algirdas syn Iozasa
Brykov, Sergey Grigorievich
Bukhvits, Iosif Iosifovich
Burlutsky, Grigory Stepanovich
Buryanenko, Vladimir Anikievich
Buyny, Anatoly Fomich
Bykadorov, Mikhail Fedorovich
Bystrov, Aleksandr Aleksandrovich
Chaly, Vladimir Anatolievich
Chavkin, Georgy Mikhaylovich
Chernenilov, Ivan Petrovich
Chernenko, Daniil Varfolomeevich
Chernogorov, Ivan Dmitrievich
Danchenko, Evgeny Petrovich
Danko, Ivan Yurievich
Davidenko, Grigory Ivanovich
Davydov, Mordkha Rakhamimovich
Dedov, Pyotr Ivanovich
Degtyarev, Arkady Petrovich
Delyagin, Nikolay Konstantinovich
Demchenko, Pyotr Ivanovich
Demidenko, Aleksandr Stepanovich
Demidov, Vasily Romanovich
Deryabin, Pyotr Sergeevich
Desyuk, Gennady Mikhaylovich
Dimitrov, Grigory Andreevich
Dimov, Zhorzh Makarovich
Dmitriev, Pyotr Arefievich
Dmitrishin, Vasily Nikolaevich
Dobrovolsky, Konstantin Avgustovich
Dobrov, Vasily Nikolaevich
Dolberg, Aleksandr Meerovich
Dolgun, Ivan Ilyich
Dolya, Ivan Yakolevich
Domansky, Nikolay Sevastyanovich
Dorofeev, Dmitry Borisovich
Dubnikov, Grigory Mironovich

Dubovsky, Adam Andreevich
Dudin, Gennady Sergeevich
Dvoenko, Aleksandr Petrovich
Dzhantemirov, Shakhim Bilyalovich
Dzyuba, Aleksey Iosipovich
Efimov, Sergey Ivanovich
Efimtsev, Mikhail Borisovich
Ellansky, Aleksandr Viktorovich
Emelyanov, Mikhail Petrovich
Epatko, Vasily Ilyich
Eremenko, Venedikt Pavlovich
Eremyan Akop Barsegovich
Ermashev, Viktor Yakolevich
Ermolin, Vasily Stepanovich
Erokhin, Evgeny Petrovich
Evdokimov, Evgeny Gerasimovich
Ezhov, Leonid Kuzmich
Fedonyuk, Viktor Klimentievich
Fedorov, Nikolay Pankratievich
Feldman, Abram Nekhamovich
Feshchenko, Vasily Ivanovich
Fomenko, Aleksandr Vasilievich
Fomenko, Vladimir Dmitrievich
Fomichev, Aleksandr Vasilievich
Fridenberg, Yanis Ansovich
Fridman, Georgy Vladimirovich
Frizen, Ivan Andreevich
Gaak, Ivan Sevostyanovich
Gadyuk, Pavel Mikhaylovich
Gaev, Aleksey Pavlovich
Galaka, Ivan Prokofievich
Galas, Maria Petrovna
Galmadze, Vsevolod Prokopovich
Gantsaev, Maksim Botievich
Garmash, Pyotr Selifanovich
Gavrilov, Eduard Anatolievich
Gavshin, Evgeny Dmitrievich
Generalsky, Mikhail Sergeevich
Genrikh, Isaak Moiseevich
Gerandokov, Zhantemir Amizhovich
Geraseev, Vladimir Mikhaylovich
Gerasimenko, Grigory Ivanovich

Gerzikorn, Vladimir Vasilievich
Geychenko, Anatoly Andreevich
Geyer, Akvilinus Ivanovich
Gil, Vilhelm Genrikhovich
Ginda, Fedor Timofeevich
Girilovich, Fedor Aleksandrovich
Glevsky, Grigory Matveevich
Gogol, Vladimir Konstantinovich
Goldfarb, Rafail Ilyich
Golitsyn, Anatoly Mikhaylovich
Golofaev, Pyotr Kirillovich
Golomytko, Pavel Alekseevich
Goloshchapov, Ivan Zakharovich
Golovchenko, Aleksey Afanasievich
Golyushev, Viktor Pavlovich
Gontarskaya, Maria
Gorbovsky, Boleslav Ivanovich
Gordeev, Sergey Sergeevich
Gordeev, Stepan Evdokimovich
Gorsky, Vladimir Pavlovich
Gorstev, Aleksey Ivanovich
Grabovsky, Boris Ivanovich
Grigoriev, Ivan Matveevich
Grigoriev, Mikhail Ivanovich
Grinyavichus, Ionas Andreyusovich
Gritsenko, Boris Pavlovich
Gromov, Pavel Ivanovich
Guselman, Iosif Andreevich
Guzenko, Igor Sergeevich
Guzenko, Svetlana Borisovna
Halling, Heyno Arnoldovich
Han, Bo-Tszun
Hartmanis, Teofil Andreevich
Hashimov, Makhamat Inoyatovich
Hubel, Enno Gustavovich
Idrisov, Garif Kharisovich
Ignaste, Lyudmila Petrovna
Ignaste, Vladimir Adrianovich
Inyakin, Sergey Aleksandrovich
Ioala, Udo Iokhannesovich
Ippolitov, Georgy Vladimirovich
Istomin, Vasily Ivanovich

Ivanchenko, Pavel Mikhaylovich
Ivanov, Aleksey Ivanovich
Ivanov, Evgeny Alekseevich
Iyelaan, Yalmar
Iygi, Kherman Petrovich
Kachur, Kuzma Emelyanovich
Kalinauskas, Zenonas Algimontas Izo
Kalinovsky, Fedor Aleksandrovich
Kallas, Vello Voldemarovich
Kalmazan, Mikhail Ivanovich
Kalmykov, Igor Borisovich
Kalmykov, Konstantin Fedorovich
Kalmykov, Pavel Vasilievich
Kanzeba, Nikolay Kuzmich
Kaplan, Gilel Davydovich
Kapotin, Nikolay
Karapetyan, Tigran Enokovich
Karatsev, Mikhail Amurkhanovich
Karpenko, Vasily Gordeevich
Kartseva, Evdokia Aleseevna
Kartsev, Konstantin Ivanovich
Kasumov, Tofik Yusuf Ogly
Kaydanov, Egor
Kayris, Andrey Andreevich
Kazakov, Aleksey Ivanovich
Kazakov, Viktor Vasilievich
Kazantsev, Vasily Maksimovich
Kaznacheev, Aleksandr Yurievich
Khabarov, Aleksey Korneevich
Khanetskiy, Aleksey Gavrilovich
Kharlamenko, Vladimir Ivanovich
Khodosov, Yury Petrovich
Khokhlov, Nikolay Evgenievich
Khudolozhko, Konstantin Pavlovich
Kibitko, Aleksey Andreevich
Kiry, Ivan Vasilievich
Kirsanov, Aleksandr Stepanovich
Klassen, Ivan Ivanovich
Klaup, Erikh syn Anny
Klimashin, Petr Fedorovich
Klimenko, Vasily Antonovich
Klimov, Grigory Petrovich

Klychko, Mikhail Antonovich
Klyuev, Ivan Andreevich
Kniga, Valentin Ivanovich
Kocherga, Pyotr Ivanovich
Kodzhamberdiev, Kudaybergen
Kogan, Aleksandr Borisovich
Kokhanovich, Vasily Ivanovich
Kokhanov, Nikolay Ivanovich
Kolbasa, Nikolay Ponkratovich
Kolegov, Ivan Vladimirovich
Kolomyets, Yarema Yakubovich
Kolosov, Lev Mikhailovich
Kolupaeva, Valentina Sergeevna
Kolupaev, Georgy Stepanovich
Komissarov, Vladislav Aleksandrovich
Konenko, Dmitry Sergeevich
Konovalenko, Aleksey Petrovich
Konovalov, Mikhail Mikhaylovich
Konstantinov, Vasily Konstantinovich
Konusenko, Vladimir Korneevich
Korkosha, Ivan Romanovich
Kornievskiy, Vasily Pavlovich
Korotkikh, Ivan
Kostiv, Dmitry Petrovich
Kovalenko, Anatoly Vasilievich
Kovalenko, Ivan Efimovich
Kovalev, Anatoly Maksimovich
Kovalev, Dmitry Petrovich
Kovrigin, Rostislav Danilovich
Kozlov, Ivan Platonovich
Krakovetskiy, Ivan Antonovich
Krasilnikov, Vladimir Andreevich
Krasnov, Nikolay Alekseevich
Krasnov, Vladislav Georgievich
Kravchenko, Pavel Andreevich
Kravtsov, Ivan Nikolaevich
Kremer, Daniil Genrikhovich
Kruk, Aleksandr Danilovich
Krusts, Maris Petrovich
Krutinskaya, Maria
Ksenofontov, Viktor Alekseevich
Kublitskas, Lenginas syn Antanasa

Kudlovskaya, Evgenia Ilyinichna
Kulagin, Ivan Makarovich
Kulagin, Vladimir Vasilievich
Kuleshov, Evgeny Vladimirovich
Kulikovsky, Dmitry Pavlovich
Kun, Aygen Rikhardovich
Kuntsyv, Mikhail Grigorievich
Kurenkov, Pyotr Efremovich
Kurynov, Viktor Nikolaevich
Kurzantsev, Viktor Mikhaylovich
Kushnarev, Nikolay Feropontovich
Kustin, Enno Augustovich
Kuz, Dmitry Ivanovich
Kuznetsov, Pyotr Kuzmich
Kuzovkin, Vasily Vasilievich
Kvashnin, Ivan Sergeevich
Larsson, Enno Lutsian Aleksandrovich
Lazarev, Nikolay Georgievich
Laklanov, Viktor Pavlovich
Lankauskas, Vladas syn Prano
Lemeshev, Egor Stepanovich
Lenchevsky, Oleg Stanislavovich
Leontiev, Timofey Dmitrievich
Leontiev, Viktor Mikhaylovich
Lepp, Aleksey Mikhaylovich
Levin, Aleksey Mikhaylovich
Levin, Shmidt Abramovich
Likhoshva, Ivan Nikiforovich
Lindstrem, Lars Yukhanovich
Lisitsyn, Gleb Aleksandrovich
Loginov, Ivan Vasilievich
Loginov, Svyatoslav Aleksandrovich
Lopatyuk, Vsevolod Vladimirovich
Loshhchagin, Evgeny Gavrilovich
Lossi, Rudolf Mikhkelevich
Ludanov, Nikolay Fedoseevich
Lukash, Stefan Davydovich
Lukyanenko, Afanasy Fedorovich
Lutsyshin, Orest Mikhaylovich
Lvov, Pyotr Andreevich
Lyasetsky, Aleksey Mikhaylovich
Lyashchenko, Ignat Fedorovich

Lybin, Arvo Yokhanesovich
Lysukhin, Ignat Fedorovich
Makara, Andrey Fomich
Makarov, Valery Ivanovich
Makshantsev, Aleksandr Nikolaevich
Malitsky, Andrey Mikhaylovich
Malyshev, Ivan Arsentievich
Manin, Stanislav Pavlovich
Manukyan, Rem Tsolakovich
Marchenkov, Aleksey Abramovich
Marchenkov, Nikolay Ivanovich
Massalov, Oleg Gavrilovich
Matkovsky, Fedor Iosifovich
Mattus, Karl Genrikhovich
Matusevich, Vladimir Borisovich
Matveev, Vasily Nikolaevich
Matyusnonok, Vasily Ivanovich
Mashtakov, Pavel Pavlovich
Maysun, Vladimir Ivanovich
Mazulans, Yanis Karlovich
Mefedovsky, Dmitry Fomich
Midny, Boris Vasilievich
Mikhelson, Anatoly Aronovich
Miklovas, Iozas syn Iozasa
Mogilny, Mikhail Minovich
Morchikyan, Pogos Petrosovich
Mordovtsev, Viktor Sergeevich
Moskalu, Ivan Leontievich
Moskalyuk, Adam Geevich
Mukutadze, Osman Muradovich
Muraviev, Vladimir Vasilievich
Muravsky, Mechislav Mironovich
Myttus, Arvo Paulovich
Myurk, Aksel Adamovich
Naaber, Tayvo Ernst-Yokhannesovich
Nashpits, Khaim Gershkovich
Nechaev, Sergey Nazarovich
Nedobezhkin, Nikolay Prokhorovich
Nendzhyan, Manvel Esaevich
Neretin, Aleksandr Vasilievich
Nesterov, Aleksandr Maksimovich
Nezhivov, Sergey Ivanovich

Nikishin, Mikhail Dmitrievich
Nikolaevsky, Kirill Dmitrievich
Nitsis, Lilia Ekabovna
Nitsis, Zhanis Yanovich
Nosenko, Yury Ivanovich
Novikov, Nikolay Mikhaylovich
Novosad, Dmitry Naumovich
Novoselchenkov, Nikifor Timofeevich
Nureev, Rudolf Khamitovich
Obrok, Vladimir Albertovich
Ofitserov, Mikhail Georgievich
Olishevich, Semyon Fedorovich
Olshvangas, Leonas Davidovich
Onuzhans, Anton Ignatievich
Open, Iosif Feyfelevich
Ore, Guntis Arvidovich
Oreshkov, Viktor Aleksandrovich
Orzhekhovsky, Yan
Oskin, Semyon Alekseevich
Ozolin'sh, Yanis-Alberts Mikelevich
Pakalka, Vintsas syn Pranasa
Palmiste, Manivald Augustovich
Pankov, Aleksandr Timofeevich
Panov, Ivan Alekseevich
Papanov, Nikolay Ivanovich
Papy, Evtikhy Isaakovich
Paranyuk, Nina Vladimorvna
Patrushev, Pyotr Egorovich
Paulauskas, Emundas syn Klemasa
Pavlichenko, Vladimir Nikolaevich
Pavlov, Grigory Fedorovich
Pavlov, Igor Fedorovich
Pelykh, Ivan Vasilievich
Penner, Yakov Yakovlevich
Pereskokov, Vladimir Fedorovich
Perlin, Sergey Naumovich
Permyakov, Ivan Karpovich
Petikyan, Andranik Karapetovich
Petrenko, Mikhail Nikolaevich
Pevny, Georgy Mikhaylovich
Pichugin, Georgy Ivanovich

Piigli, Aleksandr Karlovich
Pirogov, Pyotr Afanasievich
Pisanov, Boris Aleksandrovich
Piskov, Pyotr Ivanovich
Pleshkis, Ionas
Plon, Adolf Kazimirovich
Podlesnov, Zinovy Mikhaylovich
Podmazko, Vasily Fedorovich
Pologsyan, Vagan Saribekovich
Poletnev, Aleksandr Kuzmich
Poluektov, Aleksey Vasilievich
Polyak, Ruvin Efimovich
Pomoshchnikov, Sergey Semenovich
Popov, Alik Aleksandrovich
Popov, Semen Vasilievich
Popovich, Aleksey Andreevich
Porubov, Roman Deevich
Posylkin, Sergey Mikhaylovich
Predtechevsky, Lev Ivanovich
Prikhodko, Andrey Vasilievich
Prikhodko, Grigory Andreevich
Proletarsky, Vladimir Mikhaylovich
Pronchak, Nikolay Nikolaevich
Prutskus, Pranas syn Beneventurasa
Pruul, Aavo Vasilievich
Pshemilsky, Anatoly Stepanovich
Pulavsky, Georgy Fortunatovich
Pustovalov, Yury Aleksandrovich
Putyato, Aleksey Alekseevich
Rachek, Nikolay Ignatievich
Rak, Stepan Ivanovich
Rastvorov, Yury Aleksandrovich
Ratnikov, Pyotr Efimovich
Raudsepp, Iohannes Iohannesovich
Ravlyuk, Dmitry Mikhaylovich
Rekis, Arnold Mikelevich
Reshtein, Afanasy Gavrilovich
Reshtein, Mikhail Abramovich
Revutsky, Savely Isaevich
Romaneneko, Fyodor Stepanovich
Rose, Pyotr Bernhardovich

Rudnitsky, Grigory Mikhaylovich
Rudovsky, Arkady Veniaminovich
Ruf, Oskar Vasilievich
Rumyantsev, Pyotr Poliektovich
Runge, Evgeny Evgenievich
Rusch, Waltraud-Helga
Rusin, Mikhail Yakovlevich
Ryabenko, Aleksandr Ivanovich
Ryabov, Yury Arkhipovich
Ryakhin, Georgy Georgievich
Ryapolov, Grigory Vasilievich
Ryastas, Manivald Yuhanovich
Sablin, Vladimir Nikolaevich
Sadkov, Evgeny Alekseevich
Sadovnikov, Evgeny Vasilievich
Samokhin, Ivan Akimovich
Samusev, Georgy Ivanovich
Saramotin, Nikolay Pavlovich
Sarapuu, Hillelvi Yanovna
Satanovsky, Yakov Iosifovich
Savchina, Maria Petrovna
Savitskaya, Maria
Savyuk, Anatoly Ivanovich
Sek, Iosif Stepanovich
Semenov, Vladimir Vasilievich
Sereda, Nikolay Ivanovich
Shaltis, Drasutis Iozovich
Shelaputin, Vadim Ivanovich
Shlomov, Vladimir Ilyich
Schmidt, Nikolay Vasilievich
Sikach, Grigory Ivanovich
Skolozdra, Vasily Vasilievich
Skude, Stefen Andreevich
Skvorets, Ivan Feoktistovich
Smirnov, Nikolay Pavlovich
Smychek, Mikhail Petrovich
Sokhanevich, Oleg Viktorovich
Sokolov, Leonid Aleksandrovich
Sokolov, Nikolay Ivanovich
Sokolov, Valentin Leonidovich
Sokolovsky, Ivan Iosifovich

Solikovskiy, Vasily Aleksandrovich
Soloma, Aleksandr Nikolaevich
Solovyov, Nikolay Aleksandrovich
Sopin, Vladimir Gerasimovich
Stankaytis, Bronyus syn Antanasa
Stizhko, Viktor Mikhaylovich
Strazds, Karlis Petrovich
Stulyakov, Pyotr Grigorievich
Sumin, Kuzma Vladimirovich
Suris, Valentin Semenovich
Svaranas, Vladis Aleksandrovich
Sverdlin, Spartak Solomonovich
Svetlov, Vasily Fedorovich
Tarasenko, Ivan Sergeevich
Tarasov, Vladislav Stepanovich
Tatarnikov, Viktor Stepanovich
Tebergs, Yanis Gunarovich
Ter-Gevorkyan, Vrezh Akonovich
Termonen, Pyotr Petrovich
Teynovich, Olga Yakovlevna
Tkach-Tkachev, Nikolay Stepanovich
Tokaev, Grigory Aleksandrovich
Travkin, Nikolay Ilyich
Trifonov, Georgy Evgenievich
Tristan, Dmitry Pavlovich
Tsurtsurika, Mikhail Dmitrievich
Tsurikov, Dmitry Abramovich
Tsurikov, Dmitry Ivanovich
Tsyganenko, Vasily Karpovich
Tuklers, Andrey Yanovich
Tumanov, Oleg Aleksandrovich
Turkov, Viktor Efimovich
Tverdokhlebov, Vasily Klimovich
Udintsev, Vasily Ivanovich
Ulug-Zade, Azis Satimovich
Ulyavichus, Pranas Prano
Ushakov, Andrey Aleksandrovich
Uss, Ivan Antonovich
Uyn, Otto Karlovich
Valgre, Helmut Yurievich
Vasilchuk, Vasily Stepanovich

Vasiliev, Yury Aleksandrovich
Vaynio, Helge Eynarovich
Vaynonen, Oskar Petrovich
Vaytkyavichus, Yurgens-Ferdinandas
  Piyaus
Vdovichenko, Stanislav Konstantinovich
Velepolsky, Bogdan Leontievich
Vetlovas, Mikas Evdokimo
Vibris, Albinas
Vindi, Yaak Kaurovich
Vinogradov, Evgeny Sergeevich
Vishnyakov, Grigory Alekseevich
Vitko, Vasily Kharitonovich
Vlasko, Nikolay Ivanovich
Volkov, Lev Aleksandrovich
Volochko, Ivan Ilyich
Volodkin, Ivan Lavrentyevich
Voloshok, Fedor Fedorovich
Vorobyov, Semyon Filippovich
Vorontsov, Aleksandr Nikolaevich
Yamul, Guydo Ervinovich
Yantra, Raymund Augustovich
Yatsura, Nikolay Ivanovich
Yuzhakov, Vladimir Fedorovich

Zakharenko, Andrey Maksimovich
Zakharov, Andrey Vasilievich
Zaksenberg, Boris Ilyich
Zalipsky, Vladimir Mikhailovich
Zalishansky, Shabsay Khaymovich
Zarinsh, Lilia Indrikovna
Zaritsky, Valentin Sergeevich
Zatikyan, Zatik Migranovich
Zavadsky, Arseny Leonidovich
Zellich, Otto Adolfovich
Zhabinsky, Vladimir Ivanovich
Zhabsky, Grigory Timofeevich
Zheleznyak, Aleksey Dmitrievich
Zhluktar, Pyotr Andreevich
Zhoromskas, Cheslovas syn Antanasa
Zhukevich, Maria Mikhaylovna
Zhurbilo, Andrey Zakharovich
Zilberis, Iosif Grigorievich
Zilber, Ir Alterovich
Ziman, Evald Ioganovich
Zubov, Vasily Andreevich
Zub-Zolotarev, Ivan Pavlovich
Zyryanov, Innokenty Alekseevich

1B

THOSE MISSING FROM THE POSSEV LIST (1945–1969)

Name	Age	Occupation or Rank	Date of Defection	Country of Defection	Country of Residence	Identifying Data
Ashekhnin, Leonid	20	Sold	7/29/53	WB		
Ashkenazy, Vladimir		Pian	3/63	UK		Wife from Iceland

Name	Age	Occupation or Rank	Date of Defection	Country of Defection	Country of Residence	Identifying Data
Borzov, Anatoly		Sold	10/48	AU		Returned 1950
Dotsenko, Boris	41	Sci	10/6/67	CA		Nuclear scientist
Dukhovny, Leo		Sold	1948	AU	US	
Eltsov, Igor	39	Art	1/4/67	UK		Film director, AKA Yeltsov
Finkelshtein, Leonid		Edit	12/66	UK		AKA Vladimirov
Geroseev, Vladimir		Sci	10/17/65	UK		Gibraltar
Granovsky, Anatoly		NKVD	10/46	SW	US	
Guzenko, Yakov	24	Sold	6/17/54	AU	US	With Schlomov
Hayhanen, Reino		KGB	5/57	FR	US	
Hodokol, Yury		Sold	2/54	AU	US	
Ivanovits, Viktor	29	Sea	8/66	GR		See next entry
Ivanovits, Pyotr	26	Sea	8/66	GR		Brother of former
Jaanimets, Viktor	29	Sea	9?/60	US		Khrushchev's ship
Jarema, Anastasia	64		1/64	UK		While visiting son
Karein, Vladimir	25	Sea	9/4/66	TU		AKA Karcin; swam
Kasenkina, Oksana		Teac	8/48	US		New York; died 1960
Khachaturyan, Ashot		Engi	4/67	JA		AKA Hachaturian
Kravchenko, Viktor		Ofcl	4/44	US		Suicide? 2/66
Krotkov, Yury		Writ	9/63	UK	US	Died 12/81
Krysanov, Vladimir		Stud	9/65	FI	SW	
Kuptsov, N. V.		Sold	11/54	WG	UK	
Kushneris, Vladislav	26	Sea	6/25/65	SW		Suicide 11/67

Name	Age	Occupation or Rank	Date of Defection	Country of Defection	Country of Residence	Identifying Data
Lezhnev, Vsevolod	37	Cell	3/22/69	US		Moscow Symphony Orchestra
Martynov, Leonid	26	Lt	1/20/55	WG	UK	With Garmash
Maslakovits, Nikolay		Prof	12/16/65	GR	US	AKA Maslovich
Merrusheva, Evdokia	43	Stew	10/16/63	WG		Merkusheva?
Minin, Aleksandr	55	Prof	7/66	FI	SW	Asked U.S. help
Olonis, Adolph	21	Sea	6/23/59	CA		With Berthold
Orshansky, Boris		Capt	1947	WB		
Pavlov			1954	NO		See Markov
Petrov, Evdokia		MVD	4/54	AS		Wife of next
Petrov, Vladimir		MVD	4/54	AS		
Ponomarev, Vladimir	39	Ofcl	9/64	SW	UK	UNESCO Paris
Rudolf, Vladimir		Col	1947	WG		AKA Yurasov
Ruschat, Eduard	37	Art	1/67	WG		Moscow Circus
Rytkov, Nikolay		Actr	9/66	UK		Lenin's double; died c. 1978
Samarin, Mikhail		Teac	8/48	US		See Kasenkina
Sarmakovkai, Olga		Tour	10/22/66	LE		Sarmakovskaya? U.S.?
Schlomov, Vladimir	21	Sold	6?/54	AU	US	With Guzenko
Shcheyarkin		Sea	10/13/64	JA	US	
Shunin, Vladimir	30	Tour	9/18/63	WG		Asked asylum
Silkov, Konstantin	21	Sea	8/31/63	UK		Ship *Haapsalu*
Soloviev, Viktor		Sea	6/54	TW		U.S.; Tanker *Tuapse*
Sorokin, Vladimir		Stud		SW	WG	
Stramanis, Fricis		Fish	9/54	SW		See Arajuns

Name	Age	Occupation or Rank	Date of Defection	Country of Defection	Country of Residence	Identifying Data
Stashinsky, Bogdan		KGB	8/12/61	WB		Confessed assassin
Terskovov, Vladimir	34	Engi	11/19/67	UK		
Voyakin, Aleksey	26	Lt	3/27/54	WG	US	
Vladimirov, Leonid		Edit	12/66	UK		AKA Finkelshtein

2A

SAMPLE ENTRY OF THE KGB WANTED LIST (VLADISLAV KRASNOV)

КРАСНОВ Владислав Георгиевич, 1937 года рождения, урож. г. Перми, русский, образование высшее, бывш. редактор шведского отдела Государственного комитета при СМ СССР по радиовещанию и телевидению. Среднего роста, волосы русые, лицо овальное, рот большой, губы тонкие, нос прямой, основание носа широкое, ноздри большие, носит очки. Отец **Краснов** Георгий Николаевич. Мать **Краснова** Екатерина Ивановна, брат **Краснов** Герман Георгиевич, сестры **Краснова (Зонтова)**, Зоя Георгиевна, **Краснова (Кокинская)** Любовь Георгиевна, зять **Кокинский** Валерий Борисович проживают в г. Перми.

Находясь в Швеции в составе группы советских туристов, 26 октября 1962 г. обратился к шведским властям с просьбой о предоставлении ему политического убежища. 22 января 1963 г. в г. Стокгольме выступил на пресс-конференции перед представителями буржуазной печати с клеветническими заявлениями о советской действительности. В Швеции проживал до января 1966 г. С 1966 г. проживает в США, где учится в университете и преподает уроки русского языка. Имеются фотокарточка и образец почерка.

Розыскное дело в УКГБ при СМ СССР по Пермской обл.

SOURCE: KGB Wanted List (for a translation, see Chapter 1).

2B

ETHNIC BACKGROUND OF DEFECTORS

Ethnic Group	Number	Percentage	Adjusted Frequency Percentage
Armenian	13	2.8	3.1
Azerbaijani	2	0.4	0.5
Belorussian	15	3.2	3.5
Estonian	30	6.4	7.0
Georgian	1	0.2	0.2
Jewish	36	7.7	8.5
Latvian	21	4.5	4.9
Lithuanian	14	3.0	3.3
Moldavian	2	0.4	0.5
Russian	181	38.5	42.5
Tatar	3	0.6	0.7
Ukrainian	82	17.4	19.2
Other	26	5.5	6.1
No information	44	9.4	—
Total	470	100.0	100.0

SOURCE: Krasnov, Defstudy, p. 16.

2C

ANNUAL DISTRIBUTION OF DEFECTIONS

Year of Defection	Number	Percentage
1945	15	3.2
1946	28	6.0
1947	59	12.6
1948	60	12.8
1949	42	8.9
1950	19	4.0
1951	22	4.7
1952	11	2.3
1953	13	2.8
1954	21	4.5
1955	8	1.7
1956	11	2.3
1957	18	3.8
1958	5	1.1
1959	9	1.9
1960	8	1.7
1961	14	3.0
1962	10	2.1
1963	9	1.9
1964	10	2.1
1965	18	3.8
1966	19	4.0
1967	20	4.3
1968	17	3.6
1969	2	0.4
No information	2	0.4
Total	470	100.0

SOURCE: Krasnov, Defstudy, pp. 41–42.

2D

COUNTRIES OF DEFECTION

Country	Number of Defectors
West Germany (incl. West Berlin)	201
Austria	59
Sweden	33
Turkey	29
Canada	17
Great Britain (incl. possessions)	16
Finland	14
Denmark	10
Iran	10
Taiwan (Republic of China)	10
Japan	8
Norway	6
France	5
Switzerland	4
Greece	3
Spain	3
United States	3
Afghanistan	2
Egypt	2
Holland	2
India	2
Belgium	1
Burma	1
Cameroon	1
Dahomey	1
Guinea	1
Iraq	1
Lebanon	1
Libya	1
Philippines	1
South Korea (Republic of Korea)	1
Togo	1
Uruguay	1
Total: 33	Total: 456

SOURCE: Krasnov, Defstudy, p. 43.

2E

Countries of Residence

Country of Residence	Number	Percentage	Adjusted Frequency Percentage
Argentina	11	2.3	2.9
Australia	19	4.0	5.1
Austria	10	2.1	2.7
Brazil	5	1.1	1.3
Canada	42	8.9	11.2
Chile	9	1.9	2.4
Denmark	2	0.4	0.5
England	25	5.3	6.6
France	8	1.7	2.1
Israel	8	1.7	2.1
Italy	2	0.4	0.5
Norway	1	0.2	0.3
Sweden	28	6.0	7.4
Turkey	2	0.4	0.5
United States	107	22.8	28.5
West Germany	88	18.7	23.4
Other	9	1.9	2.4
No information	94	20.0	—
Total	470	100.0	100.0

SOURCE: Krasnov, Defstudy, p. 58.

2F

COURT SENTENCES FOR DEFECTORS

Sentence	Number	Percentage	Adjusted Frequency Percentage
Seven years	1	0.2	0.4
Ten years	8	1.7	2.8
Twelve years	1	0.2	0.4
Fifteen years	15	3.2	5.3
Twenty-five years	35	7.4	12.3
Death	224	47.7	78.9
No information	186	39.6	—
Total	470	100.0	100.0

SOURCE: Krasnov, Defstudy, p. 63.

2G

LIST OF "ANTI-SOVIET" ORGANIZATIONS ASSOCIATED WITH DEFECTORS

1. TSOPE, Tsentral'noe Ob"edinenie Poslevoennykh Politicheskikh Emigrantov (Central Alliance of Postwar Political Emigrés)

2. NTS, Narodno-Trudovoi Soiuz Rossiiskikh Solidaristov (National Labor Union of the Russian Solidarists)

3. *Possev*, a periodical affiliated with NTS

4. *Grani*, a quarterly affiliated with NTS

5. ROA, Russkaia Osvoboditel'naia Armiia (Russian Liberation Army)

6. Gvardiia Russkogo Osvoboditel'nogo Dvizheniia (The Guards of the Russian Liberation Movement)

7. Russkaia Okhrannaia Rota (Russian Guards Company)

8. Tolstovskii Fond (Tolstoy Foundation)

9. SBONR, Soiuz Bor'by za Osvobozhdenie Narodov Rossii (Alliance for the Struggle for the Liberation of the Peoples of Russia)

10. TNK, "an anti-Soviet organization abroad"

11. The Armenian Dashnaks

12. Krestovaia Troika (Three of Clubs), an Estonian nationalist organization; operated in the USSR

13. Smevor Ukrainy, a Ukrainian nationalist organization

14. Iunaki, a Ukrainian nationalist youth organization, also in the USSR

15. Various other émigré organizations (Lithuanian, Latvian, and so on), not named

16. SMISE

17. Gamburgskoe Ob"edinenie Poslevoennykh Bezhentsev (Hamburg's Union of Postwar Refugees)

18. OUN, Organizatsiia Ukrainskikh Natsionalistov (Organization of Ukrainian Nationalists)

2H

LIST OF "ANTI-SOVIET" ORGANIZATIONS SPONSORED BY FOREIGNERS

1. CIC, Counter Intelligence Corps, U.S. Army

2. CIA, U.S. Central Intelligence Agency

3. British Intelligence Service

4. French Intelligence

5. Gehlen's Intelligence, FRG

6. Various American intelligence schools: Camp King, Oberursel, Ober Ammergau, Garmisch Partenkirchen

7. Radio Free Europe
     Osvobozhdenie (Liberation)
     Svoboda (Liberty)

8. BBC

9. Amerikanskie Druz'ia Russkoi Svobody (American Friends of Russian Liberty)

10. Amerikanskii Komitet Osvobozhdenia ot Bol'shevizma (American Committee for Liberation from Bolshevism)

11. Humanity Calls, based in Los Angeles

21

DEFECTIONS BEFORE AND AFTER THE BERLIN WALL

	Number	*Percentage*
Unknown	16	3.4
Before Berlin Wall	349	74.3
After Berlin Wall	105	22.3
Total	470	100.0

SOURCE: Krasnov, Defstudy, p. 70.

2J

DEFECTIONS UNDER STALIN, KHRUSHCHEV, AND BREZHNEV

	Number	*Percentage*
Stalin	263	56.0
Khrushchev	130	27.7
Brezhnev	77	16.4
Total	470	100.0

SOURCE: Krasnov, Defstudy, p. 69.

2K

ETHNIC DISTRIBUTION OF DEFECTORS UNDER DIFFERENT RULERS (PERCENTAGE)

Ethnic Group	*Defectors Under Stalin*	*Defectors Under Khrushchev*	*Defectors Under Brezhnev*
Armenians	0.0	5.8	8.3
Estonians	2.6	10.0	16.7
Lithuanians	0.9	6.7	5.6
Latvians	3.8	6.7	5.6
Jews	11.1	5.8	4.2
Belorussians	5.1	2.5	0.0
Russians	45.3	40.0	37.5
Ukrainians	22.6	16.7	12.5

SOURCE: Based on Krasnov, Defstudy, pp. 154–55.

3

COMPOSITE LIST OF DEFECTORS (MAY 1969 TO PRESENT)

Name	Age	Occupation or Rank	Date of Defection	Country of Defection	Country of Residence	Identifying Data
Afanasiev, Valery		Pian	7/2/74	BE		
Agapov, Valentin		Sea	11/74	SW	SW	Family left
Akopian, Rafael	42	Sci	12/72	FR	US	Armenian
Alburt, Lev		Ches	7/79	WG	US	Jewish
Aleksandrov, Nikolay		Sea	8/76	US		New Orleans
Alekseychuk, Igor		Sold	1978?	WG		
Aleshin, Yury		Danc	7/30/84	JA		
Ankudinov		Scho	c. 1973	HO		
Babayan, Vigen			1978			U.S.; Armenian
Babak, Renata		Sing	11/19/73	IT		Bolshoi Theater
Bakhchevan, Stepan	32	Work	1974	FR		Stowaway
Baryshnikov, Mikhail	26	Danc	6/29/74	CA	US	Bolshoi Ballet
Belenko, Viktor		Lt	9/5/76	JA	US	Flew MIG-25
Belousova, Lyudmila	54	Sprt	9/79	SZ		With Protopopov
Belov, Mikhail	42	Tran	2/29/72	US		U.N., New York
Bezmenov, Yury	31	Dipl	2/9/70	IN	CA	Press Officer
Borzovich		Lt	10/77	TU		Crossed border
Brazinskas, Algirdas			10/15/70	TU		With father (next entry)
Brazinskas, Pranas	46		10/15/70	TU		Skyjacked AN-24

Name	Age	Occupation or Rank	Date of Defection	Country of Defection	Country of Residence	Identifying Data
Brokhis, Leonid	33	Engi	9/15/79	JA	US	Trade mission
Bublik, Viktor	32	Work	10/78	FI	SW	Crossed border
Butenko, Leonid	42	Sea	10/6/80	JA	US	2nd engineer
Butkus, Zigmas		Scho	10/8/72	US		Law scholar
Butkus, Mrs.			10/8/72	US		Former's wife
Cheskev, G.	23	Stud	4/29/77	AS		Political asylum?
Chursina, Galina		Danc	7/5/81	TU	US	AKA Tchursina
Davydenko, Vladislav	30	Sprt	9/5/69	UK	WG	Stowaway
Davydov, Anatoly		Jour	4/20/75	JA	US	Trade fair
Diosov, Vladimir		Fish	8/14/72	GR	US	With Dudnikov
Dudnikov, Pavel		Fish	8/14/72	GR	US	Led mutiny
Dzhirkvelov, Ilya	53	KGB	3/3/80	SZ	UK	TASS officer
Dzhirkvelov, Mrs.			3/3/80	SZ	UK	Former's wife, left with daughter
Egorov, Igor	26	Sea	1/84	FR	US	Not confirmed
Egorov, Yury	22	Pian	3/18/76	IT		
Faerman, Marina			1/31/79	BE		Wife of next entry
Faerman, Mikhail		Pian	1/31/79	BE		
Falin			11/84			Son of former Soviet ambassador in WG; not confirmed
Fedicheva, Kaleria		Danc	2/75	US	US	Kirov Ballet
Fedoseev, Anatoly	62	Sci	5/27/71	FR	US	Hero of USSR
Filatov, Valery	36	Sea	9/28/77	US		Texas; 3rd mate
Filipov, Aleksandr		Danc	9/70	MX		Moiseyev Ensemble
Fruman, Naum		Viol	7/15/70	AR		Argentina

Name	Age	Occupation or Rank	Date of Defection	Country of Defection	Country of Residence	Identifying Data
Gasinskaya, Liliana	18	Sea	1/17/79	AS		Waitress; swam
Gavrilov, Boris	36	Sea	11/4/80	UK		Jumped ship
Gelshtein, Garri	20	Sprt	5/20/84	FI	SW	Estonian motorcyclist
Gildebrand, Andre	20		5/20/84	FI	SW	Estonian motorcyclist
Glagolev, Igor		Scho	10/76			U.S. asylum
Geraimbekov, Sevim		Scho	8/23/82	BR		U.S. asylum
Godunov, Aleksandr	30	Danc	8/23/79	US		Wife Vlasova, S-ret
Goldgur, Leonid	26	Sea	8/28/73	JA	IS	
Gorelkin, Ivan	60	Engi	6/84	TU	CA	With six others
Grishin?		Gen?	10/83	TU		Not confirmed
Hovanesian, Artush	33	KGB	9/8/72	TU		Crossed border
Hovanesian, Mrs.			9/8/72			Former's wife
Ipatov (Itaka?), Boris		Dipl	8/12/77	UG		Uganda; U.S. asylum
Ivanov, Aleksandr		Musi	8/21/70	MX	US	With Grodetsky
Ivanov, Georgy		Work	8/8/73	FI	SW	Crossed border
Ivanov, Igor	33	Ches	7/4/80	CA		Chess master
Ivanov, Vadim		KGB	1/84	WG	US	TASS chief in Vienna
Ivashchenko, Yury	29	Sea	2/28/70	FR		Jumped ship
Jourjin, Aleksandr	27	Stud	8/79	FI	SW	Now in U.S.
Jurgutis, Aloisius			1974	YU	US	Yugoslavia
Kakauridze, Givi	33	Engi	7/31/70	JA		U.S. said no
Kaoroyko, Pyotr	26	Sea	1/3/74	JA	US	Jumped ship
Karaulov, Aleksandr	34	Scho	12/8/84	UK		Date of asylum report

Name	Age	Occupation or Rank	Date of Defection	Country of Defection	Country of Residence	Identifying Data
Kepekyan, Sogomin	17	Sprt	7/9/76	BE		Bicyclist
Kharlov, Vladislav	59	Ofcl	1/15/81	EG		Egypt
Khonenko, Ivan	23	Sea	3/27/74	US		Jumped ship
Kiselnikova, Raya	30	Dipl	3/70	MX		Mexico
Kleymenov, Anatoly		Danc	11/19/73	IT		See Babak
Kolchin, Yury	22	Stud	10/8/84	JA		Ship *Priamur'e* in the port of Otaru, Japan
Kolesnik, Anna	38	Sing	1/72	AS		Wife of next
Kolesnik, Vladimir	45	Cond	1/72	AS		Australia
Kolman, Ekaterina			10/6/76	SW	SW	Wife of next entry
Kolman, Arnosht	84	Scho	10/6/76	SW	SW	Died 1/24/79
Koloskova, Natalia	42	Viol	6/11/79	JA	US	With Markov
Komp, Einar	35		1971	SW	SW	Estonian
Kondrashin, Kirill	64	Cond	12/4/78	HO	US	Died 3/7/81
Korchnoy, Viktor	48	Ches	7/27/76	HO	SZ	
Korolyuk, Viktor	35	Tran	1/9/81	AU	WG	Talks in Vienna
Kourdakov, Sergey	20	Lt	9/7/70	CA	US	Suicide? 3/2/73
Kovalenko, Aleksandr	31	Sea	4/28/79	DE		Jumped ship
Kovalev, Vyacheslav	27	Sci	3/16/75	US	US	Jumped ship
Kozlov, Leonid	32	Danc	9/18/79	US	US	Bolshoi Theater
Kozlova, Valentina	25	Danc	9/18/79	US	US	Former's wife
Kremer, Elena		Pian	8/21/80	WG		Wife of next entry
Kremer, Gidon	23	Viol	8/21/80	WG		

Name	Age	Occupation or Rank	Date of Defection	Country of Defection	Country of Residence	Identifying Data
Kulikov, Artem	51	Scho	12/24/84	US	US	High-energy physicist on exchange in Chicago
Kurilov, Stanislav		Sea	12/74	PH		Philippines; swam
Kuum, Ya.		Sprt	7/84	DE		Estonian
Kuzichkin, Vladimir	35	KGB	10/25/82	IR	UK	Vice-consul
Kuznetsov, Anatoly	39	Writ	8/69	UK	UK	Died 6/79
Lavrov, L. G.		Scho	1980	US		Tourist
Lenghinas, Jono	45	Sci	10/17/72	IT		Missile plant
Leonskaya, Elizaveta		Pian	11/30/78	AU		Moscow
Lepaiye, Aleksandr	20	Sprt	5/20/84	FI	SW	Russian basketball player from Estonia
Leshinskys, Imants	48	Tran	9/18/78	US	US	U.N. translator
Leshinskys, Rasma			9/18/78	US	US	Former's wife
Leshinskys, Eva	20		9/18/78	US	US	Former's daughter
Lesnik, Renata		Jour	1981			Radio Moscow announcer
Levchenko, Stanislav	38	KGB	10/25/79	JA	US	Journalist
Louvich, Vladimir		Sea	3/15/83	TU	US	Captain
Lyalin, Oleg	34	KGB	9/71	UK		Trade official
Lysenko, Vladil		Fish	11/21/74	SW	SW	Captain
Lyubimov, Yury		Art	3/84	UK	UK	Theater director
Lyubimova, Katalina			3/84	UK	UK	Former's wife
Magomedov			1970s	SW		
Magomedova, Mrs.			1970s	SW		Former's wife
Makarova, Natalia	30	Danc	9/6/70	UK	US	Kirov Ballet
Markov, Valentin	43	Musi	1/11/79	JA	US	Trumpet player

Name	Age	Occupation or Rank	Date of Defection	Country of Defection	Country of Residence	Identifying Data
Matuzok, Vasily	22	Stud	11/23/84			Across DMZ to South Korea to U.S.
Mesilane, Riho		Jour	6/15/78	AU		Estonian TV
Mesokov, Aley	27	Sea	1/16/72	SP		Jumped ship
Messerer, Mikhail	31	Danc	2/6/80	JA	US	Bolshoi Ballet
Messerer, Sulamif	71	Danc	2/6/80	JA	US	Former's mother
Miller, Leila	23	Sing	8/13/84	FI	SW	Randpere's wife
Morozova, Natalia		Tran	11/26/77	CA		Interpreter, IOCA
Mullova, Victoria	23	Viol	7/5/83	FI	SW	With Zhordania
Muravin, Viktor		Sea	1970			Radio operator
Myagkov, Aleksey		KGB	2/74	WB	UK	Army captain
Nadirashvili, K. G.	31	KGB	6/75	AU	WG	Asked U.S. asylum
Nazarov, Mikhail		Tran	12/75	AL	WG	Algeria
Nazarova, Mrs.			12/75	AL	WG	Former's wife
Novikov, Vitaly	30	Sea	6/84	US	US	
Novikov, E. A.	52	Scho	9/9/83	JA		U.S. asylum?
Novikov, Yury	35	MD	6/77	FI	WG	Psychiatrist
Novitskaya, Ekaterina	26	Pian	2/22/78	HO		Married a Belgian
Oganesian, Eduard	40	Sci	12/72	FR	WG	Armenian
Okladnikov, Vladimir	32	Sea	2/10/77	US	CA	
Orionova, Galina	32	Scho	3/79	UK		Tatar
Ovsepian, Eliza			8/78			U.S. Embassy, Moscow
Palena, Daina	25	Sea	4/21/70	US		Playing sick

Name	Age	Occupation or Rank	Date of Defection	Country of Defection	Country of Residence	Identifying Data
Pavlovsky, Ivan	31	Art	6/79	FR		Belorussian
Papiashvili, Artandil	30	MD	Summer 77	AU	US	Georgian
Perkov, Dmitry	28	Art	1/75	FR	US	Suicide? 1978
Pleshchakov	42	Dipl	7/81	FR		UNESCO empl
Polyansky, Nikolay		Dipl	10/81	FR	WG	UNESCO Secretariat
Polovchak, Natalia	17	Stud	7/14/80	US	US	Left parents
Polovchak, Walter	12	Stud	7/14/80	US	US	Left parents
Ponomarenko, Igor	19	Stud	10/8/79	US		Jumped ship
Popov, Vladimir		Sing	1984	IT		Bolshoi Opera
Protopopov, Oleg	47	Sprt	9/24/79	SZ		With Belousova
Raig, Hillar	28	Ofcl	11/84	FI	SW	Secretary of Estonian Communist Youth League
Randpere, Valdo	26	Ofcl	8/13/84	FI	SW	See Miller
Redkin, Boris	36	Prof	6/7/74	JA	US	Taught Russian
Reinis, Piteris	33	Sea	9/14/73	DE		Jumped ship; swam
Reyport, Grigory		MD	1977		US	
Rezun, Vladimir		GRU	6/78	SZ		U.N. in Geneva
Rezun, Tatyana			6/78	SZ		Former's wife
Rogalsky, Ivan	27	Sea	10/70	SP	US	Convicted spy
Roosna, Raivo	20	Sprt	5/20/84	FI	SW	Estonian weightlifter
Rud, Mikhail	23	Pian	12/15/76	FR	FR	With Varvarova
Ryaguzov, Aleksandr	33	Sea	2/7/80	CA		Jumped ship
Sakalys, Vladas			1980		US	Lithuanian
Sakharov, Aleksandr		KGB			US	
Sakharov, Vladimir		KGB	1971	KU	US	Kuwait to U.S.

Name	Age	Occupation or Rank	Date of Defection	Country of Defection	Country of Residence	Identifying Data
Salesky, Lev	43	Engi	10/24/76	UK		Zelessky?
Schmidt, Boris	23		11/7/82	TU	TU	Skyjack; German
Schmidt, Vitaly	27		11/7/82	TU	TU	With former
Schneider, Viktor	25	Work	7/25/73	FI	WG	In rowboat
Schuller, Arthur	30		11/7/82	TU	TU	With Schmidts
Serega, Vladimir		Sea	2/2/78	SP		Jumped ship
Sezeman, Dmitry		Tran	10/76	FR	FR	*Novoye Vremya*
Shevchenko, Arkady		Dipl	4/27/78	US	US	U.N. official
Sheynyuk, Anatoly	43	Viol	8/8/84	FR		
Shmelyoff, Oleg	27	Engi	6/5/80	CA		Gander Airport
Shostakovich, Dmitry	19	Pian	4/11/81	WG		With father
Shostakovich, Maxim	42	Cond	4/11/81	WG		Moscow Radio
Shtepa, V.		Sci	1973?	SW		Rowed a canoe
Shtepa			1973?	SW		Former's brother
Shvyrkov, Vladislav		Scho	11/77	FI	SW	Economist
Sigl, Rupert		KGB				
Sorokin, Andrey	22	Stud	7/25/83	JA	US	Exchange student
Sorokin, Evgeny	23	Dipl	9/18/72	Laos		U.S. granted asylum?
Sosnovsky, Vasily	37	Work	3/26/77	SW	SW	Skyjacked AN-24
Stankin, Yury	32	Dipl	1/84	FR	US	Not confirmed
Stankov, Valery	37	Sea	7/12/76	US		Jumped ship
Sultan, Svetlana			10/83	IN		Soviet wife of an Afghan official
Suponitsky, Mikhail	26	Art	11/24/70	SW		Moscow Circus
Svirsky, Ivan	43	Prof	1980s	EG	US	Suicide? See Bibliography, Izvitsky

Name	Age	Occupation or Rank	Date of Defection	Country of Defection	Country of Residence	Identifying Data
Tamnick, Kristi		Sing	4/75	WG		Estonian
Tarasov, Nikolay			1977?			Suicide, 12/30/81
Tarkovsky, Andrey	51	Art	7/10/84	IT		Film director
Tarkovskaya, Larissa			7/10/84	IT		Former's wife
Teplyakova, Irina	31	Secr	9/71	UK		With Lyalin
Terekhova, Elena	22	Sea	2/7/80	CA		With Ryaguzov
Tereshkov, A. W.	31	Engi	6/21/72	IN		Bokara steel mill
Tereshkova, Mrs.			6/21/72	IN		Former's wife and two children
Tolsky, Anatoly	60	Jour	5/4/81	WG		
Tolskaya, Antonina	60	Actr	5/4/81	WG		Former's wife
Topazov, Arnold		Sold		WG	US	Convicted of bank robbery in Maryland, 1984
Toradze, Aleksandr	24	Pian	8/83	SP		See Korsakov, Boris
Trofimov, Vladimir						
Tsaryunov, Vladimir		Prof	7/15/74	UK		Taught in Nigeria
Tsaryunov, Mrs.			7/15/74	UK		Former's wife and one son
Tuomi, Kaarlo		KGB				
Turbalek, Nikolay	24	Sea	2/5/79	IT		Jumped ship
Vaguin, A.		Sci	2/19/70	SZ		At CERN, Geneva
Vaguin, Mrs.			2/19/70	SZ		Former's wife and two children
Vahtra, Aarne	40	Ofcl	1983	FR		Estonian
Valsiner, Jaan		Prof	c. 1979	SW	US	Tartu University
Valsiner, Mrs.			c. 1979	SW	US	Former's wife
Varshavsky, Aleksandr		Sci	9/8/77	FI		From conference
Varvarova, Elena		Pian	12/15/76	FR	FR	Rud's wife

Name	Age	Occupation or Rank	Date of Defection	Country of Defection	Country of Residence	Identifying Data
Vashchenko, Pyotr	51		6/78	US		Through U.S. Embassy with six others
Vashchenko, Yury	19	Sold	7/8/83	WG		From Afghanistan
Vasiliev, Pyotr	31	Pilo	6/26/73	TU		Flew a plane
Vetokhin, Yury	52	Sci	12/3/79	PH		Ship *Ilyich*; swam
Voytashevsky, Aleksandr	25	MD	1972		US	Jumped ship in Nigeria
Voslensky, Mikhail		Scho	1972	WG	WG	Academy of Sciences
Vostrikov, Gennady		Danc	9/70	MX		With Filipov
Vovchok, Maria	22	Stud	2/15/71	UK		Interpreter
Vronsky, Evgeny		Pilo	5/30/73	WG		Flew air force plane
Yakimets, Vladimir	45	Dipl	2/12/83	US		U.N. employee
Yakimets, Mrs.		MD	2/12/83	US		Former's wife
Yakushev, Aleksey	40	Scho	4/10/69	WG	US	Historian
Yakushev, Mrs.			4/10/69	WG	US	Former's wife
Yakushin, Mikhail		Tran	7/5/71	SW	SW	Interpreter
Yanin, Valery	26	Engi	8/16/73	TU		In a rubber raft
Yanyshev, Aleksandr	18	Sold	11/81			Hiding in Poland
Yurchenko, Yury		Dipl	11/12/77	VE		Venezuela to U.S.
Zakharov, Vasily		Sea	10/17/71	JA		U.S. asylum
Zamascikov, Sergey		Ofcl	7/79	IT	US	
Zelitskaya, Polina	26		5/27/71	CA		Jumped plane with two sons
Zhordania, Vakhtang	40	Musi	7/5/83	FI	SW	Now U.S.; see Mullova
Zukauskas, Arif		Sea	12/28/83	SP		Defected on the Canary Islands

3A

DEFECTING SCHOLARS AND INTELLECTUALS (1969 TO PRESENT)

Akopian, Rafael: Armenian scholar

Brokhis, Leonid: computer specialist

Butkus, Zigmas Antannas: President of the Lithuanian Jurists Union

Eltsov, Igor: film director

Fedoseev, Anatoly: electronics expert, Head of Research Institute

Geraimbekov, Sevim: political scientist from Azerbaidzhan

Glagolev, Igor: Senior Scholar, Moscow Institute of World Economy

Gorelkin, Ivan: engineer

Kakauridze, Givi Apollonovich: electrical engineer

Karaulov, Aleksandr: scholar

Kazennikov: medical doctor

Kolchin, Yury: student

Kolman, Arnosht: professor of Marxist philosophy

Kovalev, Vyacheslav: oceanographer

Kulikov, Artem: high-energy physicist

Kuznetsov, Anatoly: writer

Lenghinas, Jono Morkunas: Lithuanian engineer at a missile factory near Vilnius

Lyubimov, Yury: director of the Taganka Theater in Moscow

Lyubimova, Katalina: former's wife

Matuzok, Vasily: student

Novikov, Evgeny: physicist from the Soviet Academy of Science

Novikov, Yury: medical doctor, department head at Serbsky Institute

Oganesian, Eduard: Armenian scholar

Orionova, Galina: researcher at Moscow Institute of USA and Canada

Papiashvili, Artandil: medical doctor

Pavlovsky, Ivan Nikolaevich: Belorussian painter

Redkin, Boris P.: Russian language professor

Reyport, Grigory: medical doctor

Salesky (Zalessky?), Lev: engineer, member of delegation

Shmelyoff, Oleg: computer engineer, space research

Shvyrkov, Vladislav: economist, consumer research

Sultan, Svetlana: chemistry professor at Kabul University

Svirsky, Ivan: professor

Tarkovsky, Andrey: film director

Tarkovskaya, Larissa: former's wife

Tolsky, Anatoly: journalist

Tolskaya, Antonina: former's wife

Tsaryunov, Vladimir: Russian language professor

Vaguine, A.: nuclear physicist at CERN, Geneva, from Atomic Research Center in Serpukhov

Varshavsky, Aleksandr: guest lecturer in Helsinki, Finland

Vetokhin, Yury: computer engineer

Voslensky, Mikhail: historian, disarmament specialist at Academy of Sciences

Voytashevsky, Aleksandr: medical doctor

Yakimets, Mrs.: dentist

Yakushev, Aleksey: historian

Yanin, Valery: engineer

3B

DEFECTING MUSICIANS AND SINGERS (1969 TO PRESENT)

Afanasiev, Valery: pianist, won a Queen Elizabeth prize in 1972

Babak, Renata: opera singer, Bolshoi Theater

Faerman, Mikhail: pianist, won a Queen Elizabeth prize in 1975

Faerman, Marina: former's wife

Fruman, Naum: violinist

Ivanov, Aleksandr: trombonist

Kolesnik, Anna: prima donna, wife of next entry

Kolesnik, Vladimir: conductor

Koloskova, Natalia: violinist

Kondrashin, Kirill: conductor, Moscow Philharmonic Symphony Orchestra

Kremer, Gidon: violinist

Kremer, Elena: pianist, former's wife

Leonskaya, Elizaveta: pianist

Lezhnev, Vsevolod: cellist, Moscow Symphony Orchestra

Markov, Valentin: trumpeter

Miller, Leyla: popular Estonian singer

Mullova, Viktoria: violinist, won a Sibelius prize in 1980

Novitskaya, Ekaterina: pianist, won a Queen Elizabeth prize in 1968

Popov, Vladimir: opera singer from the Bolshoi Theater

Rud, Mikhail: pianist, won a Marguerite Long prize

Sheynyuk, Anatoly: violinist

Shostakovich, Dmitry: pianist

Shostakovich, Maxim: conductor, Moscow Radio Symphony Orchestra

Tamnick, Kristi: Estonian singer

Toradze, Aleksandr: pianist

Varvarova, Elena: pianist

Zhordania, Vakhtang: pianist

3C

DEFECTING DANCERS (1969 TO PRESENT)

Aleshin, Yury: solo dancer from a Moscow ballet company

Baryshnikov, Mikhail: ballet dancer from Kirov Ballet, Leningrad

Chursina (Tchursina), Galina: ballet dancer from Bolshoi

Fedicheva, Kaleria: ballet dancer from Kirov Ballet

Filipov, Aleksandr: folk dancer from Moiseyev Ensemble

Godunov, Aleksandr: ballet dancer from Bolshoi

Kleymenov, Anatoly: ballet dancer from Bolshoi

Kozlov, Leonid: ballet dancer from Bolshoi

Kozlova, Valentina: ballet dancer from Bolshoi, former's wife

Makarova, Natalia: ballet dancer from Kirov Ballet

Messerer, Mikhail: ballet dancer from Bolshoi

Messerer, Sulamif: ballet instructor from Bolshoi

Vostrikov, Gennady: folk dancer from Moiseyev Ensemble

3D

Defecting Seamen and Fishermen (1969 to Present)

Agapov, Valentin

Aleksandrov, Nikolay

Butenko, Leonid

Diosov, Vladimir

Dudnikov, Pavel

Egorov, Igor

Filatov, Valery

Gasinskaya, Liliana

Gavrilov, Boris

Goldgur, Leonid

Iwanschenko (Ivanchenko?), Yury

Kaoroyko?, Pyotr Nikolaevich

Khonenko, Ivan

Koshelev, Boris

Kovalenko, Aleksandr

Kurilov, Stanislav

Lysenko, Vladil
Mesokov, Aley (Meshkov, Oleg?)
Muravin, Viktor
Novikov, Vitaly
Okladnikov, Vladimir
Palena, Daina
Reinis, Piteris
Rogalsky, Ivan (convicted spy)
Ryaguzov, Aleksandr
Serega, Vladimir
Stankov, Valery
Terekhova, Elena
Turbalek, Nikolay
Zakharov, Vasily
Zukauskas, Arif

3E

DEFECTING ATHLETES AND SPORTSMEN (1969 TO PRESENT)

Alburt, Lev: chess grand master

Belousova, Lyudmila: figure skater, four-time world champion

Davydenko, Vladislav: ice hockey coach of "Dynamo," Kiev

Gelshtein, Garri: motorcyclist

Gildebrand, Andre: motorcyclist

Ivanov, Igor: chess master

Kepekyan, Sogomin: bicyclist, during World Junior Championship, Belgium, 1976

Korchnoy, Viktor: chess grand master

Kuum, Ya.: cyclist

Lepaiye, Aleksandr: basketball player

Protopopov, Oleg: figure skater, husband and partner of Belousova

Roosna, Raivo: weightlifter

Suponitsky, Mikhail: star acrobat from Moscow Circus

3F

DEFECTING SOVIET MILITARY MEN (1969 TO PRESENT)*

Alekseychuk, Igor: soldier conscript (see Bibliography)

Belenko, Viktor: air force Lt.

Borzovich (Borwsowitsch?): Jr. Lt.

Kourdakov, Sergey Nikolaevich: Ensign (Jr. Lt.), graduate of Petropavlovsk Naval Academy

Kruglov, Aleksandr: soldier conscript, entered U.S. Embassy in Kabul, Afghanistan, but "changed his mind" and returned to the USSR

Topazov, Arnold

Vronsky, Evgeny Lvovich: air force Lt.

Yanyshev, Aleksandr: soldier of Soviet occupation troops in Poland

Zasimov, Valentin Ivanovich: air force 1st Lt., returned by Iran to the USSR

Unidentified sailor conscript (Aleksandr P.?) from signal corps onboard the mine-sweeper *Dizelist* swam away and was picked up by a passing ship during a port call at Tartus, Syria, in July 1981 (see Bibliography)

Unidentified soldier, 19, serving in Pechenga, near Murmansk, crossed the border to Norway and asked for political asylum, according to *New York Times*, July 6, 1979, p. A2

Unidentified Soviet army general (Grishin?) crossed the border to Turkey, according to CBS Evening News on Saturday, October 8, 1983

Unidentified staff sergeant from Soviet troops in East Germany fled to West Germany across the fortified frontier in Niedersachsen in July 1984

---

* This list excludes those who defected or deserted from Soviet troops in Afghanistan (see Chapter 12).

3G

DEFECTING DIPLOMATS, SECURITY OFFICERS, AND OTHER OFFICIALS (1969 TO PRESENT)

Belov, Mikhail: U.N. translator, New York

Davydov, Anatoly: journalist reporting on a trade fair in Japan

Dzhirkvelov, Ilya: TASS correspondent and officer at World Health Organization in Geneva

Hohenesian (Hovanesian? Ovanesian?), Artush: a KGB Lt.

Ipatov (Itaka?), Boris: diplomat in Uganda

Ivanov, Vadim: TASS chief in Vienna; KGB

Kharlov, Vladislav: book trade representative in Egypt

Kiselnikova, Raya: commercial attaché in Mexico

Korolyuk, Viktor: chief interpreter at the troops reduction talks in Vienna, Austria

Leshinskis, Imants: U.N. conference organizer and confessed KGB officer, New York

Lesnik, Renata: Radio Moscow announcer

Levchenko, Stanislav: correspondent for *Novoe vremia* and KGB officer in Japan

Lyalin, Oleg: trade official and KGB officer in London

Mesilane, Riho: Estonian TV announcer

Morozova, Natalia: simultaneous interpreter at the International Organization of Civil Aviation, Toronto, Canada

Myagkov, Aleksey: KGB captain

Nadirashvili, Konstantin: KGB officer

Pleshchakov (also Plechshakov): employee of UNESCO secretariat in Paris

Polyansky, Nikolay: diplomat in the UNESCO Secretariat

Raig, Hillar: Secretary of Estonian Communist Youth League

Randpere, Valdo: Deputy Minister of Justice, Estonia

Rezun, Vladimir: U.N. employee and GRU officer in Geneva

Sakharov, Aleksandr: KGB officer

Sakharov, Vladimir: diplomat and KGB officer in Kuwait

Sezeman, Dmitry: translator of *Novoe vremia* in Paris

Shevchenko, Arkady: U.N. Undersecretary General in New York

Sigl, Rupert: worked for the KGB

Sorokin, Evgeny: military attaché in Laos

Stankin, Yury: member of the Soviet Trade Mission in Paris

Teplyakova, Mrs.: Lyalin's secretary

Tuomi, Kaarlo: KGB officer

Vahtra, Aarne: Estonian official

Yakimets, Vladimir: employee of U.N. Secretariat in New York

Yurchenko, Yury: commercial representative, Venezuela

Zamascikov, Sergey: party official

4

DEFECTORS WHO RETURNED OR WERE FORCED TO RETURN TO THE USSR (1945 TO PRESENT)

Alliluyeva, Svetlana, born 1926, the daughter of Stalin, defected in India on September 3, 1967, and returned from Britain to the USSR on October 23, 1984, with her American-born daughter Olga Peters, age 13.

Arutunyan, Syren, 25, an Armenian folk dancer, defected in UK in November 1975, but then told Home Office officials that he wanted to go home.

Aseev, 30, exchange scholar, defected in U.S. in 1963, returned after a few months.

Balakhonov, Vladimir, an employee of World Meteorological Organization in Geneva, asked for and was granted political asylum in Switzerland, but then returned to the USSR where he was sentenced to fifteen years in labor camps.

Barsov (AKA Borzov), Anatoly, an air force pilot, together with Pirogov, flew his plane from Kolomiye, Western Ukraine, to Linz, Austria, on October 9, 1948; the next year he fell for the enticements of Soviet Embassy officials and returned to the USSR where he was reportedly executed.

Bitov, Oleg, an editor of *Literaturnaia gazeta*, defected in September 1983 in UK; disappeared in August 1984; later appeared at a press conference in Moscow and denounced the British for "kidnapping" him.

Boytsov, crossed over to Finland during the 1970s but was returned by the Finnish authorities.

Cesiunas, Vladas, a Lithuanian canoeist and gold medal winner in the 1972 Olympics, defected in Duisburg, West Germany, in August 1979; disappeared in October 1979; the Soviets maintained that he returned to the USSR voluntarily and accused the Germans of forcing him to defect (see Chapter 13).

Chebotarev, Anatoly, a trade representative and GRU officer in Belgium, defected to U.S. in October 1971, revealed important secrets about Soviet espionage against NATO, then turned up at the Soviet Embassy in Washington and was flown back to the USSR on December 26, 1971 (see Chapter 13).

Cherkov, Nikolay, born 1935, graduate of a Physical Education College (*tekhnikum*); on September 3 and 4, 1966, swam from the tanker *Tuapse* on the Black Sea to the foreign ship *Papalios*, but Captain Kanzas returned him to the Soviets. Sentenced to two years in labor camps. Unsuccessfully applied for emigration to WG. In 1982 sentenced to three years in camps.

Derbenyov, Valentin, a radio operator, crossed over to the PRC in the early 1970s; was imprisoned by the Chinese as a suspected spy, and after nine years sent back to the USSR.

Ermolenko, Georgy, 18, a violinist and student of Moscow University, abandoned his quintet in Perth, Australia, on August 12, 1974, and asked for asylum, but changed his mind after meeting with Soviet Embassy officials.

Gilev, Nikolay, 22, a student, together with Vitaly Pozdeev, 21, skyjacked a small airplane from Kerch to Sinop, Turkey, on October 27, 1970; later the Turks returned them to the USSR, reportedly at their own decision, and they were sentenced to ten and thirteen years, respectively, in September 1972.

Golub, Aleksey, a biochemist, defected in Holland on October 8, 1961; his wife returned at once, but he returned through the Soviet Embassy only on March 27, 1962.

Grigoryan, Gegam, 29, a tenor, asked for asylum in Italy, but disappeared from a refugee camp in Padriciano, Trieste, on December 1, 1979.

Grodetsky, Yury, defected with Aleksandr Ivanov in Mexico on August 21, 1970, but later returned.

Gurov, Anatoly (see *Chronicle of Current Events*, no. 4, 9).

Istomin, Aleksandr, 31, a journalist who worked for a year as a representative of the Soviet press agency Novosti in UK, received political asylum on May 2, 1979, but on the same day took a train from Oxford to London and turned up at the Soviet Embassy.

Ivankov-Nikolov, Mikhail, born 1921, radio operator from the tanker *Tuapse*, imprisoned in Soviet mental institutions from 1956 to present.

Ivanov, Georgy, born 1945, a worker, crossed over to Finland in 1967, but was returned by the Finnish police and served fifteen months in jail. Crossed the same border in 1976 and received political asylum in Sweden.

Kaganov, Lev, 33, a ski coach, defected in Sweden on January 11, 1966, but decided to return on February 6, 1966, after talking to his mother, whom the Soviets had brought to Sweden.

Kalishenko, Pyotr, 35, landed in a walrus-skin boat on Alaska's western coast on August 7, 1965, together with Gregory Sarapushkin. On August 16, 1965, it was decided to return them to the USSR in spite of their request for political asylum.

Karpenok, Mikhail, a Ukrainian, crossed over to Turkey in 1974 or 1975, but was returned by the Turks, and from August 1976 was serving in a labor camp with Mikhail Kheifets (see latter in Bibliography). Completed his seven-year term in 1982.

Khlan, Oleg, 21, a Soviet soldier, was in the hands of Afghan guerrillas, expressed a desire to settle in the West, received political asylum in Britain at the behest of Lord Nicholas Bethell in June 1984, but returned to the USSR on November 11, 1984. (See also Igor Rykov, who defected and returned to the USSR with Khlan.)

Kondrashina, Nina, wife of the defecting conductor, returned from hiding in Holland on December 5, 1978.

Kozlov, Sergey, a Soviet mathematician who was to have spent six weeks as a guest scholar at the California Institute of Technology, disappeared from Pasadena under mysterious circumstances on April 30, 1984, after having complained to the local police that KGB agents had tried to poison him with gas. He turned up later in Washington, D.C., but refused to board a British airliner bound for Moscow. Later, in the presence of American officials, he expressed his desire to go home and was allowed to leave. The Soviets attributed his earlier complaints about the KGB and his refusal to go home to his "illness" and accused the U.S. government of raising obstacles to his return.

Kruglov, Aleksandr, 21, a soldier conscript, entered U.S. Embassy in Kabul, Afghanistan, on September 15, 1980, but a few days later agreed to return (see Chapter 13).

Kudirka, Simas, a Lithuanian radio operator from a Soviet trawler, defected to a U.S. Coast Guard cutter on November 23, 1970, but was returned by the Americans to the Soviets (see Chapter 13).

Lukashev, Valentin, a sailor, was among 20 Soviet crewmen who asked for political asylum after tanker *Tuapse* was intercepted by Taiwan in June 1954; lured by Soviet officials with four other sailors from New York on April 7, 1956.

Lysikov, Valery, asked for asylum, then "returned to aid his parents," as reported on April 25, 1955.

Mamedova, Irina, 35, defected with her daughter to an FBI office in Washington on September 25, 1981, but after twelve days "changed her mind" and returned to the Soviets (see Chapter 13).

Markov, Ivan, 30, an army lieutenant, defected in Skroitnes, near Pasvik, Norway, on November 21, 1954. The Soviets accused him of stealing several thousand rubles, and he was returned at Storskog, near Kirkenes, on December 3, 1954.

Mikheyev, Ivan, 56, a newsreel cameraman, asked for asylum in UK in December 1967; returned on October 8, 1969.

Nemtsanov, Sergey, 17, a sports diver, defected during Olympic Games in Montreal, Canada, in July 1976, then changed his mind and returned.

Novozhitsky, Andrey, defected to WG in mid-1950s, returned in 1958, sentenced to twelve years.

Pozdeev, Vitaly. See Gilev, Nikolai.

Roessini, Konstantin, 46, a veterinarian, defected from a Soviet agricultural delegation in Holland in December 1975, was granted political asylum by the Dutch, but on April 9, 1976, returned to the USSR.

Rykov, Igor, 22, a Soviet sergeant, was in the hands of Afghan guerrillas, after expressing a desire to settle in the West, received permission to stay in Britain at the behest of Lord Nicholas Bethell in June 1984, but returned to the USSR on November 11, 1984, with Oleg Khlan (see Khlan entry).

Ryzhkov, Nikolay, 19, a Soviet soldier in Afghanistan who said he defected to the guerrillas and expressed a desire to settle in the West. After Lord Bethell negotiated his release, he came to the United States in December 1983 together with Aleksandr Voronov, another Soviet defector, but returned to the USSR a year later.

Safranov, Konstantin G., 17, a sailor from the guided missile destroyer *Boiky*, leaped from his ship in Lagos, Nigeria, and boarded the British freighter *Tweedbank*. Later, on March 10, 1969, the Nigerian government handed him back to the USSR, saying that he was willing to return.

Sarapushkin, Gregory. See Kalishenko, Peter.

Shatravka, Aleksandr, born 1950, escaped with his brother (see next entry) to Finland in 1974, and soon returned by the Finns; interned in mental hospitals from four to five years. Now is in a labor camp.

Shatravka, Mikhail, born 1952, shared the fate of his brother.

Shirin, Aleksandr, a sailor from the tanker *Tuapse*, asked for asylum in June 1954; abducted from New York on April 7, 1956. See Lukashov, Valentin.

Sirodia (Siordia?), Pavel, a fisherman, defected through a mutiny onboard trawler *Vishera* on August 14, 1972, granted asylum in U.S. but returned before October 1973.

Stepanov, Yury, 32, ballet dancer, defected in Italy in January 1980; came to U.S., but then returned to the USSR.

Suslov, Aleksandr, a fisherman from the mutinied trawler *Vishera*, returned to the USSR no later than May 1973. See Sirodia, Pavel.

Tarasevich, Gennady, on May 1, 1957, swam to the Norwegian tanker *Nordfonn*, but was returned; later emigrated to U.S.

Yanin, Valery, 26, an engineer, asked for political asylum after crossing the Black Sea in a rubber raft in August 1973; later was seen in Soviet mental hospitals in 1974–78.

Zasimov, Valentin Ivanovich, a lieutenant pilot, flew his AN-2 aircraft to Iran on September 26, 1976, but was returned by the Iranians.

5

ABORTIVE DEFECTIONS (1945 TO PRESENT)*

Agapov, Valery, 33, a Moscow lawyer, tried to defect at Shannon Airport, Dublin, in June, 1984, but was sent home by Irish authorities.

Berezhkov, Andrey, 16, son of a Soviet diplomat, ran away from home on August 10, 1983, wrote letters to the *New York Times* and President Reagan asking for help in staying in U.S., but on August 18 was allowed to return to the USSR "at his own request."

Bukreev, Vladimir, an official of the ILO and one of Rezun's (see Appendix 3) colleagues in Geneva, Switzerland, was grabbed by a KGB "goon squad" and hustled on to an Aeroflot flight to Moscow on June 6, 1978.

Cherepanov, Vyacheslav, on May 15, 1981, was sentenced in Vilnius to twelve years in labor camps and three years of exile for an attempt to cross over to Finland in July 1980. The Finnish guards beat him up and handed him over to the Soviets near Hattuvara.

Chikhladze, Teimuraz, a Georgian priest, sentenced to death for a November 18, 1983, skyjack attempt (see also Kobakhidze, Iverieli, and Petriashvili).

Ehrenberg, Vadim, born 1956, on January 6, 1979, arrested with four others in Leningrad for an attempt to seize an airplane at Pulkovo airport and fly it to Oslo, Norway. Sentenced to thirteen years of labor camps; his brother, Aleksei Ehrenberg, to eight years; his wife, Ludmila Krylova, to eight years; Ms. Listvina, five years; and Mikhail Lebed, two and a half years.

Fedorov, Yury, one of the twelve *samoletchiki* who attempted to seize and fly a passenger airplane from Leningrad to Sweden on June 14, 1970. Sentenced to fifteen years in labor camps, he is one of the two still in jail. The other one is Aleksei Murzhenko, also sentenced to fifteen years.

Gakutskas, Ionas, born 1940, lived near Kaunas, Lithuania; arrested on the Finnish border during the summer of 1981 with his wife, two small children, and brother.

Gakutskas, a brother. See Gakutskas, Ionas.

Gakutskas, Mrs. See Gakutskas, Ionas.

---

* Due to the secretive nature of Soviet society, this list must be considered especially incomplete; the reader is advised to consult the *Chronicle of Current Events*, which keeps a record of human rights violations in the USSR.

Gavrilov, Mikhail, an employee of the Soviet mission in Washington, in his 50s, died of multiple internal injuries inflicted on Soviet premises in August 1977; as Washington police were not allowed to investigate the case, a defection attempt may be suspected.

Gavrilov, Evgeny, 32, a diplomat, who had just arrived at the Soviet Embassy in Washington, was found dead on the Embassy premises on January 6, 1984; as the Soviets refused to allow Washington police to investigate his death, a failed defection attempt may be suspected. (It is not known if he is related to the former.)

Gladko, Georg. (See *Chronicle of Current Events*, no. 9.)

Hlgatian, a worker from Armenia, attempted to cross over to Iran, served in labor camps, now an émigré.

Iverieli, Kakha, a Georgian medical doctor; sentenced to death.

Iverieli, Paata, also a doctor and former's brother; sentenced to death.

Kiirend, Olev, an Estonian, arrested during an attempt to cross the Baltic Sea on a raft in August 1982; in March 1983, sentenced to seven years of hard labor.

Kobakhidze, Gherman, a Georgian actor, sentenced to death for the November 18, 1983, skyjack attempt. (See Chikhladze.)

Krylova, Lyudmila. See Ehrenberg, Vadim.

Kurashvili, Merab, 36, a Soviet exchange student from Georgia, who was said to have attempted suicide while in a Soviet embassy car. He was being driven to an airport to fly him out of U.S. (See Chapter 13.)

Lebed, Mikhail. See Ehrenberg, Vadim.

Listvina, Lyudmila. See Ehrenberg, Vadim.

Makhayev, Ye. M., "an armed criminal," was killed by security guards while trying to divert abroad an airliner during its Krasnodar to Baku flight, according to a TASS report on November 15, 1978.

Martirosov, Valery, born 1960, sentenced in July 1980 to eight years for an attempt on March 20 to divert to Turkey an Aeroflot TU-134 on its flight from Baku to Yerevan. Pulled a knife on a hostess. Reported by *Bakinskii rabochii* around July 31, 1980.

Matveyev, a State Security lieutenant, around 1948–49, made an inquiry at the U.S. Embassy in Moscow and was then sentenced to five years of jail.

Mickute, Gratsina. See Simokaitis, Vitautas.

Mikheyev, Dmitry, served six years in camps for an attempt to defect in 1970. Later was allowed to emigrate to U.S.

Mkheidze, Revaz, and Orekhov, Yuri. According to *Komsomol'skaia pravda* of January 11, 1963, the two young men managed to get on board a foreign ship but were noticed by the coast guard and forcibly returned. Gulam Sulakvelidze conspired with them, but at the last moment bowed out. No punishment was reported.

Murzhenko, Aleksey. See Fedorov, Yury.

Nazarova, Natalia. See Nazarov, Vasily.

Nikitenkov, Vasily, M.D., was subjected to forcible treatment in a psychiatric hospital for visiting the U.S. Embassy in Moscow in 1971 and inquiring about the possibility of emigration.

Nikredin, Yury, commandeered a taxi into U.S. Embassy in April 1979, but was arrested by the Soviets with American help. (See Chapter 13.)

Nikulin, Viktor V., an employee of Soviet trade mission in Vienna, was forcibly taken on a train and was drugged by the Soviets, according to the *New York Times*, May 8, 1969.

Orekhov, Yuri. See Mkheidze, Revaz.

Osipov, Vladimir, was serving a prison term in Chistopol "for crossing border to Turkey," according to *Russkaia mysl'*, February 2, 1984. The date of the abortive attempt was not given.

Petriashvili, Tinatin, a Georgian student, sentenced to fourteen years for her role in the failed skyjack attempt. (See Chikhladze.)

Radygin, Anatoly, a navy officer, attempted to swim to Turkey, sentenced to ten years. Emigrated to U.S. in 1973.

Ravensky, Sasha, 16, in June 1983 attempted to cross over to Norway on foot from an area near Murmansk, but after 13 days of travail was found by Soviet border guards, and in March 1984 sentenced to two years in labor camps.

Ravinsh, Maigonis, 20, attempted to flee abroad in 1977, then served in a camp. (See Kheifets in the Bibliography.)

Sablin, Valery Mikhailovich, *zampolit*, led the mutiny on board the destroyer *Storozhevoy* on November 8, 1975, in order to run it to Sweden. Sentenced to death in May 1976, among several others. (See Chapter 12.)

Selivonchik, Galina, born in 1937, sentenced to thirteen years for an attempt to seize an airplane and fly to Finland on June 3, 1969. She was assisted by her brother, Yuri Vasiliev, and husband, Ivan, who was killed in the attempt. Vasiliev was sentenced to eleven years.

Selivonchik, Ivan. See Selivonchik, Galina.

Sheludko, Gennady, 22, was sentenced to fifteen years in November 1977 for diverting an Aeroflot TU-134 plane to Helsinki, Finland, on July 12, from its regular flight from Petrozavodsk to Leningrad. His companion was Aleksandr Zagirnyak, who received eight years. Using a dud grenade as a threat, they demanded to go to Sweden, but the pilot landed the plane in Helsinki where the two soon surrendered, overpowered by sleep.

Shinkorenko, Evgeny, 25, an engineer representing a Soviet trade mission, on December 30, 1982, was brought to a French hospital in Nanterre, where he was treated for deep knife wounds. The Soviets said he had attempted suicide.

Simokaitis, Vitautas, 34, a Lithuanian, and his pregnant wife, Tratsina, 21, attempted on November 9, 1970 to divert abroad an airplane from Vilnius. On January 14, 1971, he was sentenced to death, she to three years. The death penalty was commuted to fifteen years. The pilot was also tried.

Skachinsky, Aleksandr, born 1950, a painter, attempted on January 9, 1976, to swim to Turkey from a motorboat that departed from Gantiadi, Abkhazia. Caught and sentenced to eight years.

Sklyarova, Lidia, was sentenced to fifteen years for an attempt to seize an airplane and flee abroad, according to *Chronicle of Current Events*, January 1970.

Skubenko, Mr., was killed during his attempt in the beginning of May 1978 to divert abroad a passenger airplane from its route from Ashkhabad to Mineral'nye Vody, according to a TASS report.

Smirnova, Nina, wife of a Soviet accountant at the Soviet Embassy in Canberra, Australia, in the early 1950s made an attempt to defect but was arrested and sentenced to ten years. Her husband escaped punishment because he helped to foil her defection.

Strygin, Col., a Soviet military attaché in Rangoon, Burma, attempted to flee from a Burmese hospital on May 3, 1959.

Sulakvelidze, Gulam. See Mkheidze, Revaz.

Timoshukov, Mikhail, 22, from Kazakhstan, on May 25, 1978, entered Finnair office in Moscow armed with a hunting gun and, taking two Soviet citizens as hostages, demanded to go to Finland. In a scuffle he and, possibly, one of the hostages were wounded. The Soviet security police took him away.

Vahter, Mart E., crossed the Finnish gulf from Estonia to Finland in the summer of 1978. Disappeared somewhere in Finland while on the way to Sweden.

Vetokhin, Yury (see Appendix 3), a former naval officer and engineer, made two unsuccessful attempts to swim to Turkey, in 1964 and 1967. For the second attempt he was sentenced to ten years. In 1979 successfully defected by swimming from a Soviet liner to an Indonesian island. (See Bibliography.)

Vlasenko, Yury, 27, a merchant seaman from Ukraine, entered the U.S. Embassy on March 28, 1979, and asked them to help him emigrate. Killed by Soviet security men on the premises of the Embassy. (See Chapter 12.)

Volkov, Konstantin, vice-consul in Istanbul, Turkey, in August 1945 asked Mr. Page, the British consul general, to help him obtain political asylum in UK for himself and his wife. Because of the infiltration of the British intelligence with Burgess, Maclean, and Philby, his attempt was foiled, and he and his wife were arrested by the Soviets and taken to Moscow.

Volkov, Mrs. See Volkov, Konstantin.

Zagirnyak, Aleksandr. See Shelud'ko, Gennady.

Zhvania, Vladimir, born 1935, attempted to cross over to Turkey in 1955. Sentenced to three years.

6

Seajackings and Mutinies (1945 to Present)

1. On December 4, 1947, an Estonian, born 1925, "as captain of the fishing trawler No. 176, *Merituul*, with a crew of nine, left the port of Klaipeda, Lithuania, and fled to Sweden." Sentenced in absentia to 25 years of labor camps. (Quoted from the Hoover File, entry 265.)

2. In July 1951, a Lithuanian, born 1927, "in conspiracy with the captain [also wanted] of the trawler MRT-85, *Somum*, locked up three other crewmen, and after entering Swedish waters, escaped on a sloop to the island of Oland, Sweden." Now resides in Chicago. Sentenced to death. The captain and another sailor who had taken part in the mutiny were also sentenced to death. (Hoover File, entries 108, 207, and 271.)

3. On June 2, 1952, a Latvian trawl master, born 1929, from the fishing cooperative "Bolshevik," escaped on board a fishing boat to Sweden. He was accompanied by other fishermen (the number unspecified). Now resides in Sweden, maintains correspondence with relatives, and engages in nationalist émigré activities. (Hoover File, entry 214.)

4. On June 4, 1952, a Latvian assistant captain, born 1931, escaped on board a fishing trawler to Sweden. He, too, was from the cooperative "Bolshevik." Since 1968 he has been working in Stockholm, travels in Europe, corresponds with relatives. A 1966 photograph is on file. (Hoover File, entry 302.)

5. On January 20, 1953, a Latvian, born 1918, "as captain of a fishing boat, offered a refuge onboard to the traitors [wanted] and [wanted], with whom escaped to Sweden." Belonged to the cooperative "Bolshevik" in Liepaia. Resides in Stockholm, works in a factory, and makes broadcasts for the VOA. Apparently, four other crew members took part in the mutiny, including a Latvian electric welder and his wife. All were sentenced to death. (Hoover File, entries 408 and 468.)

6. On July 10, 1957, a Latvian mechanic, born 1933, "criminally conspired with the crewmen [wanted] and [wanted], tied up their captain, and sailed to Sweden, where abandoned the ship and stayed ashore." Resides in Sweden, maintains correspondence. (Hoover File, entry 34.)

7. On June 5, 1959, Artamonov, Nikolai Fedorovich, 31, commander of a Soviet navy destroyer stationed in Poland, escaped in a motorboat to the Swedish island of Oland. He was accompanied by his 22-year-old Polish fiancée. (About his subsequent fate, see Chapter 13.)

8. On April 6, 1961, a Lithuanian lieutenant of the Soviet navy, born 1935, "being the commander of an auxiliary vessel, went to high seas, and during the night of April 7 escaped to Sweden where asked for political asylum." Sentenced to death by a court martial. Lives in U.S., works at a computer factory, corresponds with sister. A 1967 photo is on file. (Hoover File, entry 308.)

9. On September 13, 1965, a Latvian, born 1943, "in agreement with his first cousin [wanted] seized control of the fishing boat No. 7273, *Variag*, and escaped to Sweden. Maintains correspondence and engages in anti-Soviet and nationalist activities." The cousin was an assistant captain, born 1941, and in 1968 was living in Sweden. (Hoover File, entries 437 and 200.)

10. On August 14, 1972, the trawler *Vishera*, from the Black Sea fishing fleet based in Kerch, entered the port of Piraeus, Greece, and six out of seven crew members, including captain Pavel Dudnikov, asked for political asylum. They were allowed to come to U.S. However, the next year two of them, Pavel Sirodia [Siordia?] and Aleksandr Suslov, returned to the USSR. (See Appendix 4.)

11. On November 8, 1975, part of the crew of the navy destroyer *Storozhevoy* of the Baltic fleet mutinied during a port call in Riga, seized control of the ship, and attempted to sail it to Sweden. The mutiny was led by *zampolit* (political commissar) Valery Sablin. Before reaching Swedish waters, the ship was attacked by Soviet jets and forced to return. (See Chapter 12.)

7

SKYJACKINGS AND DEFECTIONS BY AIR (1945 TO PRESENT)

1. According to Peter Pirogov, his own defection on October 9, 1948, was inspired by a previous escape of a Soviet pilot in an air force plane to Turkey.

2. On October 9, 1948, Peter Pirogov and Anatoly Barsov (AKA Borzov) flew their bomber TU-2 from Kolomiye, Western Ukraine, to Linz, Austria, where they were granted political asylum by American occupation authorities. Barsov later returned and was executed; Pirogov was sentenced in absentia to 25 years. (Hoover File, entry 16; see also Introduction.)

3. On November 10, 1948, a Russian air force mechanic, 22, flew an LI-2 plane to the Japanese island of Risiri, "where he surrendered to the Americans and gave them information about Soviet AF in the Far East." Sentenced by a court-martial to 25 years. (Hoover File, entry 282.)

4. On May 18, 1949, a Russian air force lieutenant, flew an LA-11 plane from Mogilev, Belorussia, to Tullinge, Sweden, "where declared himself a political emigre . . . and revealed to the Swedes secret information about Soviet AF." Sentenced to 25 years.

5. On July 22, 1960, the newspaper *Sovetskaia aviatsiia* reported an unsuccessful skyjack attempt by a man and a woman from the Baltic states. The two were captured and charged with "diversion," an offense punishable by death.

6. On January 7, 1961, the newspaper *Trud* reported an unsuccessful attempt to seize an LI-2 passenger plane from Tallinn airport by a demobilized pilot and a woman, both unnamed. As soon as the plane was in the air, a gun battle broke out in which one of the crew was killed. The story was timed with the unveiling of a monument to the victim, Timofei Romashkin, in Minsk.

7. On October 14, 1961, *Komsomol'skaia pravda* reported an unsuccessful attempt by three young Armenians from Yerevan to flee abroad in a stolen airplane. The culprits were caught and sentenced to be shot.

8. In August 1964, two unnamed men attempted to divert abroad a Soviet passenger plane. The pilots, in spite of the gun and knife wounds inflicted by the attackers, managed to land the plane in Kishinev, Moldavia. The attackers were brought to court.

9. In April 1966, a Soviet YAK-28 crash-landed on a lake in West Berlin in an apparent attempt to defect. Its two pilots were killed.

10. In August 1966, three people tried to skyjack a passenger plane from Batumi, Georgia, but the pilots resisted, and in the ensuing gun battle one passenger was wounded. The three were caught and tried.

11. On May 25, 1967, Epatko (also Yepatko), a Russian lieutenant engineer, 25, while participating in a long-distance group flight, changed his course and landed in West Germany, where he asked for political asylum. Resides in U.S. A 1966 photograph and handwriting sample are on file. The arrest warrant is issued. (Hoover File, entry 388.)

12. Around 1969 or 1970, the newspaper *Sovetakan Ayastan* (Soviet Armenia) carried an article, "From a Court Room," about an unsuccessful attempt by a group of Armenians to assemble a plane and fly it to Turkey. Using a discarded engine of a DOSAAF airplane, they assembled a new one near the resort city of Arnzi, but were discovered and arrested.

13. On June 3, 1969, Galina Selivonchik, her husband Ivan Selivonchik, and brother Yury Vasiliev unsuccessfully tried to seize an airplane and fly it to Finland, according to *Chronicle of Current Events*, 1970. (See Appendix 5.)

14. In the January 1970 issue of the *Chronicle* it was reported that a certain Lidia Sklyarova was sentenced to fifteen years for an attempt to skyjack an airplane and flee abroad. (See Appendix 5.)

15. On June 14, 1970, twelve people, mostly Jewish, were arrested at a Leningrad airport and charged with conspiracy to seize an AN-2 passenger plane and fly it to Sweden. (See Chapter 11.)

16. On October 15, 1970, two Lithuanians, Pranas Brazinskas-Koreivo, 46, and his son Algirdas, 16, skyjacked an AN-24 passenger plane and diverted it to Turkey from its regular Batumi-to-Sukhumi route. In the process, they killed the stewardess, Nadia Kurchenko. The Turks rejected Soviet demands to extradite the skyjackers, but sentenced them to jail.

17. On October 27, 1970, Nikolay Gilev and Vitaly Pozdeev succeeded in skyjacking a small plane from Kerch to Sinop, Turkey. (See Appendix 4.)

18. On November 9, 1970, two Lithuanians, Vitauskas Simokaitis, 34, and his pregnant wife, Gratsina, 21, attempted to divert a passenger plane from Vilnius. (See Appendix 5.)

19. On May 7, 1973, the passenger liner TU-104, on the way from Moscow to Chita, exploded in the air, killing all 100 people aboard. This happened about 100 miles from Chita, near the Chinese border. According to Dr. Samuil Pashkar, a recent émigré, the explosion occurred as a result of a skyjacking attempt by a man who demanded to be flown to China. The police interrogated all those who left the plane during stops in Novosibirsk and Irkutsk. Another version is that the plane was shot down by Soviet air force fighters after they had learned of the skyjacking attempt. Dr. Pashkar is from Chita, and he personally knew some of the victims. (See Albert Parry's article in *NRS*, November 9, 1977.)

20. On May 27, 1973, Evgeny Vronsky (at first misidentified as Lwoich), an air force lieutenant pilot, flew his Sukoi-7 fighter-bomber to West Germany. The Germans rejected Moscow's demand to extradite him but returned the aircraft, which had been wrecked during the landing. Vronsky's defection cooled the "new era" of Soviet-German détente that had been established by Brezhnev's visit a week earlier.

21. On June 26, 1973, Pyotr Vasiliev, an airline pilot, flew a small passenger plane from Rostov-on-Don to Turkey. Running out of fuel, he landed 250 meters from the sea, and 43 km away from Trabzon airport. The Turks promised to consider his request for asylum, according to Reuter.

22. Around November 1974, four young men boarded a domestic liner YAK on the flight from Domodedovo airport, near Moscow, to Minsk and, threatening the pilot with cut-off guns, demanded to be flown to Sweden. The pilot seemed to agree but suggested they stop at Vnukovo, another Moscow airport, for more fuel. Upon landing there, the plane was surrounded by MVD troops with tanks and armored cars. In the gun battle that ensued, two skyjackers and several passengers were killed, according to a recent émigré.

23. On September 5, 1976, Lieutenant Viktor Belenko flew his MIG-25 to Hakodate, Japan.

24. On September 23, 1976, Senior Lieutenant Valentin Ivanovich Zasimov flew an AN-2 to Iran and landed at airport Ahar, near Tabriz. Zasimov asked for political asylum, but was returned to the USSR at the end of October. (See Chapter 13.)

25. On May 26, 1977, Vasily Sosnovsky, 37, a worker from Belorussia, commandeered to Sweden a twin-engine AN-24 passenger plane during its normal flight from Riga to Daugavpils. Swedish J35 Dragon fighters escorted it to Arlanda airport near Stockholm. The Swedes refused to extradite Sosnovsky, but he was sentenced to a few years in jail, which he gladly served.

26. On July 10, 1977, Gennady Sheludko, 22, and Aleksandr Zagirnyak, 19, boarded an Aeroflot TU-134 on its flight from Petroyavodsk to Leningrad and, threatening with a dud grenade, demanded to be flown to Sweden. When the pilot foiled the attempt by landing in Helsinki, Finland, they kept the crew and passengers hostage for 36 hours. Overcome by sleep, they finally surrendered and were flown back to the USSR. (See Appendix 5.)

27. In the beginning of May 1978, a certain Skubenko (see Appendix 5) was killed during his attempt to divert abroad a domestic airliner from its Ashkhabad to Mineral'nye Vody flight, according to a TASS announcement.

28. On November 15, 1978, TASS announced: "E. M. Makhayev, an armed criminal, a few days ago made an attempt to hijack a passenger plane which was on a Krasnodar to Baku flight and to make it fly abroad." Security guards foiled the attempt and killed Makhayev. (See Appendix 5.)

29. On November 16, 1979, Reuter referenced a *Komsomol'skaia pravda* article about a gun battle between four skyjackers and Soviet police at a Moscow airport. The article gave no dates, and named only one skyjacker, Romanov. All four were caught, two of them wounded. There was no information provided about their subsequent fates. Also wounded were one passenger and one crew member. The seriousness of the incident was indicated by the fact that the leader of the police squad, Aleksandr Popryadukhin, was awarded the title of Hero of the Soviet Union.

30. On March 20, 1980, a certain Martirosov, in his 20s, boarded an Aeroflot TU-134 when it was approaching Yerevan from Baku and demanded to be flown to Turkey. To make his demand stick, he pulled a knife on the hostess. In the scuffle that ensued, he was overwhelmed by passengers and crew, and the hostess was wounded. He was sentenced to eight years on account of his "tender age," according to the local Soviet newspaper, *Bakinskii rabochii.* (See Appendix 5.)

31. On Sunday, November 7, 1982, three Soviet citizens of German origin—Arthur Schuller, 30; Vitaly Schmidt, 27; and his brother Boris, 23—commandeered an Aeroflot AN-25 from its regular flight from Novorossiysk to Odessa to Sinop, Turkey. (See Chapter 12.)

32. In May 1983, a Soviet AN-2 airplane, used for dusting crops, landed on the island of Gotland, Sweden. The unidentified pilot, who said that he crossed the Baltic Sea from Latvia, asked for political asylum.

33. On July 13, 1983, Soviet army newspaper *Krasnaia zvezda* reported that in the beginning of the month two unidentified Soviet citizens unsuccessfully attempted to divert abroad a domestic airliner flying from Moscow to Tallinn, Estonia. One of the skyjackers was killed, the other arrested.

34. On November 18, 1983, a group of young Georgians boarded a domestic airliner in Tbilisi, Georgia, and tried to divert it to Turkey. The attempt failed, but several crew members, passengers, and at least one skyjacker were killed in the ensuing battle. In August 1984, TASS announced death sentences for four of the skyjackers. (See Chapter 11.)

8

COMMUNIST PARTY MEMBERSHIP CARD

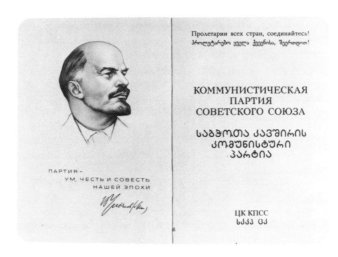

This card belongs to Konstantin Nadirashvili, a KGB officer who defected in August 1975. (Konstantin Georgievich Nadirashvili Collection, Hoover Institution Archives, Stanford, California.)

9

PASSPORT AND VISA FOR FOREIGN TRAVEL

(This document belongs to the author)

NOTES

INTRODUCTION

1. Charles Fenyvesi, "The Unwelcome Defector: An Embarrassment to Both Sides," *New Republic* 178 (April 22, 1978): 9.

2. Susan Sontag, "Communism and the Left," *The Nation* 234, no. 8 (February 27, 1982): 230–31.

CHAPTER I

1. Gordon Brook-Sheperd, *The Storm Petrels: The Flight of the First Soviet Defectors* (New York, London: Harcourt, Brace, Jovanovich, 1977).

2. Ibid., p. xi.

3. Ibid., p. 234.

4. Vernon Hinchley, *The Defectors* (London, Toronto, Wellington, Sydney: George C. Harrap, 1967).

5. Ibid., p. 8.

6. Ibid., p. 245.

7. Ibid., pp. 249–50.

8. John Barron, *KGB: The Secret Work of Soviet Secret Agents* (Toronto, New York, London: Bantam, 1974). See also Barron's *KGB Today: The Hidden Hand* (New York: Reader's Digest Press; distributed by Random House, 1983).

9. Barron, *KGB*, p. 45.

10. Alex Inkeles and Raymond A. Bauer, *The Soviet Citizen: Daily Life in a Totalitarian Society* (Cambridge, Mass.: Harvard University Press, 1959), p. 8.

11. Ibid., pp. 397–98.

12. In addition to the books reviewed in this chapter, Lois Fischer and Boris Yakovlev wrote a book that was based on interviews with the wartime refugees and defectors (*Thirteen Who Fled* [New York, 1949]).

CHAPTER 2

1. In the selection, preference was given to books and authors whose themes and topics complement, rather than duplicate, the others. A number of authors whose books may be just as important had to be excluded: Anatoli Granovsky, who defected to Sweden in 1946 and whose book, *I Was an NKVD Agent*, was published in 1962; Aleksandr Orlov, who, though a prewar defector, published two books, *The Secret History of Stalin's Crimes* and *Handbook of Intelligence and Guerilla Warfare*, in the postwar period; Svetlana Alliluyeva's *Twenty Letters to a Friend* and *Only One Year*; Sareen's *Bid for Freedom: USSR vs. Tarasov* (about Vladislav Tarasov's defection in India and his successful legal battle against extradition to the USSR); Rudolf Nureyev's autobiography; S. Iurasov's *Vrag naroda* (Enemy of the people), a fictional account of the author's defection; and A. I. Romanov's *Nights Are Longest There: A Memoir of the Soviet Security Services*, which deals with early postwar defections but was published only in 1972.

As to the post-1969 period, among the excluded authors and books are Sergei Kourdakov's *The Persecutor*, an autobiographic narration of a twenty-one-year-old KGB activist and seaman who jumped ship in Canada in September 1971, joined the Underground Evangelism, and died in an allegedly accidental shooting in San Bernardino, California, on January 1, 1973; John Barron's *MIG Pilot: The Final Escape of Lt. Belenko* and *KGB Today: The Hidden Hand*; Vladimir Sakharov and Umberto Tosi's *High Treason*; Anatoly Fedoseev's *Zapadnia* (The trap); Henry Hurt's *Shadrin: The Spy Who Never Came Back*; Viktor Suvorov's *Inside the Soviet Army*; and Michael Voslensky's *Nomenklatura: The Soviet Ruling Class*.

2. Victor Kravchenko, *I Chose Freedom: The Personal and Political Life of a Soviet Officer* (New York: Scribner's & Sons, 1946).

3. Ibid., p. 475.

4. Ibid., p. 474.

5. Ibid., p. 468.

6. John Train, "The Lonely Voice of Alexander Solzhenitsyn," *Wall Street Journal*, June 23, 1983.

7. Kravchenko, *Freedom*, p. 472.

8. Kravchenko described this trial in his second book, *I Chose Justice* (New York: Scribner's & Sons, 1950).

9. Kravchenko, *Freedom*, p. 478.

10. Igor Gouzenko, *The Iron Curtain* (New York: Dutton, 1948), p. vi.

11. Ibid., p. 73.

12. Ibid., p. 78.

13. Ibid., p. 78.

14. Michael Voslensky, *Nomenklatura: The Soviet Ruling Class* (Garden City, N.J.: Doubleday, 1984).

15. Gouzenko, *Curtain*, p. 31.

16. Ibid., p. vii.

17. Oksana Kasenkina, *Leap to Freedom* (New York, Philadelphia: Lippincott, 1949).

18. Ibid., pp. 203–4.

19. Ibid., p. 32.

20. Ibid., p. 295.

21. Peter Pirogov, *Why I Escaped: The Story of Peter Pirogov* (New York: Duell, Sloan, & Pearce, 1950), p. 31.

22. Vladimir Petrov and Evdokia Petrov, *Empire of Fear* (New York: Praeger, 1956), p. 341.

23. Pirogov, *Escaped*, p. 147.

24. Ibid., pp. 76–77.

25. Ibid., p. 276.

26. Gregory Klimov, *The Terror Machine: The Inside Story of the Soviet Administration in Germany* (New York: Praeger, 1953).

27. Ibid., p. 148.

28. Ibid., pp. 185–86.

29. Ibid., p. 386.

30. Grigory Tokaev, *Stalin Means War* (London: Weidenfeld and Nicolson, 1951).

31. Ibid., p. 135.

32. Ibid., p. 200.

33. Ibid., p. 201.

34. Grigory Tokaev, *Betrayal of an Ideal: Memoirs of the Author's Youth* (Bloomington: Indiana University Press, 1955), p. 4.

35. Grigory Tokaev, *Soviet Imperialism* (New York: Philosophical Library, 1956), pp. 72–73.

36. The term "State Security" is used here in the general sense of Soviet secret police apparatus. Unless otherwise specified elsewhere in this book, it should be understood as inclusive of its various historical stages and branches, such as the Cheka (1917–1922), GPU and OGPU (1922–1934), NKVD (1934–1946), NKGB and SMERSH (1943–1946), MVD and MGB (1946–1953), their merger to MVD during 1953–1954 when Deriabin defected, and the current binary existence as KGB and MVD since 1954. In a specific sense, State Security refers to the GB (*gosudarstvennaia bezopasnost'*) component of NKGB, MGB, and KGB. Compare John Barron, *KGB*, "History of the State Security Apparatus," app. A, pp. 457–62.

37. Peter Deriabin and Frank Gibney, *The Secret World* (Garden City, N.J.: Doubleday, 1959).

38. Ibid., p. 157.

39. Ibid., p. 70.

40. According to a *Los Angeles Times* report, these special troops of the KGB now number 300,000. See the *Sunday Peninsula Herald* (Monterey, Calif.), May 29, 1983, p. 3A.

41. Deriabin, *Secret World*, p. 94.

42. Ibid., p. 184.

43. Ibid., p. 183.

44. Ibid., p. 280.

45. Nikolai Khokhlov, *In the Name of Conscience* (New York: David McKay, 1959).

46. Deriabin, *Secret World*, p. 187.

47. Khokhlov, *Conscience*, pp. 127–28.

48. Ibid., p. 177.

49. Ibid., p. 224.

50. Ibid., p. 153.

51. Ibid., pp. 364–65.

52. Petrov and Petrov, *Empire of Fear*, p. 11.

53. Ibid., p. 9.

54. Ibid., p. 12.

55. Ibid., p. 265.

56. Ibid., p. 208.

57. Ibid., p. 341.

58. Ibid., p. 341.

59. Aleksandr Kaznacheev, *Inside a Soviet Embassy: Experiences of a Russian Diplomat in Burma* (Philadelphia, New York: Lippincott, 1962).

60. Ibid., p. 31.

61. Ibid., pp. 26–27.

62. Ibid., p. 141.

63. Ibid., p. 149.

64. Ibid., p. 105.

65. Kaznacheev also admits that his defection was spurred by an unsuccessful attempt at defection by one of his colleagues, Colonel Strygin, the military attaché at the Embassy, in May 1959.

66. Yuri Krotkov, *I Am from Moscow: A View of the Russian Miracle* (New York: Dutton, 1967). Before he died prematurely in December 1981, Krotkov published two other books, *The Red Monarch: Scenes from the Life of Stalin* (New York: Norton, 1979), and *The Nobel Prize*, a novel.

67. His reticence is probably due to the fact that he did not reveal his affiliation with

the KGB until he testified in 1969 before the Senate Internal Security Subcommittee in conjunction with his role in the entrapment of foreign diplomats in Moscow in sex scandals. (See John Barron, *KGB*, pp. 172-90.)

68. Krotkov, *Moscow*, pp. 26-27.

69. Ibid., pp. 2-3.

70. Ibid., p. 57.

71. Ibid., p. 9.

72. Leonid Vladimirov, *The Russian Space Bluff: The Inside Story of the Soviet Drive to the Moon* (New York: Dial Press, 1973).

73. Ibid., p. 10.

74. Ibid., p. 151.

75. Ibid., p. 185.

76. Ibid., p. 32.

77. Aleksei Myagkov, *Inside the KGB: An Expose by an Officer of the Third Directorate* (England: Foreign Affairs Publishing Co., 1976), pp. 15-16.

78. Ibid., p. 74.

79. Ibid., p. 113.

80. Ibid., p. 39.

81. Ibid., p. 116.

82. John Train, "The Lonely Voice of Alexander Solzhenitsyn," *Wall Street Journal*, June 23, 1983.

83. Alexander Solzhenitsyn, *Warning to the West* (New York: Farrar, Straus and Giroux, 1974), p. 41.

CHAPTER 3

1. There were altogether 26 reports under the following two titles: "The Soviet Union as Reported by Former Soviet Citizens" and "The Soviet Bloc as Reported by Former Nationals." However, I use only the former title because only four reports (nos. 20, 21, 23, and 26) deal with non-Soviet defectors. Each report consists of 10 to 35 typewritten single-spaced pages.

2. Each report is preceded by the following note: "The material included is not evaluated and no statement therein should be attributed to the Department of State or any other agency of the United States Government."

3. Report no. 18, p. 3; August 1957. Interviewees are usually identified in this book by their military rank or last position. Nationality is added for non-Russians. The date pertains to the time of the interview, not that of defection.

4. See no. 5, p. 1; September 1952.

5. No. 17, pp. 1 and 23; June 1956.

6. No. 10, p. 12; 1955.

7. No. 12, p. 16; June 1955.

8. No. 14, p. 18; August 1955.

9. No. 11, p. 14; May 1955.

10. No. 6, p. 7; November 1952.

11. No. 1, p. 23; August 1951.

12. No. 12, p. 18.

13. No. 11, p. 14.

14. No. 16, p. 2; November 1955.

15. No. 14, p. 2.

16. No. 6, pp. 4 and 17.

17. No. 18, p. 15; August 1957. See also no. 10, pp. 10–11; no. 15, p. 15; October 1955; and no. 16, p. 12.

18. No. 9, pp. 21–22; 1955. The interviewers point out, however, that the captain was "not obviously Jewish-looking" and "was thereby able to escape any untoward difficulties," that is, was not subjected to expressions of unofficial anti-Semitism.

19. There was no one to testify about the Baltic republics.

20. No. 11, p. 9.

21. No. 7, pp. 6 and 9; June 1953.

22. No. 22, abstract; August 1959.

23. No. 1, p. 16.

24. No. 6, p. 13.

25. No. 15, pp. 15 and 22.

26. No. 9, p. 22.

27. No. 15, p. 18.

28. No. 16, pp. 13 and 17.

29. No. 10, p. 15.

30. No. 12, p. 17.

31. No. 16, p. 13.

32. No. 9, p. 27.

33. No. 16, p. 13.

34. No. 10, p. 14.

35. No. 10, p. 14.

36. No. 10, p. 15.

37. No. 17, p. 22.

38. No. 9, p. 27.

39. No. 15, pp. 17 and 18.

40. No. 9, p. 28.

41. No. 16, p. 2.

42. No. 9, p. 27.

CHAPTER 4

1. This description is based on the article "O rozysknykh spiskakh KGB" (About the KGB's Wanted Lists), published in *Possev*, no. 12, December 1976, pp. 29–31.

2. See *Possev*, nos. 1, 2, 4–11, 1977, and nos. 1, 2, 4–6, 1978. See also Appendix 1A, which was drawn from the *Possev* installments.

3. *Possev*, no. 5, May 1977, p. 20, item 40. See Appendix 2A.

4. "Forcible repatriation" was often used during the first postwar years when Western authorities showed an excessive zeal in the implementation of the Yalta agreements, even though the latter did not oblige them to return defectors.

5. Nikolai Khokhlov, "Predotvratit' vozvrat k fizicheskomu terroru" (interview), *Possev*, no. 5, May 1979, p. 40.

6. See also Vladislav Krasnov, Hoover File (deposited at the Hoover Institution Archives), entry 450.

7. Hoover File, entry 75.

8. Ibid., entry 32.

9. Ibid., entry 3.

10. Ibid., entry 51.

11. Ibid., entry 180.

12. Ibid., entry 329. For the complete Russian text, see Appendix 2A.

13. Entitled "Defstudy Out 12" and dated August 28, 1981, the printout will henceforth be referred to as Defstudy. A brief explanation may be in order here to facilitate the reading of Defstudy. The input format was fixed alphanumerical. Of the eighty columns on each card, 62 were used to accommodate the 50 variables while the remaining 18 columns were reserved for special notations that did not fit any of the 50 variables. The variables roughly follow the order of their occurrence in each entry. Since each entry fills just one card, there are a total of 470 such computer cards.

CHAPTER 5

1. Defstudy, p. 12.

2. Ibid., p. 80. The variable of age was computed by subtracting the year of birth from the year of defection as they are noted in the KGB Wanted List.

3. Ibid., p. 16. See also Appendix 2B. The actual share of the Russians is probably higher because, on several occasions, the compilers of the KGB Wanted List failed to note nationality of entrants, even though circumstantial evidence indicates their Russian origin. See Chapter 4, Entry D, for an example.

4. Hoover File, entry 181.

5. Defstudy, pp. 17–18.

6. Besides the overlapping of occupations, the assigning of a professional category

to defectors from the armed forces presented a certain difficulty. As a rule, career officers were assigned the professional category of "military," while rank-and-file soldiers were assumed to be conscripts and were labeled according to their profession prior to military service.

7. Defstudy, p. 19.

8. Ibid., p. 21.

9. Ibid., p. 22.

10. Hoover File, entry 163.

11. Defstudy, p. 24.

12. Based on Defstudy, pp. 25–26, 29–30. Besides standard physical description, the KGB records note such special features as tattoos and birthmarks; since the use of fingerprinting is not common in the USSR, it is noted only in two entries, 107 and 231.

13. Defstudy, p. 32.

14. Ibid., p. 33.

15. Ibid., p. 34.

16. Ibid., pp. 35–36.

17. Ibid., p. 37. The values of this variable were not quantified; therefore, we have no breakdown between brothers and sisters and no record of their exact number.

18. See Chapter 7, n. 13.

CHAPTER 6

1. Defstudy, pp. 38–39.

2. Ibid., p. 40.

3. Ibid., pp. 41–42.

4. On June 23, 1954, the Soviet tanker *Tuapse*, while carrying jet fuel to Red China, was intercepted by nationalist Chinese naval forces and brought to Taiwan. When given the choice of returning to the USSR or remaining in the free world, as many as 20 of the 49 crewmen, more than 40 percent, chose freedom. This confirms the opinion of those State Department interviewees who insisted that discontent in the USSR was especially rife among peasants and workers, the social classes from which seamen are usually recruited. Later, 9 of the 20 were allowed to come to the United States, where they began to settle. However, on April 7, 1956, five of them were tricked by Soviet diplomatic personnel into returning to the USSR. The Senate Subcommittee to Investigate the Administration of the Internal Security Act subsequently concluded that the Soviet diplomats "used coercion, force, and duress" in returning the five sailors and that "unjustified and unnecessary concessions were made by American officials in response to Soviet pressures and truculence." (See U.S. Congress, Senate Committee on the Judiciary, "The Episode of the Russian Seamen," May 24, 1956.) By 1971, 10 of the 20 defecting sailors were still on the KGB Wanted List.

5. Defstudy, pp. 43–44. See also Appendix 2D.

6. See n. 4.

7. Hoover File, entry 52.

8. Defstudy, p. 45. In the computer programming, no distinction was made as to whether those zones referred to Germany or Austria.

9. Ibid., p. 46. A frequency count on the country of defection shows that 260 people escaped to West Germany and Austria. It can be assumed, therefore, that 31 of them did so after KGB clerks had stopped referring to these countries as Western occupation zones, some time after 1955.

10. Method of defection subsumes the data from two variables, labeled as way of defection and mode of defection. See Defstudy, pp. 46 and 47.

11. See n. 10.

12. Hoover File, entry 402.

13. Ibid., entry 420.

14. Ibid., entry 152.

15. Ibid., entries 397 and 398.

16. Defstudy, p. 48.

17. See, for instance, an official Soviet document that was smuggled from the USSR and reprinted in *Russkaia mysl'*, no. 3427 (August 26, 1982). It spells out Soviet regulations for the issuance of tourist visas for traveling abroad.

18. Hoover File, entry 26.

19. Ibid., entry 34.

20. Ibid., entry 19.

21. Defstudy, p. 58.

22. Ibid., p. 59.

CHAPTER 7

1. Based on Defstudy, pp. 49–53.

2. Hoover File, entry 111. This is one of the most specific allegations of crime in the KGB Wanted List.

3. Ibid., entry 209.

4. Ibid., entry 71.

5. Ibid., entry 123.

6. Ibid., entry 321.

7. Ibid., entry 64.

8. Ibid., entry 269.

9. Ibid., entry 66.

10. Defstudy, p. 54.

11. Ibid., pp. 55–57.

12. As legislation in the USSR is decentralized in form, the laws pertaining to defection are to be found in criminal codes of each of the fifteen Soviet republics forming the Union. However, since Soviet legislation is, in fact, totally controlled by the Communist Party, the laws in question show little variation from one republic to another and are virtually identical. Moreover, although after Stalin's death there were some legal reforms that were aimed at better protection of defendants' rights and the practice of secret trials by the three security police officials was abolished in September 1953, Soviet laws in regard to defection have changed little over time. The following Soviet legal sources were consulted: 3 editions of the *Ugolovnyi Kodeks RSFSR* (Criminal code of the Russian Federation) (Moscow, 1950, 1966, and 1983); and *Ugolovnyi Kodeks Estonskoi SSR* (Criminal code of the Estonian Soviet Socialist Republic) (Tallinn, 1968). As a commented edition, the Estonian code gives valuable information as to the interpretation of Soviet laws on defection. Also consulted was *Zakon o gosudarstvennoi granitse SSSR* (The law of the state border of the USSR), *Izvestiia*, November 26, 1982. This law, promulgated under Andropov, reflects a growing concern with the "violations" of Soviet borders.

13. With a reference to the June 8, 1934, decree, Article 58[1a] of the Criminal Code of the Russian Federation in the 1950 edition (see n. 12) defines "the betrayal of the Fatherland" as "acts, committed by citizens of the USSR, which harm the military might, sovereignty, and territorial inviolability [of the USSR], such as espionage, passing of military or state secrets, going over to the enemy side, and escape or flight [*begstvo ili perelet*] abroad." The gravity of these crimes was emphasized in that they head the list of "counterrevolutionary" state crimes. The penalty prescribed is execution by a firing squad (*rasstrel*) with confiscation of all property or, "if there are extenuating circumstances," ten years of "deprivation of liberty" (*lishenie svobody*) with confiscation of all property. If the same crimes are committed by military personnel, the only punishment is death, says Article 58[1b]. Article 58[1c] stipulates that the adult members of a defector's family are to be punished by five to ten years of prison, with confiscation of property, if they contributed to the escape plan in any way or even just knew about it but failed to report it. The other adult members of a defector's household are to be exiled to the "remote regions of Siberia," for five years. Finally, Article 58[1d] stipulates that the crime of "nonreporting" (*nedonesenie*) escape plans on the part of military personnel is to be punished by ten years of prison.

Both the 1966 and 1983 editions of the Criminal Code of the Russian Federation trace their legal basis to the legislation passed by the Supreme Soviet of the Russian Federation on December 25, 1958; October 27, 1960; and July 25, 1962. It can be assumed, therefore, that the main provisions of the 1950 code in regard to defectors were in effect until at least 1958. Both editions carry an identical Article 64, "The Betrayal of the Fatherland." Placed at the top of the section, "Especially Dangerous State Crimes," it substantially retains the 1950 definition of defection. However, a "refusal to return from abroad" is now added to the former "escape abroad." The punishment remains the same, but the order and, presumably, the emphasis are changed: first goes the "ten to fifteen years" prison term, then follows the death penalty. "Freedom from persecution" is promised to those who, having been recruited by foreign intelligence services, decide to report their contacts. There are no provisions for the punishment of a defector's family members. Finally, unlike the 1950 edition, the later editions differentiate between "escape abroad" and "illegal departure" from the

USSR. The latter is treated in Article 83, which stipulates a more lenient punishment of from one to three years of "deprivation of freedom."

The Estonian Criminal Code of 1968 is virtually identical to the Russian ones. It treats "betrayal" in Article 62 and "illegal departure" in Article 81. The comment to the latter says that it differs from the former in its "subjective aspect," that is, whether one escapes to harm the interests of the USSR or to engage in such personal activities as smuggling or visiting relatives. The KGB Wanted List apparently excludes those accused of "illegal departure" alone.

14. Defstudy, p. 63.

15. Military defectors are usually punished more harshly; see n. 13.

16. Hoover File, entry 106.

17. Ibid., entry 134.

18. Ibid., entry 410.

19. Ibid., entry 234.

20. Ibid., entry 6.

21. Ibid., entry 130.

22. Ibid., entry 380.

23. Defstudy, pp. 94–96.

24. Ibid., pp. 99–100.

25. Ibid., p. 62.

26. Based on Defstudy, p. 102.

27. Hoover File, entry 187.

28. Ibid., entry 186.

29. Ibid., entry 199.

30. Ibid., entry 383.

31. Ibid., entry 91.

32. Ibid., entry 53.

33. Ibid., entry 316.

34. Defstudy, pp. 60–61.

35. Hoover File, entry 410.

36. Ibid., entry 416.

37. Defstudy, p. 64.

38. On the tasks of the PK service (Russian acronym for *perliustratsiia korrespondentsii*, perlustration of correspondence), see Aleksei Myagkov, *Inside the KGB* (England: Foreign Affairs Publishing Co., 1976), apps.

39. Hoover File, entry 59.

40. Ibid., entry 66.

41. Ibid., entry 176.

42. Ibid., entry 306.

43. Ibid., entry 387.

44. Ibid., entry 53.
45. Ibid., entry 339.
46. Defstudy, pp. 65–66.
47. Hoover File, entry 305.
48. Ibid., entry 74.
49. See n. 13.

CHAPTER 8

1. Defstudy, pp. 19 and 21.
2. Ibid., p. 23.
3. Ibid., p. 62. See also Chapter 9.
4. Ibid., pp. 49–53. See also Chapter 7, n. 14.
5. Hoover File, entry 27.
6. Ibid., entry 345.
7. Ibid., entry 78.
8. Ibid., entry 321.
9. Ibid., entry 10.
10. *Dallas Morning News*, January 20, 1977, p. 21A; see *Novoe russkoe slovo* (hereafter, *NRS*), December 31, 1977, about Rogalsky's mental problems and his letter to the editor; and *New York Times*, September 19, 1978, II, 6:3.

CHAPTER 9

1. Based on Defstudy, p. 223.
2. Ibid., pp. 238–39.
3. Ibid., p. 267.
4. Ibid., pp. 264–65.
5. Ibid., pp. 285–87.
6. Ibid., p. 235.
7. Ibid., p. 233.
8. Ibid., based on pp. 231–32.

CHAPTER 10

1. The table is based on Defstudy, p. 146.
2. Defstudy, pp. 41–42. See also Appendix 2C.

3. See Chapter 7, n. 13.

4. See John B. Dunlop, *The New Russian Revolutionaries* (Belmont, Mass.: Nordland, 1976). This monograph is devoted entirely to the VSKhSON.

5. See, *e.g.*, F. J. M. Feldbrugge, *Samizdat and Political Dissent in the Soviet Union* (Leyden, Holland: Sijthoff, 1975), p. 40; and Peter Reddaway, ed., *Uncensored Russia: Protest and Dissent in the Soviet Union* (New York: American Heritage Press, 1972).

6. Ibid., p. 130.

7. Defstudy, pp. 156–57.

8. The only exception is medical doctors, because under Stalin many of them defected from Soviet occupation forces.

9. Although the Federal Republic of Germany became fully sovereign in 1954, the KGB compilers continued to refer to it as Western occupation zones well into the 1960s. Computer cards merely reflect the language of the compilers.

10. Defstudy, p. 190.

11. Ibid., p. 192.

12. Ibid., p. 197.

13. Ibid., pp. 199–201.

14. Ibid., pp. 209–10.

15. Ibid., p. 82.

16. Ibid., p. 148.

17. Ibid., p. 173.

18. See Chapter 6, n. 17.

19. See Barron, *KGB*, chap. 13.

CHAPTER 11

1. For more data see, *e.g.*, Jerome M. Gilison's paper, "Soviet Jewish Emigration 1971–1980: An Overview," in *Soviet Jewry in the Decisive Decade, 1971–1980*, Robert O. Freedman, ed. (Durham, N.C.: Duke University Press, 1983). Presently, the flow of thousands has diminished to the lucky hundreds to whom the Soviets issue exit visas.

2. For more about the incident, see Joshua Rubenstein, *Soviet Dissidents: Their Struggle for Human Rights* (Boston, Mass.: Beacon Press, 1980), pp. 169–74. Two of those sentenced to fifteen years, Yury Fedorov and Aleksey Murzhenko, were not due to be released until 1985.

3. Albert Parry, "Ugon sovetskikh samoletov" (On the skyjacking of Soviet airplanes), *NRS*, September 15, 1977. See also issues for September 13, 14, 16; November 9; and December 22, 1977.

4. Ibid., December 22, 1977.

5. Ibid., September 15, 1977.

6. Ibid., September 15, 1977.

7. He died ten years later in London of a heart attack.

8. Andrei D. Sakharov, *My Country and the World* (New York: Vintage Books, 1975), p. 58.

9. Eduard Kuznetsov, "Desiat' let nazad, 15 iiunia" (Ten years ago, on June 15), *NRS*, June 25, 1980.

CHAPTER 12

1. *Christian Science Monitor*, July 20, 1981.

2. These figures were released to me by Mr. Krister Killander, bureau director at Sweden's Immigration Office. In France, I interviewed Mr. Jacques Fouchet, director, Office Français de Protection des Réfugiés et Apatrides, Ministère des Affaires Etrangères. See also Elena Sokolova's article "Beg," *NRS*, November 8, 1984. She cites a United Nation's Refugee Commission report, according to which in 1983 there were 21 Soviet citizens who were granted the status of political refugees in Yugoslavia alone.

3. See Robert C. Tucker's interview in G. R. Urban, ed., *Stalinism: Its Impact on Russia and the World* (New York: St. Martin's Press, 1982), p. 174.

4. *NRS*, August 16, 1979.

5. *NRS*, September 16, 1979.

6. *Possev*, no. 10, October 1979, p. 5.

7. *Japan Times*, January 9, 1981.

8. *New York Times* (hereafter, *NYT*), July 11, 1976.

9. *Japan Times*, January 9, 1981.

10. *Japan Times*, August 21, 1980.

11. Associated Press (AP) report, July 10, 1983.

12. Los Angeles Times Service, *Monterey Peninsula Herald*, November 23, 1983.

13. United Press International (UPI), August 15, 1984.

14. *International Herald Tribune* (hereafter *IHT*), April 22, 1970.

15. *IHT*, June 4, 1971.

16. *NRS*, January 19, 1979.

17. *NYT*, October 7, 1976, 4:3.

18. See interview with Alekseychuk in *Possev*, no. 11, November 1978, pp. 52–56.

19. *IHT*, September 2, 1969, quotes a UPI report about the defection of a 19-year-old soldier near Helmstadt; DPA, a West German news agency, reported the defection of an 18-year-old soldier near Niedersachsen in September 1976; and it also reported on September 25, 1976, about the defection of a Soviet army officer "three years ago." On July 13, 1984, AP reported that a 20-year-old staff sergeant from Soviet combat troops in East Germany fled to West Germany across the fortified frontier in Niedersachsen.

20. Richard Gabriel quotes this incident in his book, *The New Red Legions: An Attitudinal Portrait of the Soviet Soldier* (Westport, Conn.: Greenwood Press, 1980), p. 171. See also the *Los Angeles Times*, March 24, 1972, p. 4.

21. *Dallas Morning News*, June 20, 1978.

22. AP report, dateline Oslo (August 7, 1970); and *NYT* (UPI), July 6, 1979.

23. *Christian Science Monitor*, November 25, 1977.

24. *Possev*, nos. 3 and 4, 1977.

25. The following discussion of the incident is largely based on Lt. Gregory D. Young's unpublished master's thesis, "Mutiny on *Storozhevoy*: A Case Study of Dissent in the Soviet Navy," defended at the Naval Postgraduate School, Monterey, California, March 1982.

26. Lieutenant Young (see above) lists several of them, most notably "A Meeting Before Execution," *Chronicle of Current Events*, no. 48, March 14, 1978; *samizdat* document no. M2767 (anonymous letter dated July 1976); "Drama in the Baltic Sea," *Laiks*, May 12, 1976; and "Mutinied Soviet Destroyer Dispatched on Long Voyage," *Christian Science Monitor*, June 29, 1976, 4.

27. Young, "*Storozhevoy*," p. 39.

28. *Krasnaia zvezda*, December 24, 1974.

29. Young, "*Storozhevoy*," p. 84.

30. *Japan Times*, June 12, 1980, p. 1.

31. *NRS*, February 1, 1980, p. 1.

32. *NRS*, February 18, 1982.

33. *Possev*, no. 2, February 1983, pp. 18–21.

34. AP, November 12, 1984.

35. AP, December 18, 1984.

36. *Russkaia mysl'*, September 8, 1983, p. 2.

37. *NRS*, May 22, 1984.

38. According to a 1982 *samizdat* document, several factory workers in the city of Pavlovo (near Gorky) tried to evade induction into the Soviet armed forces, saying, "We shall not shoot at the Poles and will not let others." See *Possev*, no. 9, September 1983, 6.

39. Viktor Suvorov, *Inside the Soviet Army* (New York: Macmillan, 1982), p. 245.

40. Ibid., p. 162.

41. Even though the Soviets managed to avoid a direct confrontation with the Solidarity movement in Poland, at least one soldier from Soviet occupation forces, Aleksandr Yanyshev, deserted in the fall of 1981 and has since been hiding among the Solidarity people in Poland. See *NRS*, May 25, 1984.

42. A number of American students of the Soviet military come to similar conclusions. In his book, *The New Red Legions*, which is based on interviews with recent Soviet immigrants, Richard A. Gabriel writes: "What we know of the performance of Soviet troops in Eastern Europe between 1953 and 1968 suggests that their reliability in 'foreign' environments is open to question. There are numerous stories told by soldiers who actually were involved in Poland, Hungary, or Czechoslovakia that report incidents of Soviet units mutinying, deserting or refusing to fight. In Hungary, for example, in the town of Lyov, an entire Soviet regiment refused to leave its garrison and attack

Hungarian civilians . . . Other instances abound." Professor Gabriel comes to the conclusion that "these conditions place significant limits on the use of the Soviet Army as an instrument of state policy and provide Western defense planners with considerable advantages—if only they come to recognize them" (2: 233–34). Robert Bathurst and Michael Burger, whose booklet, *Controlling the Soviet Soldier: Some Eyewitness Accounts*, is also based on interviews with recent Soviet immigrants, notes "a basic distrust commanders and political leaders have of Soviet soldiers." Noting that only "fear of surveillance and secret police informers keep possible dissent in check" (p. 18), Professor Bathurst arrives at a more cautious conclusion: "if the danger of marching forward becomes as great as the danger of disobeying orders and going back, the behavior of soldiers, in the absence of clear motivation for self-sacrifice, becomes dangerously unpredictable" (p. 24).

43. *Russkaia mysl'*, March 25, 1982.

44. Lee Seligson, "The Defectors: Life Under Red, White, and Blue," *Newsday Magazine*, July 4, 1982, pp. 12–17.

45. Andrei Amalrik, letter to the editor, *NRS*, April 27, 1979.

46. Mahmet Kulmagambetov, "Vozvrashchentsy" (Returners), *Kontinent*, no. 39 (1984): 295–321; *Russkaia mysl'*, February 2, 1984; and "Moriaki s tankera *Tuapse*," *NRS*, June 9, 1984.

47. Vladimir Bukovsky, *To Build a Castle: My Life as a Dissenter* (New York: Viking, 1979), pp. 215–16.

48. UPI, August 23, 1976.

49. UPI, November 26, 1977.

50. England's Keston College, a research center on Christianity under communism, estimates that as many as 30,000 Soviet Pentecostalists, that is, about one-fifth of the total, would leave the USSR if given a chance. (*Time*, January 25, 1982.)

51. This victory was due to the efforts of many human rights activists in the West. In the U.S., *e.g.*, Reverend Blahoslav Hruby and his wife Olga tirelessly publicized the plight of the "Siberian Seven" in their magazine, *Religion in Communist Dominated Areas*, and elsewhere.

52. Actually, a precedent was created earlier, but it was never publicized. In August 1978, an Armenian woman, Eliza Ovsepian, and her two sons entered the U.S. Embassy and were allowed to stay there for 82 days until the Soviets relented and granted them permission to emigrate. The Soviets made the exception only on the condition that the U.S. Embassy would do nothing to publicize the case. The Soviets then treated the case as falling within their policy on family reunification, and the three family members left for the United States, where they joined their relatives in Los Angeles. (*NRS*, April 28, 1979.)

53. AP, March 29, 1979.

54. Ilya Levin, letter to the editor, *NYT*, April 10, 1979, A18:4; and Andrei Amalrik, letter to the editor, *NRS*, April 27, 1979.

55. *NYT*, May 7, 1979, A20:4.

56. In July 1983, Cheslav Lisovsky, a 27-year-old Baptist from Grodno, Belorussia,

was arrested when he tried to enter the U.S. Consulate in Leningrad. It was reported that he would be put on trial. (*Possev*, no. 4, April 1984, p. 7.)

On March 19, 1984, Eduard Gudava from Tbilisi, Georgia, was arrested when he tried to enter the British Embassy. He had been unsuccessfully trying to obtain an exit visa for himself, his mother, and two brothers. (*NRS*, April 8, 1984.)

On May 17, 1984, Natalia Khmelnitskaya, 53, was arrested at the doors of the French Embassy after trying to deliver a letter to President Mitterrand. In the letter she requested that she, her husband, Mark Volchonok, and their son be allowed to emigrate to France. After the arrest she was confined to a mental hospital for a month and was released only after an official French protest. (AP, June 16, 1984.)

On June 9, 1984, the Soviets accused two American journalists of allegedly helping a Soviet citizen, A. I. Rukosuev, flee to the West. The man was caught, charged with the "betrayal of the Fatherland," and sentenced to an unspecified jail term. (UPI, June 10, 1984.)

57. See, for instance, the case of Yuri Nikredin, as reported by the AP on April 29, 1979.

CHAPTER 13

1. Algis Ruksenas, *Day of Shame: The Truth About the Murderous Happenings Aboard the Cutter Vigilant During the Russian-American Confrontation off Martha's Vineyard* (New York: David McKay, 1973); and Simas Kudirka and Larry Eichel, *For Those Still at Sea* (New York: Dial, 1978).

2. *IHT*, January 13, 1972.

3. Smith Simpson, "One Day in the Life of Simas Kudirka and the State Department," *Foreign Service Journal*, September 1979, pp. 17–34.

4. Ibid., p. 20.

5. Ibid., p. 22.

6. *NYT*, October 17, 1971, 17:1.

7. *NYT*, December 28, 1971, 13:1.

8. *IHT*, January 13, 1972.

9. Jack Anderson, "Will the Russians Return the Man She Loves?" *Parade* (*Dallas Times Herald*), August 28, 1977.

10. Henry Hurt, *Shadrin: The Spy Who Never Came Back* (New York: McGraw-Hill, Reader's Digest Press, 1981).

11. *Time*, October 22, 1979, p. 59.

12. Barron, *KGB*, pp. 430–31.

13. AP, September 13 and October 3, 1978.

14. On August 7, 1978, DPA reported the disappearance of a Soviet defector (who claimed to be a locksmith) who had come to Hamburg as a stowaway on a Soviet freighter and had asked for political asylum. At a meeting with Soviet officials, attended

by Hamburg officials, he refused to return to the USSR. He was never seen again after the meeting.

15. Barron, *KGB*, p. 431.

16. Simpson, "One Day," p. 22.

17. Charles Fenyvesi, "The Unwelcome Defector: An Embarrassment to Both Sides," *New Republic* 178 (April 22, 1978): 9.

18. Quoted from a Radio Liberty teletype report datelined Washington, D.C., September 21, 1977 (Special/Lyle).

19. *Asahi Evening News*, November 14, 1980.

20. *Dagens Nyheter*, May 25, 1979. It was also reported that a high-ranking police officer in Austria was sentenced to two years in prison for informing the Romanian KGB about Romanian defectors in Austria. (*Possev*, no. 2, February 1982, p. 17.)

21. Robert G. Kaiser and Bob Woodward, "The Soviet Wife Who Came In from the Cold—and Out Again," *Washington Post*, January 22, 1982, p. 1.

22. A better explanation was offered by a recent Soviet defector quoted in the above article. According to him, "those first days after a defection are filled with emotional strain, and that a new defector—particularly a wife and mother with no strong political feelings and very few ties to American life—would have to be handled with great delicacy by American counterintelligence officials." The unnamed defector concluded that "the pressures just may have been too great, particularly if Mrs. Mamedova felt in any way misunderstood by her new protectors."

23. *San Jose Mercury News*, November 5, 1982.

24. *NYT*, August 19, 1983, p. 6.

25. *NYT*, August 20, 1983, p. 16.

26. The most recent incident involved Sergei Kozlov, a Soviet mathematician and guest scholar at the California Institute of Technology. In late April 1984, Kozlov complained to American authorities in Pasadena, where he was staying at a hotel, about being in trouble with the KGB. Soon after he was put on a flight to Washington by Soviet officials, who escorted him. However, at Dulles Airport he refused to board another plane bound for Moscow. Although he did not ask for asylum, State Department officials insisted on interviewing him to ascertain his wishes. During the interview they were satisfied that he wanted to return to the USSR. They admitted, however, that at no point could they talk to him privately because a Soviet official was always present. Insinuating that Kozlov was insane, the Soviets finally were allowed to fly him out of the country (*Monterey Peninsula Herald*, May 3, 1984).

27. Simpson, "One Day," p. 24.

Conclusion

1. Charles Fenyvesi, "The Unwelcome Defector: An Embarrassment to Both Sides," *New Republic* 178 (April 22, 1978): 9.

2. Robert C. Tucker, in G. R. Urban, ed., *Stalinism: Its Impact on Russia and the World* (New York: St. Martin's Press, 1982), p. 174.

3. *Japan Times* (UPI), February 3, 1981.

4. Warren Christopher, "Political Asylum" (an address before the Los Angeles County Bar Association), *Department of State Bulletin*, January 1980, p. 37.

5. Susan Sontag, "Communism and the Left," *The Nation* 234, no. 8 (February 27, 1982): 230.

6. Actually, one such organization, The Jamestown Foundation, began its operations in Washington, D.C., while this book was being written. For its address, see the Questionnaire for Defectors at the end of this book.

BIBLIOGRAPHY

Agabekov, Georges. *OGPU, The Russian Secret Weapon*. Trans. Henry W. Bunn. Westport, Conn.: Hyperion, 1931.

Agursky, Mikhail. "Klaus Barbie i Ivan Daragan." *Kontinent*, no. 40, 1984. 1984, pp. 239–49. Confirms Victor Kravchenko's characterization of Daragan, who has now emigrated to Israel, as one of the NKVD henchmen.

Alburt, Lev. "Eshche odna popytka pokhishcheniia" (Another attempt at abduction: About Tania Lemachka). *Novoe russkoe slovo* [hereafter, *NRS*], February 1, 1985.

Alekseychuk, Igor'. "Polozhenie sovetskikh chastei v GDR" (Conditions of Soviet troops in the GDR). *Possev*, no. 11, 1978, pp. 52–56. An interview.

Alliluyeva, Svetlana. *Only One Year*. New York: Harper & Row, 1969.

———. *Twenty Letters to a Friend*. Trans. Priscilla Johnson. New York: Harper & Row, 1967.

Bakhchevan, Stepan. "Prostoi sovetskii perebezhchik" (A simple Soviet defector). *NRS*, April 3, 1982.

Barghoorn, Frederich C. *Detente and the Democratic Movement in the USSR*. New York: Macmillan, 1976.

Barmine, Alexander. *Memoirs of a Soviet Diplomat: Twenty Yeras in the Service of the USSR*. 1938. Reprint. Westport, Conn.: Hyperion, 1973.

Barron, John. *KGB: The Secret Work of Soviet Secret Agents*. Toronto, New York, London: Bantam, 1974.

———. *KGB Today: The Hidden Hand*. New York: Reader's Digest Press; distributed by Random House, 1983.

———. *MIG Pilot: The Final Escape of Lt. Belenko*. New York: Reader's Digest Press; distributed by McGraw Hill, 1980.

Bathurst, Robert, and Burger, Michael. *Controlling the Soviet Soldier: Some Eyewitness Accounts*. College Station: Texas A&M University, Center for Strategic Technology, 1981.

Bathurst, Robert; Burger, Michael; and Wolffe, Ellen. "The Soviet Sailor: Combat Readiness and Morale." A typewritten study, dated June 30, 1982, and submitted to Office of Naval Research, Arlington, Va.

Beloff, Nora. "Escape from Boredom: A Defector's Story." *Atlantic*, November 1980. The story of Galina Orionova.

Besedovskii, Grigorii Z. *Revelations of a Soviet Diplomat*. 1931. Reprint. Westport, Conn.: Hyperion, 1977.

Bethell, Nicholas. *The Last Secret*. London: Deutsch, 1974.

Bezmenov, Yuri. "Confessions of a Subverter." *Our Canada* (Toronto), October 1980. See also Schuman, Thomas.

Bialoguski, Michael, M.D. *The Case of Colonel Petrov: How I Weaned a High MVD Official from Communism*. New York, Toronto, London: McGraw Hill, 1955.

Bloch, Sidney, and Reddaway, Peter. *Russia's Political Hospitals: The Abuse of Psychiatry in the Soviet Union*. London: Gollancz, 1977.

———. *Soviet Psychiatric Abuse*. London: Golancz, 1984.

Borovik, Genrikh. "Zagnannykh loshadei pristrelivaiut, ne tak li?" (They shoot worn-out horses, don't they?). *Literaturnaia gazeta*, August 17, 1977, p. 14. A Soviet journalist writes about the disappearance of Nicholas Shadrin (pseudonym of Artamonov).

Brook-Shepherd, Gordon. *The Storm Petrels: The Flight of the First Soviet Defectors*. New York, London: Harcourt, Brace, Jovanovich, 1977.

Bukovsky, Vladimir. *I vozvrashchaetsia veter*. New York: Khronika, 1979.

———. *To Build a Castle: My Life as a Dissenter*. New York: Viking, 1979.

Burg, David. *New York Times Sunday Magazine*, April 13, 1969, sec. 6, p. 34. An article on Mikhail Dyomin (penname of Soviet writer and defector Georgii Trifonov).

Christopher, Warren. "Political Asylum," *Department of State Bulletin*, January 1980. Address before the Los Angeles County Bar Association on November 6, 1979.

Code of Federal Regulations: Aliens and Nationality. Revised as of January 1, 1981. Published as a special edition of the Federal Register.

Custance, George. "Why People Flee to the West." *New York Times*, October 19, 1979, p. 34.

Deriabin, Peter. *Watchdogs of Terror: Russian Bodyguards from the Tsars to the Commissars*. New Rochelle, N.Y.: Arlington House, 1972.

Deriabin, Peter, and Gibney, Frank. *The Secret World*. Garden City, N.J.: Doubleday, 1959.

Dulles, Allen, ed. *Great True Spy Stories*. New York: Harper & Son, 1966.

Elliott, Mark. *Pawns of Yalta: Soviet Refugees and America's Role in Their Repatriation*. Urbana: University of Illinois Press, 1982.

———. "The War of the Moles." *New York*, v. 11, February 27, 1978: 28–38, March 6: 55–59.

Epstein, Edward Jay. *Legend: The Secret World of Lee Harvey Oswald*. New York: Reader's Digest Press, 1978.

Epstein, Julius. *Operation Keelhaul*. Old Greenwich, Conn.: Devin-Adair; Stanford: Hoover Institution Press, 1973.

Fedoseev, Anatoly. *Zapadnia: Chelovek i sotsializm* (The trap: Man and socialism). 2nd ed. Frankfurt/Main: Possev, 1979.

Feldbrugge, F. J. M. *Samizdat and Political Dissent in the Soviet Union*. Leyden, Holland: Sijthoff, 1975.

Felshtinsky, Yuri. "Delo Volkova" (The Volkov affair). *NRS*, February 16, 1983.

Fenyvesi, Charles. "The Unwelcome Defector: An Embarrassment to Both Sides." *New Republic* 178 (April 22, 1978): 9. Discusses Arkady N. Shevchenko.

Fischer, Lois, and Yakovlev, Boris. *Thirteen Who Fled*. New York, 1949.

Fisher, George. *Soviet Opposition to Stalin: A Case Study in World War II*. Cambridge, Mass.: Harvard University Press, 1952.

Freedman, Robert O., ed. *Soviet Jewry in the Decisive Decade, 1971–1980*. Durham, N.C.: Duke University Press, 1983.

Freeman, Neal B. "The Current Wisdom: As Shevchenko Sees It." *National Review* 33 (August 21, 1981).

Freemantle, Brian. *KGB*. New York: Holt, Rinehart, and Winston, 1982.

Gabriel, Richard A. *The New Red Legions: An Attitudinal Portrait of the Soviet Soldier*. Westport, Conn.; London, England: Greenwood Press, 1980.

Gaucher, Roland. *Opposition in the USSR: 1917–1967*. New York: Funk & Wagnalls, 1969.

Gavrilov, Vladimir. "Vy chto, protiv sovetskoi vlasti?" (Are you against the Soviets?). *Possev*, no. 7, July 1976, pp. 39–42. A recent émigré describes unrest in the Soviet northern fleet in the 1960s.

Gitelman, Zvi. "Soviet Political Culture: Insights from Jewish Emigres." *Soviet Studies* 29, no. 4 (October 1977): 543–64.

Goldhamer, Herbert. *The Soviet Soldier: Soviet Military Management at the Troop Level*. New York: Crane, Russak & Co., 1975.

Golitsyn, Anatoliy. *New Lies for Old: The Communist Strategy of Deception and Disinformation*. New York: Dodd, Mead and Co., 1984.

Golovskoy, Valeri. "Dezinformatsiia v kvadrate" (Disinformation in square root). *NRS*, November 6, 1984.

Gouzenko, Igor. *The Fall of a Titan*. Trans. Melvin Black. New York: Norton, 1954.

———. *The Iron Curtain*. New York: Dutton, 1948.

Gramont, Sanche de. *The Secret War: The Story of International Espionage Since World War II*. New York: Putnam & Sons, 1962.

Granovsky, Anatoli. *I Was an NKVD Agent*. New York: Devin-Adair, 1962.

Heitman, Sidney. "Soviet German Emigration and Soviet Foreign Relations." Paper read at the AAASS conference, Washington, D.C., October 1982.

Hinchley, Vernon. *The Defectors*. London, Toronto, Wellington, Sydney: George G. Harrap, 1967.

Hoover File. "The KGB Wanted List." Vladislav Krasnov Collection, Hoover Institution Archives, Stanford, California. (*See also*, Krasnov.)

Hurt, Henry. *Shadrin: The Spy Who Never Came Back*. New York: Reader's Digest Press, McGraw-Hill, 1981.

Huss, Pierre J., and Carpozi, George, Jr. *Red Spies in the UN*. New York: Coward-McCann, 1965.

Inkeles, Alex, and Bauer, Raymond A. *The Soviet Citizen: Daily Life in a Totalitarian Society*. Cambridge, Mass.: Harvard University Press, 1959.

"In War, in Peace: Flight from Communism Goes On." *U.S. News and World Report*, January 17, 1977, pp. 38–40.

Iurasov, S. [Rudolf]. *Vrag naroda* (Enemy of the people). New York: Chekhov Publishing House, 1952. A novel.

Izvitsky, Roman. "Glotok svobody tsenoiu v zhizn'" (A gulp of freedom worthy of a life). *NRS*, November 3, 1984. The defection and suicide of Ivan Svirsky.

Karlowich, Robert A. *Young Defector*. New York: J. Messner, 1982. Refers to the defection of Walter Polovchak.

Kasenkina, Oksana. *Leap to Freedom*. New York, Philadelphia: Lippincott, 1949.

Katkov, George. *The Khokhlov Case*. St. Anthony's Papers on Soviet Affairs. Oxford, 1954.

Kaznacheev, Aleksandr. *Inside a Soviet Embassy: Experiences of a Russian Diplomat in Burma*. Philadelphia, New York: Lippincott, 1962.

Kellar, Stephen. "Defections of Soviet Ballet Artists in the Postwar Period: A Synopsis." *New York Radio Liberty Research*, RL 71/80, February 18, 1980.

Kheifets, Mikhail. *Mesto i vremia: Evreiskie zametki* (Place and time: Jewish notes). France: Tret'ia volna, 1978.

———. "Shpion. Begletsy." *Russkaia mysl'*, March 25, 1982, p. 10.

Khokhlov, Nikolai. *In the Name of Conscience*. Trans. Emily Kingberry. New York: David McKay, 1959.

———. *Pravo na sovest'*. Frankfurt/Main: Possev, 1957.

———. "Predotvratit' vozvrat k fizicheskomu terroru" (To prevent a return to physical terrorism). *Possev*, no. 5, May 1979, pp. 36–40. An interview.

Klimov, Gregory. *Berliner Kreml*. Köln: Kiepenheuer und Witsch, 1951.

———. *Berlinskii Kreml'*. Frankfurt/Main: *Possev*, 1953. Camouflaged as *Graf Monte Kristo*.

———. *Imia moe—legion* (My name is legion). New York: Slaviia, 1975.

———. *Kniaz' mira sego* (Prince of this world). New York: Slaviia, 1971. A novel.

———. *Kryl'ia kholopa* (The wings of a slave). New York: Rossiia, 1972. 2nd ed. of *Berlinskii Kreml'*.

———. *The Terror Machine: The Inside Story of the Soviet Administration in Germany.* Trans. H. G. Stevens; Introd. Edward Crankshaw and Ernest Reuter, Burgomaster of Berlin. New York: Praeger, 1953.

Konev, Yevgenii. "Chto proizoshlo s Olegom Bitovym" (What happened to Oleg Bitov). *NRS*, September 21, 1984.

Konstantinov, D. "O Sokrate i ob izmene rodine" (About Socrates and high treason). *NRS*, November 26, 1977.

Kourdakov, Sergei. *The Persecutor.* Old Tappan, N.J.: Fleming H. Revell, 1973.

Kozlovsky, Vladimir. "Marsh-brosok sem'i Gorelkinykh." *NRS*, September 20 and 21, 1984. Ivan Gorelkin tells about his escape, with six other members of his family, across the border to Turkey in June 1984.

Krasnov, Vladislav. "Begushchie na Zapad." *NRS*, October 13, 1981.

———. "Begletsy iz Sovetskogo Souiza v rozysknykh spisakh KGB." *Russkaia mysl',* November 19, 1981.

———. "Defectors: A Profile." *New York Times,* October 25, 1981, sec. 4, p. 21.

———. *Defstudy* (Computer printout). Vladislav Krasnov Collection, Hoover Institution Archives, Stanford, California. (*See also*, Hoover File.)

Kravchenko, Victor. *I Chose Freedom: The Personal and Political Life of a Soviet Official.* New York: Scribner's & Sons, 1946. An abridged Russian-language version appeared as *Ia izbral svobodu* (New York, n.d.).

———. *I Chose Justice.* New York: Scribner's & Sons, 1950.

———. "Protsess V. A. Kravchenki." *Russkaia mysl'* (Paris), 1948.

Kravchenko versus Moscow. Introd. Sir Travers Humphreys. London, New York: Wingate, 1950. The report of the famous Paris case.

Krivitsky, Walter G. *In Stalin's Secret Service: An Expose of Russia's Secret Police by the Former Chief of the Soviet Intelligence in Western Europe.* 1939. Reprint. Westport, Conn.: Hyperion, 1980.

———. *I Was Stalin's Agent.* London: H. Hamilton, 1940.

Krotkov, Yuri. *I Am from Moscow: A View of the Russian Miracle.* New York: Dutton, 1967.

———. *The Red Monarch: Scenes from the Life of Stalin.* New York: Norton, 1979.

Kudirka, Simas, and Eichel, Larry. *For Those Still at Sea.* New York: Dial, 1978.

Kulmagambetov, Mahmet. "Moriaki s tankera *Tuapse*" (Sailors from the tanker *Tuapse*). *NRS*, June 9, 1984.

———. "Vozvrashchentsy" (Returners). *Kontinent,* no. 39 (1984): 295–321. Another installment appeared in *Russkaia mysl',* February 2, 1984.

Kurilov, Stanislav. "Odin v okeane" (Alone in the ocean). *NRS*, July 11, 1976.

Kustovtsev, R. "Nelegal'nye ukhody iz SSSR" (Illegal departures from the USSR). *Possev,* no. 7, July 1978.

Kuznetsov, Anatoly. "I Could No Longer Breathe." *Time,* August 8, 1969.

Kuznetsov, Eduard. "Desiat' let nazad, 15 iiunia" (Ten years ago, on June 15). *NRS*, June 25, 1980.

————. "Iubileinaia, skorbnaia: K 10-letiiu leningradskogo protsessa 'samoletchikov' " (The 10th anniversary of the Leningrad trial). *NRS*, December 30, 1980.

Levkov, Il'ia. "Novye amerikantsy v anfas i v profil' " (New Americans profiled). *Vremia i my*, no. 68–69, 1983.

Lipman, Samuel. "The Russian Wave." *Commentary* 69 (February 1980): 68–73.

Lysenko, V. "Bespravie, ekspluatatsia, lozh'!" *Possev*, no. 9, September 1977, pp. 47–53. Defecting captain of Soviet merchant marine writes about living conditions of Soviet sailors.

————. *Poslednii reis: Zapiski kapitana* (The last voyage: Captain's notes). Frankfurt/Main: Possev, 1982.

————. "Zhizn' moriaka v usloviiakh svobody." *Possev*, no. 10, October 1977; pp. 46–50. A comparison with the Swedish merchant marine.

Manakov, Anatolii. "Uchast' izmennika" (A traitor's fate). *Literaturnaia gazeta*, no. 12, March 21, 1979, p. 15. Story of Dmitrii Per'kov.

Martin, David C. *Wilderness of Mirrors*. New York: Harper & Row, 1980. Contains information on Anatoli Golitsyn.

Myagkov, Aleksei. *Inside the KGB: An Expose by an Officer of the Third Directorate*. England: Foreign Affairs Publishing Co., 1976; New Rochelle, N.Y.: Arlington House, 1977.

O'Brien, Maureen. "Bringing Sanity to the Laws of Asylum: The Kudirka Affair." *Human Rights* 8 (Winter 1980): 30–43, 56.

Oglesby, Carl. "The Man Who Came in from the Cold. Maybe." *Boston Magazine* 71 (October 1979): 45–48, 51–52, 56–59.

Orionova, Galina. See Beloff, Nora.

Orlov, Alexander. *Handbook of Intelligence and Guerilla Warfare*. Ann Arbor: University of Michigan Press, 1963.

————. *The Secret History of Stalin's Crimes*. New York: Random House, 1953.

P., Alexander. "Krasnoznammenyi Chernomorskii: Rasskaz voennogo moriaka" (A navy sailor tells about the Black Sea fleet). *Possev*, no. 6, 1983, pp. 37–42.

Parrott, Jasper, with Ashkenazy, Vladimir. *Ashkenazy: Beyond Frontiers*. New York: Atheneum, 1985.

Parry, Albert. "Eshche dva ugona" (Two more skyjackings). *NRS*, November 9, 1977.

————. "Opiat' ob ugonakh sovetskikh samoletov" (Once again about Soviet skyjacking). *NRS*, December 22, 1977.

————. "Ugon sovetskikh samoletov" (On the skyjacking of Soviet airplanes). *NRS*, September 15, 1977.

Petrov, Vladimir, and Petrov, Evdokia. *Empire of Fear*. New York: Praeger, 1956.

Pirogov, Peter. *Why I Escaped: The Story of Peter Pirogov*. New York: Duell, Sloan, & Pearce, 1950. (Translation of *Za kurs!* [New York: Chekhov, 1952].)

Polianski, Nicolas. *M.I.D.: Douze ans dans les services diplomatiques du Kremlin*. Paris: P. Belfond, 1984.

"Political Asylum." *U.S. Department of State Bulletin* 80 (January 1980): 35–37. Transcript.

"Ponimaiut li eto amerikantsy?" (A statement by a group of Soviet military defectors.) Hoover Institution Archives, Nicolaevsky Collection, container 236/3, outcard no. 507, ID no. 29.

Reddaway, Peter, ed. *Uncensored Russia: Protest and Dissent in the Soviet Union*. New York: American Heritage Press, 1972. Drawn from the *Chronicle of Current Events*.

————. See Bloch, Sidney.

Roitman, Lev. "Pochemu ugoniaiut sovetskie samolety?" (Why do they hijack Soviet planes?). *NRS*, May 27, 1978.

————. "A Chronology of Attempted and Successful Hijackings of Soviet Aircraft." *New York Radio Liberty Research*, RL 393/81, September 30, 1981.

Romadinov, Dora. "Cyril Kondrashin: Why He Defected." *High Fidelity* 29 (October 1979): MA26–28.

Romanov, A. I. [pseud.]. *Nights Are Longest There: A Memoir of the Soviet Security Services*. Trans. by Gerald Brooks. Boston, Toronto: Little, Brown & Co., 1972.

Rubenstein, Joshua. *Soviet Dissidents: Their Struggle for Human Rights*. Boston, Mass.: Beacon Press, 1980.

Ruksenas, Algis. *Day of Shame: The Truth About the Murderous Happenings Aboard the Cutter Vigilant During the Russian-American Confrontation off Martha's Vineyard*. New York: David McKay, 1973.

Sakharov, Andrei D. *My Country and the World*. New York: Vintage Books, 1975.

Sakharov, Vladimir, and Tosi, Umberto. *High Treason*. New York: Putnam's Sons, 1980.

Sareen, C. L. *Bid for Freedom: USSR vs Tarasov*. Englewood Cliffs, N.J.: Prentice Hall, 1966.

Schuman, Thomas [Bezmenov]. "My Role in the Subversion of India." *Speak Up*, April 1981. Interview with Kaneko Magayoshi of Sekai Nippo, Japan.

————. "Soviet Defector Tomas Schuman." *Review of the News* 20 (March 7, 1984): 31–35, 37–40.

Sedykh, Andrei. "Pochemu oni begut?" (Why do they escape?). *NRS*, September 25, 1979.

————. "Vokrug nas shpiony" (There are spies around us). *NRS*, February 12, 1980.

Seligsohn, Leo. "The Defectors: Life Under Red, White, and Blue." *Newsday Magazine*, July 4, 1982, 12–17.

Semyonov, Vasily. "Radi chego rabotaiut liudi na sudakh zagranplavaniia?" (Why do they become merchant mariners?). *Russkaia mysl'*, January 17, 1985.

Shadrin, Nicholas [Artamonov]. See Borovik, Genrikh, and Hurt, Henry.

Shatravka, Aleksandr. "Pis' mo iz lageria" (Letter from a labor camp). *Russkaia mysl'*, October 18, 1984.

Shevchenko, Arkady. See Freeman, Neal.

————. *Breaking with Moscow.* New York: Knopf, 1985.

Shmelyoff, Oleg. "Anatomy of a Soviet Defection." *MacLeans* 93 (September 8, 1980): 16–18. Interview.

Shostakovich, Maxim. "I Bring the Blood of Shostakovich to Freedom: Maxim Shostakovich Tells Why He Left the Soviet Union." *High Fidelity* 31 (November 1981): MA 18–19.

Shtepa, V. "Kak pereplyvaiut more" (How to cross a sea). *Possev*, no. 9, September 1978, pp. 53–59.

Shultz, Richard H., and Godson, Roy. *Dezinformatsia: Active Measures in Soviet Strategy.* Washington, D.C.; New York: Pergamon, 1984.

Simpson, Smith. "One Day in the Life of Simas Kudirka and the State Department." *Foreign Service Journal*, September 1979, pp. 11–34.

Sokolova, Elena. "Beg" (Flight). *NRS*, November 8, 1984.

————. "Begletsy i vozvrashchentsy" (Defectors and Returners). *NRS*, February 8, 1985.

Solzhenitsyn, Alexander. *Warning to the West.* New York: Farrar, Straus and Giroux, 1974.

Sontag, Susan. "Communism and the Left," *The Nation* 234, no. 8 (February 27, 1982): 230–31.

Sosnovsky, Vasilii. "A chto mne bylo delat'?" *Possev*, no. 5, May 1979, pp. 36–40. About a successful skyjack of a Soviet plane.

Suvorov, Viktor. *Inside the Soviet Army.* New York: Macmillan, 1982.

————. *The Liberators: My Life in the Soviet Army.* Norton, 1983.

Thorne, Ludmilla. "The Littlest Defector." *National Review* 35 (March 18, 1983): 314, 316, 318–320, 341.

Thorwald, Jurgen. *The Illusion: Soviet Soldiers in Hitler's Armies.* New York: Harcourt, Brace, Jovanovich, 1975.

Tokaev, Grigory. *Betrayal of an Ideal: Memoirs of the Author's Youth.* Introd. David Kelly, former British ambassador to Moscow; trans. Alec Brown. Bloomington: Indiana University Press, 1955.

————. *Comrade X.* London: Harville, 1956.

————. *Soviet Imperialism.* Ed. Virpsha, E.S., and Sykes, E. New York: Philosophical Library, 1956.

————. *Stalin Means War.* London: Weidenfeld and Nicolson, 1951.

Tol'sky, A. "Lager' Shenek" (Camp Schönek). *NRS*, May 12, 16, 18, and 19, 1984.

————. "Prichina moego nevozvrashcheniia" (The reason for my nonreturning). *NRS*, March 16, 1984.

————. "V nemetskoi provintsii" (In a German province). *NRS*, September 6, 7, and 9, 1984.

Tolstoy, Nikolai. *The Secret Betrayal.* New York: Scriber's Sons, 1977.

Train, John. "The Lonely Voice of Alexander Solzhenitsyn." *Wall Street Journal*, June 23, 1983.

Ugolovnyi kodeks Estonskoi SSR (Criminal code of the Estonian Soviet Socialist Republic). Tallinn, 1968.

Ugolovnyi kodeks RSFSR (Criminal code of the Russian Federation). Moscow, 1950, 1966, 1983.

Urban, G. R., ed. *Stalinism: Its Impact on Russia and the World*. New York: St. Martin's Press, 1982.

U.S. Congress. Senate Committee on the Judiciary. "The Episode of the Russian Seamen" (From Soviet tanker *Tuapse*). Washington, D.C.: U.S. Government Printing Office, May 24, 1956.

―――. *Murder International, Inc.: Hearing Before the Subcommittee to Investigate the Administration of the Internal Security Act*. See esp. testimony of Peter Deriabin, George Karlin [Yuri Krotkov], and Yevgeny Runge.

U.S. Department of State, Office of Intelligence Research. "The Soviet Union As Reported by Former Soviet Citizens." August 1951 through August 1960. Deposited at the Hoover Institution Archives.

Vasil'ev, O. "Metnulsia v'rai'." (Gone to a "paradise"). *Komsomol'skaia pravda*, May 28, 1968. Concerning Vladislav Kushneris.

Verbitsky, A. "Opasnye sviazi" (Dangerous connections). *NRS*, November 9, 1982, p. 3.

―――. "Raskol'nikov." *NRS*, May 11, 1982.

Vetokhin, Yuri. *Sklonen k pobegu* (Inclined to defect). P.O. Box 16084, San Diego, California.

Vladimirov, Leonid. *Rossiia bez prikras i umolchanii*. Frankfurt/Main: Possev, 1969.

―――. *The Russians*. New York, Washington, London: Praeger, 1968.

―――. *The Russian Space Bluff: The Inside Story of the Soviet Drive to the Moon*. New York: Dial Press, 1973.

Voinovich, Vladimir. "Koe-chto o begletsakh" (Something about defectors). *NRS*, November 11, 1984.

Volkov, Solomon. "Pamiati Kondrashina: Artisticheskaia svoboda dirizhera" (In memory of Kondrashin). *NRS*, March 7, 1982.

Von Laue, Theodore H. "Rash U.S. Cheers for Soviet Defectors." *New York Times*, October 10, 1979, p. A26.

Voslensky, Michael. *Nomenklatura: The Soviet Ruling Class*. Trans. Eric Mosbacher; preface by Milovan Djilas. Garden City, N.J.: Doubleday, 1984.

Wishnevsky, Julia. "Svetlana Returns." *New York Radio Liberty Research*, 1984.

Young, Gregory D. "Mutiny on *Storozhevoy*: A Case Study of Dissent in the Soviet Navy." M.A. thesis, Naval Postgraduate School, Monterey, Calif. March 1982.

Yurchenko, Yuri. "Sovetskii Soyuz: Peremeny neizbezhny" (Soviet Union: Changes are inevitable). *NRS*, April 16, 1982.

Zakon o gosudarstvennoi granitse SSSR (The Law of the State Border of the USSR). *Izvestiia*, November 26, 1982.

Zolotarev, Aleksandr. "Rasskaz 'Vozvrashchentsa'" (A story of a "returner"). *Russkaia mysl'*, June 28, 1984.

INDEX

QUESTIONNAIRE FOR DEFECTORS

Confidential. Only for statistics. Any question may be left unanswered.

1. _____
   Last Name   First   Patronymic

2. _____
   Month   Date   Year of Birth

3. _____
   City (Village)   Raion   Oblast'   Republic of Birth

4. _____
   Nationality (acc. to Soviet passport);   In your opinion

5. _____
   What languages did you speak before defection?   After?

6. Education (circle):
   nachalnoe, nepolno-srednee, srednee, tekhnikum,
   vysshee tekhn., vysshee gumanitarnoe,
   other:

7. Military service (circle):
   Army, Navy, Air Force, none, other:

8. Military education and training (circle):
   at university, institute, tekhnicum

9. Member of (circle):
   VLKSM, Communist Party, Candidate (at time of defection)

10. Civil status (before defection): single, married, divorced

11. Any children? (before defection): _____

12. Place of work (before defection): _____

13. Position (before defection): _____

14. _____
    Month   Date   Year of Defection

15. _____
    Country   City   Place of Defection

16. Method of defection (circle):
    nevozvrashchenets, cherez granitsu, s sudna, vplav',
    other:

17. If you were legally abroad, what type of visa did you have?

18. In which country did you first seek asylum?

19. In which country were you granted asylum?

20. Reasons for defection (circle):
    political, ideological, religious, national, personal,
    others:

21. Was your defection reported abroad? (circle):   Yes   No   Don't know

22. Was your defection reported in USSR? (circle):   Yes   No   Don't know

23. If yes, the name and date of main publication, please:

24. Did you describe your defection?
    When?
    Where?

25. Of what country are you now a citizen? Or resident?

26. Place and position of your present work or study:

27. Your present civil status (circle):
    single, married, separated, divorced

28. Present address and telephone (if you so wish):

Please fill out and mail to:
    The Jamestown Foundation
    1708 New Hampshire Avenue, N.W.
    Washington, D.C. 20009
    Tel. (202) 483-8888